Into the
WILDERNESS
with the
ARMY
of the
POTOMAC

Into the
WILDERNESS
with the
ARMY
of the
POTOMAC

ROBERT GARTH SCOTT

INDIANA UNIVERSITY PRESS • BLOOMINGTON

Library of Congress Cataloging in Publication Data

Scott, Robert Garth, 1957–
Into the Wilderness with the Army of the
Potomac.

Bibliography: p.
Includes index.
1. Wilderness, Battle of the, 1864.
2. United States.   Army of the Potomac—History.
I. Title.
E476.52.S39   1985   973.7'36   84-48251
ISBN 0-253-14326-8

1 2 3 4 5   89 88 87 86 85

For my father,
who has a good sense of history

Contents

ILLUSTRATIONS

MAPS

PREFACE

Never in recorded military history has there been a battle quite like the one fought in the Wilderness of northern Virginia on May 5–6, 1864. The terrain of that now-famous battlefield is what, above all else, made the engagement unique in warfare. Neither before the Civil War nor after have two opposing forces been compelled to operate in such a thicket. Not even the overgrown field of Chancellorsville, four miles to the east, could compare to the impenetrable second growth of scrub oak and pine that was abundant in the Wilderness.

When the battle began on May 5, the problems of maneuvering troops through this brush were quickly realized. Entire brigades stumbled through the woods, losing all organization and direction, and before long the battle was raging out of control. Many units lost sight of their officers and, as a result, the outcome of the fight fell into the hands of the common soldiers.

These men, the volunteers, and not necessarily the military movements, make war worth studying. Although the actions of one brigade against another are important to any campaign history (and they are given in this book), the human element in battle shines above all else. That is what we remember most; whether it be the young man from South Carolina who, at the climax of a desperate assault, picks up his regiment's colors and carries them on to certain death or a boy from Ohio who offers comfort to a wounded foe. Such actions reassure us that, even in the midst of turmoil, men are still men, often rising above themselves in devotion to duty and compassion toward their fellow human beings.

Unlike many other battles of the war, the Wilderness lacked pageantry. Rarely were the defending lines of one army able to see the enemy's flag snapping defiantly in the breeze as the opposing troops formed for the charge; the brush prevented it. This, however, does not indicate that the engagement lacked in heroic assaults, for quite the opposite is true. The charge of the 20th Massachusetts on the afternoon of May 6 and the Confederate assault against the strongly entrenched Union lines along Brock Road, later in the same day, remain two of the most desperate attacks of the war; yet, for some reason, they have been largely ignored by historians. In fact, in the 121 years since the battle, only two in-depth studies have been written about the entire Wilderness campaign—Morris Schaff's *The Battle of the Wilderness* (1910) and Edward Steere's *The Wilderness Campaign* (1960).

Into the Wilderness with the Army of the Potomac is a modest attempt to bring some of the limelight back into the woods, where, for two bloody days, so many Americans were called upon to give the ultimate sacrifice. Although the narrative focuses primarily on the Army of the Potomac, Confederate accounts are given in certain phases of the battle that are either lacking in Federal accounts or are particularly interesting when seen from the Confederate point of view. I have, to the best of my ability, remained impartial, and the reader will note that both praise and criticism are given to the deserving troops, regardless of the side on which they fought. I can only hope that this book has done justice to the memory of the men, North and South, who fought in the Wilderness and that perhaps it will enlighten someone somewhere.

ROBERT GARTH SCOTT

ACKNOWLEDGMENTS

Because no historical work could ever be the result of the efforts of any single person, the author is greatly indebted to the following people and institutions that contributed greatly to the publication of this book. First and foremost among the individuals who assisted me is my father-in-law, Ronald F. Carlson, who not only aided me in the preparation of the maps but also photographed the modern views of the battlefield that appear throughout the text. My brothers-in-law, Mark Carlson and David Carlson, were also instrumental in preparing the maps, and for their help I am deeply grateful. No lesser amount of thanks is due to my wife, Karen, who twice traveled with me to Virginia while I was researching the book and was a constant source of support and inspiration. I am also extremely thankful to the staff at Indiana University Press.

Many of the wartime and early postwar photographs were obtained through the efforts of Michael J. Winey, curator of the United States Army Military History Institute at Carlisle Barracks, Pennsylvania (cited throughout as USAMHI). These photographs are a part of the collection of the Military Order of the Loyal Legion, Massachusetts Commandery, U.S. Army Military History Institute. The remainder of the early photos appear through the courtesy of the Prints and Photographs Division of the Library of Congress and the Still Picture Branch of the National Archives. Much credit must also be given to David A. Lilley, a historian at the Fredericksburg-Spotsylvania National Military Park, who so kindly replied to an endless stream of letters I sent to him, answering many questions concerning the Wilderness battlefield.

I would also like to acknowledge the services of Mary Ann Neary of the State Library of Massachusetts, in Boston; Cathy Carlson of the Museum of the Confederacy, in Richmond; Monique Leroux of the Virginia State Library, in Richmond; as well as the staffs of the Division of Manuscripts in the Library of Congress; the University of Michigan Graduate Library, in Ann Arbor; the Detroit Public Library; the Michigan State Library, in Lansing; and finally the Flint Public Library.

Into the
WILDERNESS
with the
ARMY
of the
POTOMAC

CHAPTER ONE

Shadows of the Past

1. The New Commander

By the spring of 1864 America was embroiled in the largest and bloodiest civil war the world had ever known, and an end to the conflict was nowhere in sight. It had only been three years earlier (although it seemed an age ago) that the nation had so cheerfully (and naively) paraded down the road to war with banners flying and bands playing. Now, however, those banners were bullet-torn, the bands were playing dirges, and the people of the country, North and South, were faced with the grim reality of something they had neither expected nor prepared for—total warfare.

For the Union, in particular, the war had been going badly. In the eastern theater the nation's number one fighting force, the Army of the Potomac, had been plagued by a long series of defeats. Strategically positioned between Washington, D.C., and Richmond, Virginia, it was this army's duty to protect the Federal capital while simultaneously attacking the Confederate capital. As a result, the Army of the Potomac, more than any other Federal force, attracted the attention of the nation; moreover, somewhat unfairly, it was the Army of the Potomac that was expected to win the war for the Union.

The popular misconception that pervaded the North was that if the Confederate capital could be taken the war would be over. "On to Richmond!" had been the cry from the beginning, but the nation's hopes were not being met. The Army of the Potomac had been defeated in every major campaign into which it had ventured, with the exceptions of Antietam and Gettysburg—two victories that had been gained by defensive fighting during Robert E. Lee's two invasions of the North.

Blame for the army's successive losses, however, did not rest solely with the troops. They were inexperienced, to be sure, but so were the Confederates. Responsibility, for the most part, rested with the commanders of the Army of the Potomac. From the time it was officially organized after the disastrous defeat at Bull Run until just prior to the Battle of Gettysburg, the Army of the Potomac had seen three commanding generals come and go. Although they had been educated in the art of war at the United States Military Academy at West Point and had previously seen service in the Mexican War, each of these men had been, in one way or another, unfit for high command. Unfortunately, the only way to determine if an officer was capable of leading over 100,000 men in battle was through the slow and costly process of trial and error.

The first of the army's commanders had been Major General George B. McClellan, who was also burdened with the role of general-in-chief of the Union Armies, the nation's highest command. Lieutenant General Winfield Scott had previously held the title of general-in-chief, but the infirmities of old age had forced him to turn the army over to a younger man. McClellan did a fine job of organizing the army, yet, before he was willing to commit the army to the field, everything had to be "just so." If he felt he was lacking a few pieces of artillery or mounts for his cavalry, he preferred to delay the campaign a few weeks rather than move without them—an attitude that cost the army precious time and eventually cost McClellan his title of general-in-chief, reducing him to commander of the Army of the Potomac. When, at last, the army was in the field, another problem developed. McClellan, believing he was outnumbered when he actually had the superior force, became hesitant to attack the enemy. Overestimating the strength of the Confederates while underrating the power of his own troops was his worst mistake. "Little Mac," beloved in the hearts of his men, was finally put on the shelf.

After the departure of McClellan, Major General Ambrose E. Burnside was ordered to assume command of the Army of the Potomac. If ever there was a more dilatory general than McClellan, it was Burnside. His slowness and indecisiveness allowed the Confederates to occupy the heights above the town of Fredericksburg, Virginia, which, on December 13, 1862, resulted in one of the most futile battles of the war. The Army of the Potomac suffered over 12,000 casualties as it hopelessly assaulted, head on, the heavily entrenched Confederate position.

After the Fredericksburg disaster, the army was encamped on the east bank of the Rappahannock River, directly opposite the town and the defiant foe that guarded its hills. No sooner had the army finished licking its wounds, however, than Burnside had it on the march in an effort to skirt the town and cross the Rappahannock at one of its upper fords. Shortly after the movement started, the winter rains set in, quickly turning the roads into quagmires. Horses, cannons, and men became stuck, in some cases lost, in the mud. All hope of continuing the march was, of course, abandoned, and the army—cold, wet, and humiliated—struggled its way back to its camps and went into winter quarters. The devastating losses of Fredericksburg, combined with the fiasco of the "Mud March," brought morale in the Army of the Potomac to a record low, prompting President Lincoln to relieve Burnside. Once again a new commander for this hard-luck army was summoned; perhaps this time the right man for the job would be found.

Handsome, hard-fighting, hard-drinking Major General Joseph Hooker was Lincoln's choice to replace Burnside, and, at the time, it seemed the right choice. Hooker looked like a general; in fact, he seemed the epitome of a hard-bitten warrior. He spoke confidently of taking Richmond and of crushing Lee, but in fact Hooker was uncertain and uncomfortable in his new position. In spite of his uneasiness, however, "Fighting Joe" pulled off a feat of strategic brilliance in the early spring of 1863 that amazed everyone, but no one more than himself.

After leaving a portion of his force behind to keep an eye on the Confederates across the river, Hooker forded the Rappahannock above Fredericksburg and concentrated the majority of the army at a little crossroads known as Chancellorsville. He had succeeded in placing his army squarely on the left and rear of Lee's army, thus compelling the Confederates to abandon their untenable Fredericksburg defenses and make a hasty retreat across the front of the Federal position. With a portion of the Federal army left behind to press Lee's front and the majority of its force directly on the rebel flank, the Army of the Potomac was in an ideal position to deliver a crushing blow to the Army of Northern Virginia. Unfortunately, that is as far as it went, for, although Hooker had maneuvered the army with a keen military deftness, when the showdown came, poor old Joe lost his nerve. To the horror of his subordinate officers, Hooker abandoned the initiative, ordered the army to take up a defensive position, and, in the end, barely escaped annihilation himself.

(Throughout military history, at least as many battles have been won through the intervention of chance as by sheer preponderance of force. In the heat of conflict, however, opportunity may only present itself for a moment, and, once it has passed, is gone forever. The one characteristic of a great commander is the ability to recognize that opportunity in the confusion of battle, to seize it, and to take the fullest advantage of it. Washington had this ability, as did Napoleon, and, as was becoming more and more apparent to the Union commanders, Lee also had this ability.)

Grasping the initiative that Hooker was so quick to abandon, Lee gambled on the Federal commander's ineptness and split his forces, sending the legendary "Stonewall" Jackson on his final and greatest assignment. On the morning of May 2, 1863, Jackson embarked through the woods on a circuitous route across the front of the Federal army, with the intention of turning Hooker's right flank. Through great skill and daring, Jackson's force reached its attack point late that afternoon, still undetected by the bluecoats. The resulting attack achieved such surprise that it nearly obliterated one Federal corps entirely. Only the fall of darkness and the mortal wounding of Jackson spared the rest of Hooker's army a similar fate. The sole choice left to Hooker was an inglorious retreat across the Rapidan in the face of a hostile enemy—a risky business at best. In fact, the only thing that prevented the Army of the Potomac from being driven into the river was the ferocity of the rear-guard action fought by a portion of its troops.

As spring wore into summer, both the Army of the Potomac and the Army of Northern Virginia left the heavily wooded region of Chancellorsville. Little could anyone have realized at the time that they would return the following year to fight a similar battle on nearly the same ground. In 1863, however, they had an appointment in Pennsylvania at a little town with an equally unfamiliar name—Gettysburg. There the Army of the Potomac fought its greatest battle and won its greatest victory, but not under the command of the hapless Hooker. He was replaced just prior to that great event by a man in whom Lincoln learned to have much confidence—Major General George Gordon Meade. At long last the slow and costly process of trial and error came to an end for the army that had experienced more than its share of defeat.

As countless historians have pointed out in the past, Gettysburg was the turning point of the war, but only insofar as it restored the confidence of the Northern population in the Federal cause—a desperately needed measure. Lee's army, of course, never again imposed as great a threat to the Union as it had at Gettysburg, but this could not have been foreseen. In 1863 the war for the Republic could still be lost.

When one looked at the grand picture of military operations at the end of 1863, one thing was clearly evident. The war in the east had been going wretchedly for the Union, while the war in the west was running a different course entirely. The great Mississippi River had been reopened for navigation and the Confederates had been pushed from western Kentucky into the far reaches of Mississippi and from Tennessee into Georgia. The logical thing for Lincoln to do, it seemed, was to give the top command to the man who, more than any other, was responsible for the victories in the west. That man was Ulysses S. Grant, and, on March 9, 1864, in a little ceremony at the White House, Grant accepted his commission as lieutenant general. He now outranked every American general in history except George Washington.[1]

The previous general-in-chief had been Major General Henry W. Halleck, who had replaced McClellan as commander of all the Union forces. Halleck was an intellectual soldier; in fact, he had gained the nickname of "Old Brains" through his reputation. He knew what the books said on leading an army, but, when he actually tried to take charge of such a large force, things just did not work out. Halleck, who was more comfortable behind a desk than in the field in any case, was relieved of command and given a position at the War Department on March 12, 1864, as army chief of staff.

After assuming command as the Federal general-in-chief, Grant had originally intended to return to the west and operate from there; after more careful consideration, however, he decided that the Union commander belonged in the east and so chose to make his base with the Army of the Potomac. Grant knew that the western troops were in good hands under the command of his friend, Major General William T. Sherman. The Army of the

Lieutenant General Ulysses S. Grant. *Courtesy National Archives.*

Potomac had been having some hard luck and he wanted to personally see to it that, from that point on, things would be different.

On March 10, 1864, the day after accepting his new commission, Grant arrived at Brandy Station, Virginia, where the Army of the Potomac was in its winter quarters. Having spent his entire Civil War career in the west, Grant arrived as a stranger among strange troops, and, as a result, his reception was rather cool. This, however, did not seem to bother him in the least, and, after setting up his headquarters at nearby Culpeper Court House, the new Federal commander immediately set to work.

If ever there was a better organizer than McClellan, it was Grant. Having served as a quartermaster during the Mexican War, Grant knew from experience how the complex military supply system worked to prepare an army for a campaign, and, shortly after his arrival, the massive gears of the Federal army began to move. New equipment arrived at Brandy Station and the troops had more drilling and target practice than ever before. The idle troops that had been serving as heavy artillery and cavalry in the Washington defenses were issued rifles and turned into infantry—a move that pleased the other foot soldiers very much, since these troops had been living the good life in comfortable barracks. Grant was using every available resource to turn the army into a more effective fighting unit.

Due to the heavy losses suffered by the army at Gettysburg, another major change was made in the ranks of the Army of the Potomac under orders from the War Department. On March 23, 1864, the five corps of the army were consolidated into three, eliminating the First and Third corps entirely. The Second Corps now consisted of its original troops, re-formed into two divisions, and the remnants of the old Third Corps, also consisting of two divisions. The soldiers of the Fifth Corps were also formed into two divisions and were joined by the two divisions of the old First Corps. The Sixth Corps was kept as it was, except a division that had joined the defunct Third Corps on July 9, 1863, was transferred back to the Sixth Corps, becoming its third division. In an attempt to lessen the impact this change had on troop morale, each unit was allowed to retain its old corps and division badges.[2]

During that spring of 1864 a relationship developed between Lincoln and Grant that had not previously existed between the President and his commanding generals. In a candid conversation,

Lincoln told one of his secretaries, William O. Stoddard, what he thought about Grant: "Stoddard, Grant is the first general I've had! He's a general!" Stoddard asked Lincoln what he meant. The President replied:

> I'll tell you what I mean. You know how it's been with all the rest. As soon as I put a man in command of the army he'd come to me with a plan of campaign and about as much say, "Now, I don't believe I can do it, but if you say so I'll try it on," and so put the responsibility of success or failure on me. They all wanted me to be the general. It isn't so with Grant. He hasn't told me what his plans are. I don't know, and I don't want to know. I'm glad to find a man who can go ahead without me.[3]

Lincoln also stated that Grant was the first general he had who did not continually ask for more cavalry, artillery, or anything else in short supply and complain that he could not proceed with the campaign until he got what he wanted.

The Confederates probably had a good idea of the type of general they were now up against. General James Longstreet, commander of the First Corps in the Army of Northern Virginia, asked a fellow officer, who spoke confidently of being able to whip the new Federal commander, if the officer knew Grant. The young man indicated that he did not and Longstreet replied:

> Well I do. I was in the corps of cadets with him at West Point for three years, I was present at his wedding, I served in the same army with him in Mexico, I have observed his methods of warfare in the west, and I believe I know him through and through; and I tell you that we can not afford to underrate him and the army he now commands. We must make up our minds to get into line of battle and to stay there; for that man will fight us every day and every hour till the end of this war. In order to whip him we must out maneuver him, and husband our strength as best we can.[4]

As supreme commander of all the Union forces, Grant had decided on a new strategy. Previously, each branch of the army had acted independently of the others, enabling the Confederates to send support troops from an unopposed force to one that was under attack. Grant was determined to put a stop to this practice by having all of the Federal armies act in concert with one another. General Sherman was to move into Georgia, against Joseph E. Johnston's Army of Tennessee; General Franz Sigel was to move his force up the Shenandoah Valley to Staunton, where he could then proceed east toward Richmond; General Benjamin Butler had been ordered to move his Army of the James up the south bank of the James River and to attack the rebel capital; while the Army of the Potomac was to move south of the Rapidan River against Lee's Army of Northern Virginia, eventually linking up with Butler's force.[5]

When April arrived, the only question left unanswered was the route to be taken by the Army of the Potomac in crossing the Rapidan. If it moved by its left (Lee's right), the connecting waterways along the Virginia coast would offer a suitable route for a supply line that could support the army in any position it might take between the Rapidan and the James. Brandy Station could continue to be the base of supplies for the army until another was established on the York or James rivers. This route, however, would also make it possible for Lee to ignore Richmond and go north on a raid.

In a movement by the right flank (Lee's left), Lee would be cut off from taking his army north, but Grant would be unable to connect with Butler. Also, the army would be forced to abandon its supply line and carry with it everything it would need for the campaign. The latter idea was eventually abandoned, and the final decision was made for the army to move by its left.[6]

Someone once asked Grant about the art of war and the general replied that it really was quite simple: "find out where your enemy is, get at him as soon as you can and strike him as hard as you can and keep moving on."[7] This was exactly what Grant was about to do; when he met Lee, however, it was soon discovered by both parties that there would be no easy victories.

In the spring of 1864, the war took a new turn and the country entered the final and most bitter year of the conflict. Grant first struck Lee's army in the Wilderness of northern Virginia and there the world first caught a glimpse of how the rest of the war would be fought. From May 5, 1864, to April 9, 1865, the Army of the Potomac and the Army of Northern Virginia remained in close and bloody contact.

2. *Crossing the River*

Shortly after midnight on May 4, the Army of the Potomac pulled out of its camps at Brandy Station and filed out into the

Major General George G. Meade. *Courtesy USAMHI.*

road. The great blue host was heading south for the fifth time since
the innocent days of 1861, when young men enlisted because they
believed that wars were glorious and the men who fought them
were gallant; no one entertained ideas of chivalry any longer. This
war had brought an end to all that. Such illusions were smashed in
front of the stone wall at Fredericksburg and in the wheat field at
Gettysburg. As the men marched down the dark road, some sang
while others walked silently, thinking of home or of the days
ahead. None expected this campaign to be any different from the
others. Most of the men figured that "Bobby" Lee's army would
once again send them back across the river in utter defeat.

At about five o'clock that morning, the commanding general of
the Army of the Potomac, forty-eight-year-old Major General
Meade, joined the march. Meade was a West Point graduate who
had seen service in the Mexican War as a member of the elite Corps
of Engineers. He had been given command of the Army of the
Potomac just prior to the Battle of Gettysburg, where he won
eternal fame as the victor in that engagement. He was known for
his furious temper, and, whenever it surfaced, his staff officers
learned to keep their distance. Even the men in the ranks were no
strangers to Meade's sharp tongue, for he came to be known to
them as that "damned old goggle-eyed snapping turtle."

During this campaign, Meade was forced to operate under
Grant's shadow, and, although it has often been claimed that this
was an awkward situation, such was not the case. All of Grant's
orders to Meade throughout the campaign were general in nature,
giving Meade a free hand to conduct his army the way he saw fit.
Also, Major General Burnside's Ninth Corps was supporting
Meade's army in this campaign, and, since it was not officially a
part of the Army of the Potomac, its orders had to come directly
from the general-in-chief himself. This situation required Grant's
presence with the army, in the event that an emergency situation
arose that would require the supreme commander to make a quick,
on-the-spot decision and to dispatch orders promptly to the Ninth
Corps. (Meade, however, did suffer in the long run because of
Grant's presence with the army. He never received the recognition
he so richly deserved for the role he played in the campaign of
1864–65.)

When Grant first arrived at Brandy Station, Meade stated that
he was under the impression that Grant wished to have a West-

erner, perhaps Sherman, commanding the Army of the Potomac. Meade indicated to the new Federal commander that if this were the case, he would certainly understand and would tender his resignation without regret. Realizing the importance of the coming campaign, General Meade stated that no individual should stand in the way of selecting the right men for all positions. This unselfish attitude so impressed Grant that he later wrote "This incident gave me even a more favorable opinion of Meade than did his great victory at Gettysburg the July before. It is men who wait to be selected, and not those who seek, from whom we may expect the most efficient service."[8]

Meade's army consisted of the Second Corps, under Major General Winfield Scott Hancock, a soldier in every sense of the word; the Fifth Corps, under Major General Gouverneur Kemble Warren, distinguished at Gettysburg as the savior of Little Roundtop; the Sixth Corps, commanded by the amiable Major General John Sedgwick; and the Cavalry Corps, led by the feisty Major General Philip H. Sheridan, who had come east with Grant. The artillery was under the direction of Brigadier General Henry Hunt, who had helped in the defense of Cemetery Ridge in the Battle of Gettysburg. The total manpower of the three infantry corps plus Sheridan's cavalry and Hunt's artillery came to 99,438 men. When combined with Burnside's 19,331 troops in the Ninth Corps, Grant's force was brought to 118,769. If we subtract from this figure the 2,276 engineers with the Army of the Potomac, who were noncombatants, along with General Edward Ferrero's division of colored troops from the Ninth Corps, who numbered 3,095 and were not used for combat at the time, we get a total effective fighting force of 113,398.[9]

Accompanying these troops on the march were 274 pieces of artillery, 675 caissons and battery wagons that traveled with the combat trains that followed each corps, 835 ambulances, and 609 "ordinary army wagons." The combat trains, mentioned above, carried ten days of rations as well as extra ammunition and forage. The remainder of the supplies were carried in hundreds of large wagons known as great trains, which followed the army. Several thousand head of cattle also moved with the army, to be slaughtered as needed.[10]

The movement of such an immense force was indeed a spectacle to behold. Sylvanus Cadwallader, a newspaper correspondent who witnessed the march, stated that the train, in one continuous line,

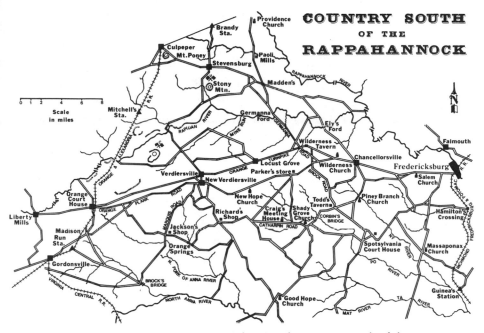

Theater of Operations, May 1864, showing the country south of the Rappahannock.

would have stretched from the Rapidan to Petersburg, a distance of over seventy-five miles.[11] Confederate signal stations on nearby Clark's Mountain, south of the Rapidan, could also see the Federal column as it approached the river crossings, and they kept the Confederate high command apprised of the developing situation.

In order to effect the quickest possible crossing of the Rapidan, the Army of the Potomac marched in two parallel columns, following two roads that were no more than five miles apart. The road on the right of the army led to the crossing at Germanna Ford, and the one to the left led to Ely's Ford.

The column of troops on the right was led by Sheridan's 3d Division of cavalry, commanded by Brigadier General James H. Wilson. It was about 2:00 A.M. when these troopers reached the bluff overlooking Germanna Ford, and Wilson immediately dispatched the 3d Indiana Cavalry to disperse a few pickets from the 1st North Carolina Cavalry, which had been guarding the crossing. This was done with little trouble on the part of the Federals, and the pontoniers were then ordered to lay the canvas bridge.

Following Wilson's cavalry was Warren's Fifth Corps. The 1st

Division, under Brigadier General Charles Griffin, was at the head of the corps and was followed by Brigadier General Samuel Crawford's 3d Division of Pennsylvania Reserves. Next came the corps artillery, forty-eight guns under Colonel Charles S. Wainwright, which in turn preceded the 4th and 2d divisions, commanded by brigadier generals James S. Wadsworth and John C. Robinson, respectively. John Sedgwick's Sixth Corps followed Warren's line of march, with Brigadier General George Getty's 2d Division in the lead, accompanied by one battery of artillery. Brigadier General Horatio G. Wright's 1st Division marched closely behind Getty, and Brigadier General James B. Ricketts's 3d Division brought up the rear.[12]

Warren's leading division reached Germanna Ford at about 6:00 A.M., and a wooden pontoon bridge was laid as the rest of the corps came up. By 7:00 A.M., the infantry of Griffin's division were ordered to break cadence and began crossing the river behind Wilson's horse soldiers.

The column on the left of the army was marching for Ely's Ford, just a short distance down river (east) from Germanna Ford. Sheridan's 2d Division of cavalry, led by Brigadier General David M. Gregg and accompanied by a section of the canvas pontoon train, rode at the head of the column. Reaching the ford at about dawn, the pontoniers with this advance unit set to work building a bridge.

Hancock's Second Corps marched immediately behind the cavalry. As it arrived at the river crossing, the wooden bridge that traveled with it was put into the water. The four divisions of the Second Corps, each taking a section of the corps artillery, advanced in the following order: Brigadier General Francis C. Barlow's 1st Division; Brigadier General John Gibbon's 2d Division; Major General David B. Birney's 3d Division; and the remainder of the Second Corps reserve artillery and Brigadier General Gershom Mott's 4th division.[13] The great trains and the reserve artillery of the Army of the Potomac followed the march of the Second Corps, crossing the Rapidan at Ely's and Culpeper Mine fords.

Burnside's Ninth Corps had by far the longest march of the day. It had been guarding the Orange and Alexandria Railroad and, when it began the march at midnight, was just northeast of Bealton. As a result, it had to march about ten miles farther than the rest of the army. As soon as the Ninth Corps was up, it was scheduled to cross the river at Germanna Ford, as was Brigadier General A. T. A. Torbert's 1st Division of cavalry, which brought up the rear of the army.[14]

Grant was up late the night of May 3 making some final preparations for the march, and, as a result, he did not join the rest of the army until about 8:00 A.M. on May 4. He rode his big bay horse Cincinnati this day, and, since the general was only 5'8" in height, he must have appeared out of proportion astride such a large animal. Grant, however, was an excellent horseman; he was, in fact, noted for his skill and had once considered entering the cavalry. He liked to ride along at a rather fast clip, leaving his staff trailing far behind.

The lieutenant general must have thought the beginning of this campaign was an extremely special occasion, because he decided to dress up for it. On this day he wore the full-dress uniform that was appropriate for his rank. It consisted of a dark-blue felt hat with a gold officer's cord around it, a dark-blue frock coat that he wore unbuttoned over a dark-blue waistcoat, and a pair of dark-blue trousers, which he tucked into a pair of knee-high riding boots. He was also trimmed at the waist with a sash and a sword and wore a pair of cotton thread gloves. For once, he looked every bit a general. Grant usually wore a simple private's uniform, with his shoulder straps tacked to the coat to indicate his rank. Colonel Wainwright, chief of artillery in the Fifth Corps, described Grant's appearance as "stumpy, unmilitary, slouchy and western looking; very ordinary in fact."[15] Indeed, he was so plain looking that he was often stopped by guards around the camps and compelled to identify himself before being permitted to pass. Herman Melville wrote of the new general-in-chief at the outset of the campaign:

> The May-weed springs; and comes a Man
>   And mounts our Signal Hill;
> A quiet Man, and plain in garb—
>   Briefly he looks his fill,
> Then drops his gray eye on the ground
>   Like a loaded mortar he is still:
> Meekness and grimness meet in him—
>   The silent General.[16]

As Grant and his staff approached Germanna Ford they halted for a short time to watch the troops cross the river. Lieutenant

This photograph by Timothy O'Sullivan was taken during the late afternoon of May 4, 1864. The troops are probably those of Ricketts's division of Sedgwick's Sixth Corps, crossing the Rapidan at Germanna Ford. Note the engineers in the distance taking up the canvas pontoon bridge. *Courtesy Library of Congress.*

This photograph by Timothy O'Sullivan shows a Federal infantry regiment (probably a part of Sedgwick's Sixth Corps) crossing the Rapidan River at Germanna Ford during the late afternoon of May 4, 1864. *Courtesy Library of Congress.*

Morris Schaff, an ordnance officer with the army, described the scene:

> Under the open pines on the bluff we found Warren, Meade, and Grant, with their headquarters colors. They and their staffs spurred and in top boots, all fine-looking fellows, were dismounted and standing or lounging around in groups. Grant was a couple of hundred yards back from the ford, and except Babcock, Comstock, and Porter, he and all of his staff were strangers to the officers and the rank and file of the army. His headquarters flag was the national colors; Mead's *(sic)* a lilac-colored, swallow-tailed flag having in the field a wreath inclosing an eagle in gold; Warren's Fifth Corps a blue swallow-tail, with a Maltese cross in a white field.
>
> Down each of the roads, to the bridges that were forty or fifty feet apart, the troops, well closed up were pouring. The batteries, ambulances, and ammunition trains followed their respective divisions.[17]

At about noon Grant and Meade, along with their respective staffs, crossed the river and set up their headquarters in front of an old abandoned farmhouse that was situated on the bluff overlooking the Rapidan.

Although the Army of the Potomac consisted of many veterans, there was also a substantial number of raw recruits. At the beginning of the march, most of these green troops were loaded down with heavy haversacks containing such extravagances as coffeepots, frying pans, and so forth, but, as the warm Virginia sun climbed higher into the sky, these unnecessary items were discarded along the road.

The new troops had not yet learned to travel like the seasoned veterans, who carried only essentials. The experienced soldiers did not carry a haversack, but instead wore what was known as a "horse collar": half of a pup tent (their partner carried the other half) with a gum blanket on top, rolled up tightly and tied together at the ends with a piece of twine. Any extra clothing was rolled up inside, along with a three-day supply of hardtack, salt pork, and coffee. The whole thing was worn over the shoulder and certainly did resemble a horse collar. Of course every soldier also carried his rifle, forty rounds of cartridges (which were in a cartridge box attached to a strap worn over one shoulder), and some percussion caps in a box that was hooked to a waist belt.

Private Frank Wilkenson, who was with the reserve artillery following in the rear of the Second Corps, described the scene along his line of march:

> The heavy-artillery regiment of Germans serving as infantry, which had been encamped to our left during the winter, fell into line. We light artillery men laughed to see the burdens these sturdy men had on their backs. Jellet, the gunner of the piece I served on, joined me as I stood leaning against a cool gun. He smiled, and said, significantly: "They will throw away those loads before camp tonight."

After the troops crossed the river at Ely's Ford they had to climb a steep bank on the other side, and the Germans began to unload their burdens. Private Wilkenson continued: "Spare knapsacks, bursting with richness, were cast aside near its base. Near the top of the hill we found many well-filled haversacks, and we picked up every one of them and hung them on the limbers and caissons and guns."[18]

So the men in blue crossed the Rapidan, and for many of them it was their last river. On the other side was an area of dense, second-growth timber that reeked of death—an area with a name many families and veterans, both North and South, would have preferred to forget. The region was known as the Wilderness, and the Battle of Chancellorsville had been fought on its eastern border just a year earlier; the bones of many of its victims were still lying in the woods as a grim reminder of what had been and what was yet to be.

Germanna Ford Road ran south from the Rapidan straight through the heart of the Wilderness, to a point just south of an old building known locally as Wilderness Tavern. At the tavern Germanna Road intersected with the Orange Turnpike, which ran east from Orange Court House, twenty miles west of the tavern, to Chancellorsville, five miles east of the tavern, then on to Fredericksburg. A little south of the intersection, Germanna Ford Road merged with Brock Road, which ran southwest from a point just east of Wilderness Tavern. After merging with Germanna Road, Brock Road continued in a southwesterly direction, intersecting with Orange Plank Road, which ran parallel to the turnpike and

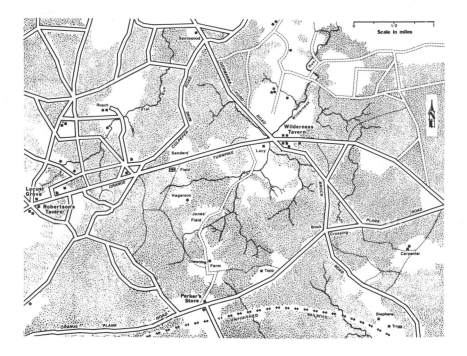

The Wilderness battlefield as it appeared in May 1864.

also ran east from Orange Court House to Chancellorsville. After crossing Plank Road, Brock Road continued southward to Spotsylvania Court House, crossing a few small roads in between.

Wilderness Tavern, which is referred to in many dispatches written at the time of the battle, was a two-story house made of hewn logs. It was abandoned prior to the battle and the once-lovely yard surrounding it had become weedy. The building was located in the southeastern corner of the intersection of Germanna Road and Orange Turnpike and was part of a larger complex of five or six other buildings, all of which were built around 1800. The tavern itself survived the Civil War, only to burn in 1977. (The ruins are still there on the south side of the turnpike, but anyone driving past who is not familiar with the battle would never realize that the building ever existed.)[19]

By 3:05 that afternoon, the entire Fifth Corps was at the tavern and, as ordered, went into camp there for the night. At 6:00 P.M. Sedgwick's Sixth Corps was across the river and making camp just

Wilderness Tavern in 1886. The road in the foreground is Orange
Turnpike. *Courtesy USAMHI.*

View of the intersection of Orange Turnpike
with Germanna Ford Road, looking west
down the turnpike. The old Wilderness Tavern
can be seen at the left of the photograph. *Courtesy USAMHI.*

south of the crossing. General Barlow's leading division of Hancock's Second Corps arrived at Chancellorsville around 9:50 that morning and by two o'clock in the afternoon the remainder of the corps was going into bivouac on the old battlefield:

> In glades they meet skull after skull
> Where pine-cones lay—the rusted gun,
> Green shoes full of bones, the mouldering coat
> And cuddled-up skeleton;
> And scores of such. Some start as in dreams,
> And comrades lost bemoan:
> By the edge of those wilds Stonewall had charged—
> But the year and the man were gone.[20]

After the soldiers had briefly rested, washed their tired feet, and had a cup of coffee, they were called to order and the following message was read to them by their company or regimental commanders:

SOLDIERS: Again you are called upon to advance on the enemies of your country. The time and the occasion are deemed opportune by your commanding general to address you a few words of confidence and caution. You have been reorganized, strengthened, and fully equipped in every respect. You form a part of the several armies of your country, the whole under the direction of an able and distinguished general, who enjoys the confidence of the Government, the people, and the army. Your movement being in co-operation with the others, it is of the utmost importance that no effort should be left unspared to make it successful. Soldiers! the eyes of the whole country are looking with anxious hope to the blow you are about to strike in the most sacred cause that ever called men to arms.

Remember your homes, your wives and children, and bear in mind that the sooner your enemies are overcome the sooner you will be returned to enjoy the benefits and blessings of peace. Bear with patience the hardships and sacrifices you will be called upon to endure.

Have confidence in your officers and in each other. Keep your ranks on the march and on the battlefield, and let each man earnestly implore God's blessing, and endeavor by his thoughts and actions to render himself worthy of the favor he seeks. With clear consciences serve the Government and the institutions handed down to us by our forefathers—if true to ourselves—victory, under God's blessing, must and will attend our efforts.

GEO. G. MEADE
Major-General Commanding.[21]

Over at Chancellorsville, General Hancock, surrounded by his staff, lay under the apple trees in the orchard of the old Chancellor homestead, where Union artillery had fired just a year ago that very day. Hancock, tapping his boot with his whip, chatted of the year gone by—a subject that could hardly be avoided that day, for the men of the Second Corps found that they were surrounded everywhere by shadows of the past. Many of the regiments discovered that they were occupying the same rifle pits that they had been in the year before, and the bones of their comrades were all around.

Understandably, the scene was an upsetting one for many of the men, and it left a marked impression on them for the rest of their lives. A member of the 116th Pennsylvania wrote, nearly forty years later,

> In the evening, after resting, when the rations had been distributed, officers and men strolled around examining the ground on which they had been fighting that day a year ago. The apple trees and lilies bloomed again. Pink and white roses struggled to life in the trampled garden of the old homestead and the fragrance of May filled the air. The old members of the Regiment *(sic)* took great pleasure in imparting to the new men the particulars of the battle and showing them how the battery was saved. The boys, fresh from home, who had not yet heard the sound of a hostile gun, were full of curiosity and took great interest in everything. The evidence of the fight was so strongly visible that the scene impressed them deeply. The burnt and crumbling buildings, trees torn and rent, the ground strewn with debris, told in mute, but terribly strong, language of the carnage and storm. The shallow graves of the men of the brigade were discovered and, much to the delight of the men, found overgrown with wild flowers and forget-me-nots. When Lieutenant-Colonel Dale noticed the profusion of the little blue flower he was deeply affected. He stood gazing upon the ground, wrapped in thought, and spoke in a strangely poetic strain of the goodness of the Creator in covering with beauty and perfume the last resting places of those brave men. He lingered there on that sweet spring evening and talked of

the matter for a long time, and finally began writing a letter to a Pittsburg paper, describing the scene and telling of the forget-me-nots. Gentle, noble soul! Within ten days he also filled a soldiers grave, and if God who sends the flowers in spring casts them over the last resting place of brave men in proportion to the soldier's merits, then indeed the unknown grave of Colonel Dale must be covered with the choicest bloom that nature yields in very great abundance.[22]

The scene described above was a familiar one that evening throughout the Second Corps, as many of the veterans described the past battle to some of the army's newcomers. One of the latter was Private Wilkenson, who later recalled the scene around his campfire that night:

> It grew dark and we built a fire at which to light our pipes close to where we thought Jackson's men had formed for the charge, as the graves were thickest there, and then we talked of the battle of the preceding year. One veteran told the story of the burning of some of the Union soldiers who were wounded during Hooker's fight around the Wilderness, as they lay helpless in the woods.
> "This region," indicating the woods beyond us with a wave of his arm, "is an awful place to fight in. The utmost extent of vision is about one hundred yards. Artillery cannot be used effectively. The wounded are liable to be burned to death. I am willing to take my chances of getting killed, but I dread to have a leg broken and then to be burned slowly; and these woods will surely be burned if we fight here. I hope we will get through this chaparral without fighting," and he took off his cap and meditatively rubbed the dust off the red clover leaf which indicated the division and the corps he belonged to.[23]

As the sun began to sink slowly below the treetops, most of Grant's force was already bedding down for the night; however, the great trains of the army, along with Burnside's Ninth Corps, were still strung out on the roads leading to the river crossings. Although Stevenson's leading division of Burnside's force was nearing Germanna Ford, the rest of the corps was far behind, in the vicinity of Rappahannock Station, twenty miles from the river. In order to avoid the possibility of these units getting too far behind the main body, an early halt of the army was necessary.[24]

That evening the pontoniers picked up the canvas bridges, which were then returned to their respective corps, leaving the wooden bridges for the Ninth Corps and the trains. The movement of the army had gone well. The Second, Fifth, and Sixth corps had marched about twenty miles each and had crossed the Rapidan with virtually no opposition, except for a few scattered pickets.

Earlier in the day, Grant had spoken to a member of his staff, Colonel Horace Porter, regarding the success of the day's advance: "Well, the movement so far has been as satisfactory as could be desired. We have succeeded in seizing the fords and crossing the river without loss or delay. Lee must by this time know upon what roads we are advancing, but he may not yet realize the full extent of the movement. We shall probably soon get some indication as to what he intends to do."[25]

3. A Formidable Foe

The Army of Northern Virginia, with the exception of Longstreet's First Corps, had spent the winter in the vicinity of Orange Court House. General Longstreet and his men had been sent west after Gettysburg to reinforce Braxton Bragg's Army of Tennessee, but they rejoined Lee's army in time for the spring campaign.

The men of Lee's army truly rejoiced with the arrival of spring. The hardships brought on by the Union blockade were felt everywhere in the Confederacy, but nowhere as severely as in the Army of Northern Virginia. Many of these loyal Confederates had suffered through the winter without shoes or blankets, and food had been scarce. More than once a comparison has been made between Lee's ragged veterans and Washington's army at Valley Forge. The condition of the army was so severe by January that Lee was compelled to take it upon himself to write the Confederate quartermaster general:

> General: The want of shoes and blankets in this army continues to cause much suffering and to impair its efficiency. In one regiment I am informed that there are only fifty men with serviceable shoes, and a brigade that recently went on picket was compelled to leave several hundred of its men in camp who were unable to bear the exposure of duty, being destitute of shoes and blankets.[26]

The Federal blockade was, of course, the major cause of the Confederates woes, but it could in no way bear all of the blame, for the very issue in which the Confederacy had its roots—states' rights—was slowly breaking its back. Due to the lack of a strong central government (something the Confederacy needed desperately to survive), it was up to the states to provide their troops with the clothing needed, and, as a result, some states had an overabundance of supplies while others had nothing. North Carolina alone is said to have had some 92,000 pairs of shoes in various warehouses, but Governor Vance refused to share his state's vast supply with the rest of the Southern states. Consequently, many rebel troops were forced to the loathsome task of stripping dead Federals after a battle in order to provide themselves with proper equipment. This practice was, in fact, exercised to such an extent that by the end of the war it was often difficult to judge from appearance to which army a soldier belonged.[27]

Although the Confederates suffered many hardships that winter, their morale remained high. They had been encouraged by their many victories over the Army of the Potomac and regarded the defeats of Antietam and Gettysburg as nothing more than bad luck. Moreover, they never lost confidence in Lee, who was fast becoming a legend to the people of the South, in addition to being highly respected by the folks in the North.

Although Lee was deemed a legend, he was, nevertheless, human. At the beginning of the spring campaign he was fifty-seven years old, and the hard campaigning was starting to take a toll on his body. In March 1863 he began to complain of pains in his chest, arms, and back, and, although this was diagnosed as rheumatism at the time, it is now believed that the general was actually suffering from the heart condition that would eventually be the cause of his death in 1870. Lee, however, showed no signs of this illness in May 1864.[28]

During the afternoon of May 3, Confederate lookouts on Clark's Mountain spotted clouds of dust across the river, indicating the movement of some of the Union army. This was probably only the Federal cavalry moving closer to the river crossings, but it was enough to convince Lee that Grant was about to advance. His troops were issued three days of rations and all unnecessary baggage was sent to the rear. That night the lookouts could catch glimpses of the Union troops as they marched past the large fires that had been built on the north side of the Rapidan, and it appeared that General Lee's prediction of a Federal advance that evening had proved correct.

General Robert E. Lee, C.S.A. *Courtesy USAMHI.*

Early on the morning of May 4, it became certain that the Yankee force was heading for the lower fords on the Rapidan, and the Confederate corps commanders were given their orders. The Second Corps, under Lieutenant General Richard S. Ewell, who had lost a leg at Groveton, began moving east down the Orange Turnpike toward Locust Grove. Major General Jubal A. Early's division was in the lead, followed closely by the divisions of major generals Robert Rodes and Edward Johnson. Stephen Ramseur's brigade of Rodes's division had been detached, along with one regiment from each division, to guard Raccoon Ford (which was up river, to the left and rear of Lee's army) and to reconnoiter in the direction of Culpeper Court House. Also, Robert Johnston's brigade of Rodes's division, was at Hanover Junction and would not be up until May 6. That night, as Ewell's men set up camp at Locust Grove, they were just a short march (5½ miles) from Warren's Fifth Corps at Wilderness Tavern.[29]

Lee's cavalry corps, which was commanded by the flamboyant Major General James E. B. (Jeb) Stuart, was moving down Orange Plank Road toward the little village of New Verdiersville, minus Fitzhugh Lee's division, which was near Hamilton's Crossing, just south of Fredericksburg.

Marching directly behind Stuart was the Third Corps of the Army of Northern Virginia, led by the ailing Lieutenant General Ambrose Powell (A. P.) Hill. (All that is known about Hill's illness is that it was some type of intestinal disorder.) Major General Henry Heth's division led the Third Corps's march that morning, followed closely by the troops belonging to the division of Major General Cadmus Wilcox. Richard Anderson's division had been left behind to cover the rear.[30]

General Lee, astride Traveller (a horse that had become as familiar a figure to the Confederates as the general himself), rode alongside Hill at the head of the Third Corps. Later that evening, after reaching New Verdiersville, Hill's men set up camp, just fourteen miles from the intersection of Plank Road with Brock Road. Lee himself had established Confederate headquarters nearby, in some woods near the farmhouse of a Mrs. Rodes.

By the morning of May 4, Longstreet's First Corps (minus George Pickett's division, which was on detached duty near Petersburg) was in the vicinity of Gordonsville, nearly forty miles southwest of Parker's Store. (This little hamlet was located on

Plank Road, three miles west of Brock Road.) At 4 o'clock that afternoon, the corps began its long trek northward, reaching Brock's Bridge early the next morning, still twenty-five miles from Parker's Store.[31]

Lee's entire force, including Stuart's cavalry and all artillery-men, amounted to approximately 62,000 men. Hundreds of white-topped wagons, along with about 224 pieces of artillery, followed at the rear of the army.[32] The Army of the Potomac outnumbered Lee's army nearly two to one, and it is probably for this reason that Lee did not oppose Grant's crossing of the Rapidan.

At about eight o'clock that evening, as the following dispatch to Ewell indicates, the Confederate high command was still uncer-tain as to the direction Grant would take after crossing the river:

> General: General Lee directs me to inform you that he will be found in the woods opposite this house (Rodes') tonight. He wishes you to be ready to move on early in the morning. If the enemy moves down the river, he wishes you to push on after him. If he comes this way, we will take our old line. The general's desire is to bring him to battle as soon now as possible.[33]

In effect, Lee was telling Ewell to attack Grant's rear if he moved toward Fredericksburg or to reoccupy the old Mine Run trenches if Grant turned his army west. No arrangements were made, however, in case Grant should elect to keep heading south and pass through the center of the Wilderness, which, of course, was what he was about to do.

Under a starry sky in front of the farmhouse where they had spent the afternoon, Grant and Meade stood around a campfire, smoking cigars. Their staff officers had gone off to a fire of their own, leaving the two men to a private conversation. No one knows what was said by these two soldiers that evening as they stood gazing into the cheery little fire, and probably no one ever will. One thing, however, is certain: the spring offensive was in the back of their minds.

As the two opposing armies settled down for the night, the soldiers on both sides talked of what the next day might bring. Uneasiness prevailed in the blue ranks, felt even by the veterans, for the men were now in enemy territory, far from their homes and families. This state of Virginia was totally foreign to boys from such places as Wisconsin, Vermont, or Maine. (In those days, before the automobile, few men traveled beyond their native states.) One Union soldier recalled that the men felt "a sense of ominous dread which many of us found almost impossible to shake off." Another soldier, who was encamped near Chancellorsville, prodded one of the skulls that were abundant in the area and grimly remarked: "This is what you are all coming to, and some of you will start toward it tomorrow."[34]

CHAPTER TWO

A Battle Develops

1. Projected Movements

The morning of May 5 came in clear and the low-hanging fog of the night before was swept away by the first warm rays of the rising sun. The pleasant smell of coffee was drifting through the camps even before daylight, as the bluecoats arose, stiff and sore from spending the night on the hard ground. After having spent the winter in relatively comfortable quarters at Brandy Station, it took the men some time to readjust themselves to the rigors of campaigning. One soldier in the Second Corps remembered the scene of that morning: "At daybreak, the reveille sounds, and as far as the bounds of the open plain one can see men arising from amidst the stack of arms. No dressing is required. A little water from the canteen, poured on the hands and transferred to the face, completes the most fastidious toilet, and all are ready for breakfast, hastily prepared by each in his own way."[1]

Each of the men seemed to react differently to the beginning of the day that many sensed would be their last. Private Theodore Gerrish recalled:

> Some (of the men) were laughing and cracking jokes about hunting for the Johnies through the forest, of the grand times we should have marching down to Richmond and entering the rebel capital, how when the war was over "we would hang Jeff Davis to the sour apple tree" and then go marching home.
> Another class, more thoughtful . . . were lying upon the ground, silent, alone . . . with compressed lips, seeming not to notice what was transpiring around them. They were thinking of wives and little ones far away, and wondering if they would ever see them again. Others were leaning against trees, writing letters.[2]

Before further examining the developments of the day, it is first necessary to give a description of the country in which the battle was fought. The area known as the Wilderness is roughly bordered on the north by the Rapidan, on the south by Spotsylvania Court House, on the east by Chancellorsville, and on the west by Locust Grove. The virgin timber that had once grown in abundance here had been cut down years earlier to provide fuel for the nearby iron smelting furnaces. By 1864 a dense second growth had sprung up. The ground within this brush was uneven, forming numerous knolls and ravines. A tributary of the Rapidan, known as Wilderness Run, flowed southwest through the Wilderness, crossing Germanna Road and the Orange Turnpike at their junction, then branching off into several smaller streams that ran off into the low-lying areas, creating several marshes. Colonel Horace Porter stated that this region "is well described by its name. It was a wilderness in the most forbidding sense of the word."[3]

From the center of this tangled thicket it was impossible to see more than a few feet in either direction. There were, however, a few clearings in the area. The immediate vicinity of the old Wilderness Tavern was fairly void of trees and brush, and, if one walked west from the tavern by way of the Orange Turnpike, in the first half-mile he would see the open fields of the Lacy plantation off to the left, on the south side of the road. Another half-mile down the turnpike was Sanders' Field (sometimes referred to as Palmer's Field), which extended for several hundred yards on either side of the road. This field was probably the largest in the area, and another clearing, belonging to a Mrs. Hagerson, adjoined its southern border. Continuing south from Hagerson's land was Jones' Field, the southernmost tip of which connected with the high, open ground of the Chewning farm. A small cattle trail led southeast from Chewning's property to the little farm of the Widow Tapp. This field was the smallest in the area and was situated on the north side of the Plank Road, slightly over a mile west of the Brock-Plank intersection.

As soon as breakfast was finished, camp was broken, and by 5:00 A.M. the apprehensive soldiers of the Army of the Potomac were resuming the march through the Wilderness. Riding at the head of the Second Corps, as cheerful and alert as always, was General Hancock, leading his men on to their assigned destination at Shady Grove Church. This little meeting house was located on Catharpin Road, which was about four miles south of Plank Road and ran roughly parallel to it.

The Second Corps (Gibbon's division in the lead, followed by Birney, Mott, and Barlow) marched south on the road from Chancellorsville for about half of a mile, until it reached Furnace Road. Here the men turned to the right (west) and followed it to the point where it struck Brock Road. Moving south down Brock Road for another half-mile, Hancock's infantry reached Todd's Tavern, where they turned west on Catharpin Road and continued on to Shady Grove Church.

General Warren's Fifth Corps was moving toward Parker's Store by way of Parker's Store Road (which, in actuality, was little more than a trail), which led southwest from the Lacy farm to the store. Crawford's division of Pennsylvania Reserves was at the head of the corps, followed by Wadsworth and Robinson, with Griffin's division bringing up the rear. Pickets, under the direction of Colonel David Jenkins, had been thrown well out on the Turnpike in order to cover Warren's right flank.

Sedgwick's Sixth Corps had the shortest scheduled march for the day. It was ordered to simply move up to Wilderness Tavern from its position just south of the river. General Getty's division took the point, followed directly by the divisions of Wright (minus Shaler's brigade, which was guarding the trains) and Ricketts.[4] As stated previously, General Stevenson's division of Burnside's corps was approaching Germanna Ford, but the rest of the Ninth Corps was not expected to begin crossing the river until sometime around noon, except for Ferrero's division, which was not due to arrive until the morning of May 6.

Wilson's cavalrymen had spent the previous night in the vicinity of Parker's Store, after a brief clash with Confederate outposts near New Hope Church on Plank Road, midway between Lee's headquarters at New Verdiersville and Parker's Store. At 5:00 A.M. Wilson's troopers saddled up and headed south down a trail through the woods, toward Craig's Meeting House, a little church on Catharpin Road, four miles west of Shady Grove.

General Wilson had previously been ordered to leave some of his cavalry patrolling down the turnpike and Plank Road before moving on to Craig's Meeting House, but the only detachment that had been assigned to this duty was Lieutenant Colonel John Hammond's 5th New York Cavalry, at Parker's Store. There were no troopers at all on the turnpike, leaving only 600 pickets between Meade's right flank and Ewell's Confederate corps. The primary function of scouting cavalry was to act as the eyes and ears of an army, but here Wilson, by directly disobeying orders, left Meade both deaf and blind as to the developments on the turnpike.[5]

In the meantime, Torbert's cavalry was tied up in the traffic jam of wagons at Ely's Ford. Originally scheduled to cover the right rear of the army and cross the river at Germanna Ford, this division was under new orders to cross at Ely's Ford and accompany Gregg's division of horse soldiers to Hamilton's Crossing, where Fitz Lee's division of rebel cavalry was believed to be. Unknown to the Federals, however, Fitz Lee had already left the area and was on his way to rejoin the rest of Stuart's cavalry. As a result, Torbert and Gregg were off on a wild goose chase.

2. *Surprise Meeting on the Turnpike*

Shortly before 6:00 A.M., General Warren mounted his big gray horse and, accompanied by his staff, struck out to follow the divisions of Crawford and Wadsworth, which were just marching past the Lacy house. Shortly after leaving his camp on the south side of the turnpike near Lacy's farm, Warren was approached by an aide who galloped up and saluted as he pulled his horse to a halt in front of the general. The officer explained that General Griffin had sent him to tell Warren that the enemy had been spotted advancing in force on his picket line. Morris Schaff, who was with Warren at the time, later wrote: "I do not believe that Warren ever had a greater surprise in his life, but his thin, solemn, darkly sallow face was nowhere lighted by even a transitory flare—Hancock's open, handsome countenance would have been all ablaze."[6]

After hearing the news of rebels on the turnpike, the Fifth Corps commander quickly wrote the following dispatch to General Meade:

> General: General Griffin has just sent in word that a force of the enemy has been reported to him coming down the turnpike. The foundation of the report is not given. Until it is more definitely ascertained no change will take place in the movements ordered. Such demonstrations are to be expected, and show the necessity for keeping well closed and prepared to face toward Mine Run and meet an attack at a moments notice.[7]

Major General Gouverneur K. Warren. *Courtesy USAMHI.*

It seems that Warren was truly alarmed by the sudden appearance of Confederate troops in front of Griffin. Certainly Schaff's description of the general's reaction upon receiving the news seems to point in that direction. Also, the above dispatch seems to indicate that Warren wanted to shrug off the sighting of these troops as nothing more than a small reconnaissance force, or perhaps just some rebel pickets. Just as he was about to send off the dispatch to Meade, however, a message arrived at Fifth Corps headquarters from Brigadier General Joseph Bartlett, commanding Griffin's advance brigade. This note informed Warren about what was happening in his front, forcing the Fifth Corps commander to deal more seriously with the situation. Bartlett's dispatch was added as a postscript to the one stated previously and both were sent by courier to Meade at 6:20 A.M.: "General Bartlett sends in word that the enemy has a line of infantry with skirmishers out advancing. We shall soon know more. I have arranged for General Griffin to hold the pike until the Sixth Corps comes up, at all events."[8]

After sending the message to Meade, Warren ordered General Griffin to push out a reconnaissance force against the enemy to determine the size of the force in his front. After receiving Warren's instructions, Griffin referred the orders to General Bartlett, who in turn ordered Colonel Joseph Hayes of the 18th Massachusetts to advance with his regiment and the 83rd Pennsylvania to find out what the rebels were up to.

Colonel Hayes advanced cautiously down the turnpike and through the woods on either side until his men discovered a strong line of Confederates busily engaged in constructing breastworks. A brief skirmish ensued, in which eighteen-year-old Charles Wilson of the 18th Massachusetts was killed by one of the whizzing Minié balls. He was the first of many young men to fall in the battle that was now developing. Unable to bear the heavy fire being dealt to them by an obviously superior force, the two regiments fell back and rejoined the rest of the brigade.[9]

Shortly before seven o'clock, Meade was riding down Germanna Road from the farmhouse near the ford, when he was approached by the courier bearing Warren's dispatch of 6:20 A.M. After quickly reading it, Meade and his staff galloped on to Fifth Corps headquarters where General Warren sat waiting. Meade walked over to the Fifth Corps commander and exclaimed: "If there is to be any fighting this side of Mine Run, let us do it right off." Meade then penned this message to Grant:

> The enemy have appeared in force on the Orange pike, and are now reported forming line of battle in front of Griffin's division, Fifth Corps. I have directed General Warren to attack them at once with his whole force. Until this movement of the enemy is developed, the march of the corps must be suspended. I have, therefore, sent word to Hancock not to advance beyond Todd's Tavern for the present. I think the enemy is trying to delay our movement, and will not give battle, but of this we shall soon see. For the present I will stop here, and have stopped our trains.[10]

General Grant, who was still at his headquarters near the old farmhouse, received Meade's dispatch at 7:30 A.M. and replied at 8:24 A.M. with the following: "Your note giving the movement of the enemy and your dispositions received. Burnside's advance is now crossing the river. I will have Ricketts division relieved at once, and urge Burnside's crossing. As soon as I can see Burnside I will go forward. If any opportunity presents itself for pitching into a part of Lee's army, do so without giving time for disposition.[11]

Grant's dispatch displayed his eagerness to bring Lee to battle as soon as possible. This disproves the long-expressed belief that Grant wanted to march through the Wilderness as quickly as possible and thus avoid a collision there. It is reasonable to assume, however, that Grant would have preferred to fight Lee on more open ground, where he could make more effective use of his overwhelming army. But if Lee wanted an engagement here, then here it would be. Grant was simply not the sort to refuse battle. Adam Badeau, who served as Grant's military secretary during the campaign, recalled: "It was not his (Grant's) objective to avoid the enemy; not even, as some have supposed, to pass beyond him; he did not desire to out-flank the rebel army, in a purely strategic sense, so much as to bring it to speedy battle . . . Grant really compelled either immediate battle or the immediate retreat of Lee."[12]

At about 7:30 A.M., after Meade had arrived on the scene, Warren sent two aides off to the divisions of Crawford and Wadsworth and then rode up to the Lacy house, where he re-established Fifth Corps headquarters. This house was quite large and sat a few hundred feet back from the turnpike. (It is still standing today.)

After arriving at his new headquarters, General Warren directed his assistant adjutant-general, Colonel Fred Locke, to pen a message to Griffin at 7:50 A.M.: "GENERAL: Have your whole division prepared to move forward and attack the enemy, and await further instructions, while the other troops are forming. Keep us informed of everything going on in your front."[13]

The couriers that had been sent to Crawford and Wadsworth bore messages for them to halt their divisions and close up with the troops on their right. Crawford's command was to connect with Wadsworth's left and Wadsworth himself had been ordered to connect with Griffin's left. This movement, of course, would prevent any Confederate attack from breaking through Warren's ranks and sending the entire Fifth Corps off in a rout.

By the time Warren's aide reached Crawford's division, however, it had already advanced as far south as the Chewning farm, quite a distance to the left of the rest of the corps; in fact, a gap of nearly a half-mile existed between his division and that of General Wadsworth. If the Confederates decided to advance they would certainly find this gap in the Union lines and take advantage of it; therefore, it became urgent for Crawford to retrace his steps and make contact with Wadsworth at once.

The Chewning farm, as has been previously stated, was situated on relatively high ground, and any force that occupied it would, by right, command a large area of the country in every direction. Because of the nature of the position his division now held and also because of unfolding developments on Plank Road (which we will examine later), Crawford found himself faced with a difficult situation. He knew that he should not abandon the Chewning farm heights, yet, at the same time, he realized that it was imperative to close the gap between his command and that of Wadsworth. Finally, believing that retention of the Chewning farm was most important, Crawford sent the following dispatch to Fifth Corps headquarters at 8:00 A.M.: "I have advanced to within a mile of Parker's Store. There is brisk skirmishing between our own and the enemy's cavalry. The general's order is received, and I am halted in a good position."[14]

The skirmishing that Crawford refers to in his dispatch was not between opposing cavalry, as he believed, but between Colonel Hammond's 5th New York Cavalry and the advance of Hill's entire corps of infantry, led by Brigadier General William Kirk-

The Chewning farm heights, facing south. *Photo by Ron Carlson.*

land's North Carolina brigade of Heth's division. Not realizing that they were opposed by nothing more than one regiment of cavalry, the Confederates moved cautiously down Plank Road, while Hammond's dismounted troopers fought valiantly to hold off Kirkland's entire brigade.

Meanwhile, back at Fifth Corps headquarters, Colonel Locke received Crawford's message at 9:00 A.M. Warren, however, was not present at the time, as he was out examining Griffin's front, so Locke forwarded the dispatch to General Meade, who received it shortly after nine o'clock. This was the first indication Meade had of the presence of Confederates on Plank Road.

At 11:15 A.M. another message was received at Fifth Corps headquarters from General Crawford, who was now asking if he should abandon his position. General Warren had by this time returned to the Lacy house and replied curtly to Crawford's dispatch: "You will move to your right as quickly as possible."[15] It probably seemed to Warren at the time that he had the last word on the matter, but he quickly learned otherwise. Major Washington Roebling, an aide-de-camp to Warren, was out visiting Crawford's front and saw the desperateness of the situation. He had been to see Colonel Hammond, who told him that he could perhaps hold on for another fifteen minutes but no longer. Roebling hurried back to Crawford, but by the time he reached the Chewning farm it was too late. The rebels had pushed the Federal cavalry past Parker's Store and down Plank Road to the left and rear of Crawford's division. Roebling then sent an urgent note to Warren, pleading with him to let Crawford stay where he was: "It is of vital importance to hold the field where General Crawford is. Our whole line of battle is turned if the enemy get possession of it. There is a gap of half a mile between Wadsworth and Crawford. He cannot hold the line against attack."[16]

By 11:30 A.M. Crawford reported to Warren that the firing had ceased along his front and that the Confederates were passing up Plank Road to his rear. Hammond's cavalry was still trying desperately to hold them off, but sooner or later his small force would be overwhelmed and forced to give way.

Warren was faced with a tough decision. He knew that Plank Road had to be held at all costs, otherwise the right of the entire army would be in danger; however, at the same time he could not afford to leave a hole of a half-mile in the center of his command.

As a result, he ordered Crawford to close up with Wadsworth's left. If Plank Road was to be saved, it would have to be done by Hancock.

3. *Grant Comes Up*

The general-in-chief had indicated to Meade in his dispatch of 8:24 A.M. that he intended to stay at his headquarters near Germanna Ford until he spotted Burnside's main force crossing the river. Grant, however, was one who preferred to be at the front and the longer he sat waiting for Burnside, the more impatient he became. Burnside, who had commanded the Army of the Potomac during the Battle of Fredericksburg, was well known for his tardiness. He had been late in crossing the river on the left of the army at Antietam, he was late in crossing the Rappahannock at Fredericksburg, and it seemed he was going to be late in crossing the Rapidan. According to Grant, as related in his memoirs: "Burnside was an officer who was generally liked and respected. He was not, however, fitted to command an army. No one knew this better than himself."[17]

By 8:40 A.M. Burnside was still nowhere in sight; Grant, anxious to move on, sent the Ninth Corps commander a message giving him details on crossing the river and telling him to close rapidly with the Sixth Corps. As soon as this task was completed, Grant mounted Cincinnati and struck out with his escort down Germanna Road to join Meade and the rest of the army.[18]

After riding down the road for about a mile, Grant and his staff were approached by Colonel Thomas Hyde, of Sedgwick's staff, who bore a message for the general-in-chief from Meade. Reining his sweating horse alongside Grant, Hyde saluted his commander and explained: "General Meade directed me to ride back and meet you, and say that the enemy is still advancing along the turnpike, and that Warren's and Sedgwick's troops are being put in position to meet him." Upon hearing this, Grant pressed ahead at a gallop, arriving at the turnpike shortly afterward, at about ten o'clock. Meade, who was standing along the roadside when Grant arrived, walked over and, after Grant had dismounted, the two men briefly discussed the situation they faced.

Shortly thereafter Grant established his headquarters, along with that of General Meade, on a little knoll located in the northwest corner of the intersection of Germanna Road with the turn-pike, directly across the road from the Lacy farm. Except for a sparse scattering of scrub oaks and pine, this knoll was located on fairly open ground as compared to the rest of the surrounding country. (Time has left little mark on this portion of the battlefield, and the knoll today appears much as it did during the war.)[19]

The scene at army headquarters was a hectic one as the Federals prepared for battle, with excited young staff officers scampering around, issuing and receiving dispatches, amid a constant stream of arriving and departing mounted couriers. To anyone visiting Grant's headquarters that morning, the general-in-chief must have looked oddly out of place as he sat with his back against a tree, calmly whittling on a stick, seemingly unaffected by all that was transpiring around him. This display of Grant's cool demeanor in a time of crisis completely amazed Meade's staff officers, who were standing nearby, especially after having been subjected for so long to the irascible temper of Meade, who could discharge like a loaded gun even when things were running smoothly. Grant's even tem-perament continued to make a marked impression on these men for months to come.[20]

By the time of Grant's arrival at the front, Meade was pretty much aware of the development of affairs on the turnpike, but the events that were unfolding on Plank Road were still, for the most part, a mystery to him. This, however, should not have been the case. Wilson's cavalry, which was supposed to act as a screen and intelligence arm for the left of the army, was engaged in a pointless fight with Confederate cavalry on Catharpin Road.

It was about 8:00 A.M. when Wilson's troopers ran into Brigadier General Thomas Rosser's brigade of Virginia cavalry, which had been scouting eastward on Catharpin Road. Colonel George Chapman's brigade of Wilson's division was positioned a short distance east of Craig's Meeting House, while Timothy Bryan's brigade was halted on the trail from Parker's Store. The 3d Vermont Cavalry, which had been thrown well out in front of Chapman's main force, attacked and successfully drove back Ros-ser's advance; however, Rosser's main body of horsemen quickly galloped to the support of the Confederate advance and a hot fire fight ensued, continuing for nearly three hours. As Chapman threw in the rest of his brigade, the men of both sides dismounted and continued to fire their hot carbines into the opposing ranks;

Major General J. E. B. Stuart, C.S.A. *Courtesy National Archives.*

neither side, however, was able to gain any advantage over the other.

At about noon, General Stuart, who was riding down Plank Road at the head of Hill's advance, heard the firing off to the south and, sensing trouble, immediately rode to Rosser's aid. As the rebel buglers sounded the charge, Stuart's troopers drove into Chapman's Federals and pushed them with great force back down the road; however, at the home of Mrs. Faulkner, just west of the meeting house, two batteries of horse artillery were waiting for the oncoming Confederates. As soon as Chapman's men had safely passed, the guns roared into action, spraying the rebel horsemen with canister. Horses and men tumbled to the ground as the iron tore through their ranks. At the height of the disorder, Wilson and his headquarters detachment, sabers drawn, charged forward in a desperate attempt to buy enough time for the rest of the division to withdraw safely to Todd's Tavern. The gamble paid off, and at about 2:45 P.M., Wilson's exhausted men and horses reached the tavern, where they fortunately encountered Gregg's fresh division of troopers, which had just arrived on the scene. Gregg took in the situation at once and led his men forward in a countercharge against the Confederates, who had rallied since Wilson's attack and were advancing down the road once more. The opposing cavalry came to close quarters on the east side of Corbin's Bridge and continued to fight until nearly 6:00 P.M., when the Confederates were forced to pull back to Shady Grove Church.[21]

By dawn of May 5, it at last became apparent to General Lee that the Union army was not moving east toward Fredericksburg or west toward Mine Run but was in fact heading south, directly through the center of the Wilderness. As he breakfasted with some of his staff that morning, Lee expressed his surprise that Grant had taken up nearly the same position as Hooker had the past spring. He hoped that the new Federal commander would meet with the same great disaster that Hooker had experienced. In short, General Lee was hoping for a repeat of Chancellorsville. His high hopes, however, were never realized; if Lee thought Grant was anything like Joe Hooker, he soon found out differently.

That morning, after breaking camp at Locust Grove, Ewell was ordered to push his corps down the turnpike and to regulate his march with that of Hill's corps, on Plank Road. Johnson's division was at the head of Ewell's Confederate Second Corps that morning, and, at about 8:00 A.M., after advancing to within two miles of Wilderness Tavern, Johnson's pickets reported that they had seen Federal troops on the road in front of them. Johnson, of course, sent word to General Ewell at once, and the march of the corps was halted.

After notifying General Lee of the situation, Ewell received orders to avoid a general engagement until Longstreet was up. Just the night before, Ewell had been informed that Lee wished to bring Grant to battle as soon as possible. It is thus obvious that during the past twelve hours Lee had changed his mind regarding the course of action he would take against the advancing Federals. It seems that Lee's first impulse was to attack, as was his nature; however, his better judgment prevailed in the long run, and he decided it would be best to wait until Longstreet was in supporting distance before committing his army to battle—a wise decision when one considers the size of the force he was dealing with. Fate, however, was to have the final word, and Lee's plans were soon thrown to the wind.

Heth's division, with Kirkland's brigade in front, led the march of A. P. Hill's Third Corps on this day, followed closely by Wilcox's division. Hill had most likely been given the same orders as Ewell about not bringing on a fight, but when two rival forces are marching toward each other on the same stretch of road, there is little anyone can do to prevent them from pitching into each other. Hill was marching straight toward Brock Road, and, if he reached it, it was just possible that he could turn the entire Union army and drive it back across the river from whence it came. Meade could not let this happen at any cost; therefore, a fight was going to take place on Plank Road, a battle almost entirely separate from the one that was about to break out on the turnpike.

CHAPTER THREE

Tempest in the Woodland

1. Getty Saves the Intersection

The war had been slowly rolling across the country like a dark cloud, its violent winds touching many little villages that had been left to themselves for over a century. Places with unfamiliar names like Bull Run, Mechanicsville, Shiloh, and Gettysburg were indelibly etched into the nation's consciousness. Virginia had experienced the worst of the storm, and, even in the spring of 1864, after three years of war, an end was nowhere in sight. The dark clouds were once again roiling over that state, this time just west of Chancellorsville, and they were about to release their tempestuous winds on the quiet woodland.

The people living in the area had previously known nothing but peace and were, for the most part, cut off from the problems experienced by the rest of the country; all this, however, changed within the short span of two days. The little farm of the Widow Tapp, with all the others that had been built in the Wilderness, was about to become a piece of the country's history, to be forever haunted by the memories of the men who fought there. There was nothing that anyone could do to prevent it:

> The foe that held his guarded hills
> Must speed to woods afar;
> For the scheme that was nursed by the Culpepper hearth
> With the slowly-smoked cigar—
> The scheme that smouldered through winter long
> Now bursts into act—into war—
> The resolute scheme of a heart as calm
> As the Cyclone's core.[1]

The men of the Second Corps were marching down Furnace Road, and, whether or not any of them thought of it at the time, they were moving down the same road that Stonewall Jackson had taken a year earlier, during his march around Hooker's army. At 9:00 A.M. General Hancock received the following order, written by Meade's chief of staff, Andrew A. Humphreys, directing him to halt his command at Todd's Tavern: "The enemy are on the Orange pike about 2 miles in front of Wilderness Tavern in some force. Until the matter develops the major-general commanding desires you to halt at Todd's Tavern."[2]

At the time Hancock received these instructions, his leading division (Gibbon's) was about a mile west of the tavern, while the rest of the Second Corps was still strung out on Furnace Road. Hancock sent a courier at once to Gibbon, with orders for him to stop his march and await the arrival at the tavern of the other three divisions.

At 10:30 A.M., Humphreys penned another order to Hancock, this time directing the Second Corps commander to move his entire force up Brock Road to the Plank Road intersection. Hancock received this dispatch at 11:40 A.M. and immediately set his corps into motion: "The major-general commanding directs that you move up the Brock road to the Orange Court-House plank road, and report your arrival at that point and be prepared to move out the plank road toward Parker's Store."[3]

In the meantime, Kirkland's brigade was driving Hammond's cavalry farther and farther down Plank Road, and something had to be done quickly. One regiment of cavalry could not hold off an entire brigade of infantry for very long.

At 10:30 A.M. the Sixth Corps was still making its way down Germanna Ford Road, except for General Getty's division, which was massed near the Wilderness Tavern, awaiting orders. Shortly before eleven o'clock, Lieutenant Colonel Theodore Lyman, of Meade's staff, delivered an order to Getty, instructing him to hasten to the Brock-Plank junction and support Hammond's troopers.

Getty was one man who could be counted on in an emergency. According to Brigadier General Hazard Stevens, Getty's chief of staff, Getty was a man of "prompt decision and readiness of resource in emergencies." He also stated that he could not point out "a single emergency where he failed to act precisely as he should have acted."[4]

Shortly after receiving his orders, Getty had his division hurrying off for the intersection, which it reached at about 11:30 A.M. Stevens later recalled:

> The division marched at once and rapidly. Just as its commander, preceding it some distance, reached the cross-roads, a detachment of cavalry came flying down the Plank Road strung out like a flock of wild geese, and were soon out of sight, a few barely pausing to cry out that the rebel infantry were coming down the road in force, a statement corroborated by a few musket shots heard in the woods in front. Getty instantly hurried back an aide to bring his troops up at the double-quick. Surrounded by his staff and orderlies, with his headquarters flag flying overhead, he took post directly at the intersection of the roads. Soon a few gray forms were discerned far up the narrow Plank Road moving cautiously forward, then a bullet went whistling overhead, and another and another, and then the leaden hail came faster and faster over and about the little group until its destruction seemed imminent and inevitable. But Getty would not budge. "We must hold this point at any risk," he exclaimed, "our men will soon be up." In a few minutes, which seemed an age to the little squad, the leading regiments of Wheaton's brigade, the 1st, came running like greyhounds along the Brock Road until the first regiment passed the Plank Road, and then, at the commands "Halt!" "Front!" "Fire!" poured a volley into the woods and threw out skirmishers in almost less time than it takes to tell it. Dead and wounded rebel skirmishers were found within thirty yards of the cross-roads, so nearly had they gained it, and from these wounded prisoners it was learned that Hill's corps, Heth's division in advance, supported by Wilcox's division, was the opposing force.[5]

Brigadier General Frank Wheaton's brigade went into action astride Plank Road with Colonel Lewis Grant's Vermont brigade on its left and Brigadier General Henry Eustis's brigade on the right. Had these troops reached the Brock-Plank junction just a few minutes later, the Battle of the Wilderness might possibly have had a different outcome.[6]

The importance of that now-famous intersection cannot be overstressed, for, if the Confederates had gained possession of it, they would have succeeded in cutting the Army of the Potomac in half. Hill's troops could then have moved straight up Brock Road and hit Warren's left flank, forcing him back across the Rapidan with the aid of Ewell's corps. Then, with a force left to guard the

The Brock-Plank intersection as it appears today, looking west down Plank Road. Much of the bitter fighting on the Union left was over this key point of the battlefield. The Confederates of A. P. Hill's corps had so nearly gained possession of the crossing during the early fighting on May 5 that their dead and wounded were found within thirty yards of the junction. *Photo by Ron Carlson.*

Group of Federal veterans standing in Plank Road several years after the war. *Courtesy USAMHI.*

Orange Plank Road as it appeared during the war. The planks, which paved one side of the road, are visible in the lower right-hand corner of the photograph. *Courtesy USAMHI.*

river crossing, Lee could have turned his attention toward Hancock. This, of course, is pure conjecture, as an endless amount of factors are involved, but it does emphasize the strategic importance of the crossing.

Getty's men sparred with Hill's advance until about two o'clock, when the fighting temporarily died down. Meanwhile, at 12:45 P.M., General Hancock and his staff reached Plank Road. Upon his arrival, Hancock became the senior officer in the area and thus commanded this wing of the army.

General Hancock was, without a doubt, the best corps commander the army had, and, although he was a little flamboyant (a characteristic he shared with many other officers in this war), he was a capable leader who flourished in battle. His commanding nature and heroic actions had earned him the sobriquet "Hancock the Superb," which described him so well. He had been wounded in the leg at Gettysburg while directing his men in the defense of Cemetery Ridge, and the leg still bothered him, although he was not the sort to admit it. Meade had given him official permission to ride in an ambulance, but he chose to ride his horse this day. After reaching Plank Road, Hancock went over to see Getty, who informed him of the situation in his front. Hancock assured him that the Second Corps would soon be up and the Confederate advance would be firmly checked.

Birney's division was now leading the Second Corps march, but was still some distance behind Hancock's cavalcade. Directly behind Birney were the divisions of Mott, Gibbon, and Barlow, with Colonel Paul Frank's brigade covering the rear. It is about a five-mile march from Todd's Tavern to Plank Road, and, as a result, it was nearly 2:00 P.M. before the van of the Second Corps arrived at the intersection.

As Getty's men threw up log and earth breastworks in the woods and across Plank Road, Hill's Confederates were also preparing for battle. By 2:00 P.M. all of Heth's division was up and entrenching while Wilcox's division, which was near Parker's Store, was up shortly thereafter.[7]

General Lee and his staff, who had been riding with Heth's command, pulled off into the Tapp farm clearing at about noon. This farm consisted of a small house, corncrib, and log stable and was located in the northwest corner of the field. (The farmhouse burned sometime after the battle but the clearing is still there.) In this field Lee's aides pitched his tents and set up the Confederate command post.[8]

Lieutenant Colonel William Poague, commanding one of Hill's artillery battalions, posted his twelve guns along the edge of the woods on the west side of the field, while the remainder of the Confederate Third Corps artillery went into park, along with the trains, at Parker's Store. In the meantime, the ringing of axes and occasional skirmish firing along Plank Road was nearly drowned out by the sharp rattle of musketry to the north, where a major battle was underway on the turnpike.

2. *Fifth Corps Action Begins*

It takes time to maneuver great masses of men in such twisted brush as faced the armies in the Wilderness, and, as a result, it was nearly one o'clock before Warren's line of battle went forward— over five hours after Meade's decision to engage the enemy. By noon General Crawford's division was finally moving to the right to establish contact with General Wadsworth; Colonel William McCandless's brigade led the march, followed by Colonel Joseph Fisher's troops. It was, however, some time before Crawford was able to make the connection with Wadsworth, who had been in position on Griffin's left, awaiting word to advance, since 10:30 A.M.

Wadsworth's line of battle, formed in the woods just east of Hagerson's Field, was anchored on the left by the brigade of Brigadier General James Rice; in the center by Colonel Roy Stone's Pennsylvanians; and on the right, under Lysander Cutler, by the remnants of the old Iron Brigade, which had been nearly obliterated at Gettysburg. Colonel Andrew Denison's Marylanders, from Robinson's division, were formed in line of support to the rear of the Iron Brigade, while Robinson's remaining two brigades were massed in reserve near the Lacy house.

Griffin's division, meanwhile, defended the extreme right of the Fifth Corps and was deployed along the eastern edge of Sanders' Field, covering both sides of the turnpike. Joseph Bartlett's brigade occupied the south side of the road, with Colonel Jacob Sweitzer's brigade supporting his rear.[9]

Formed in the woods on the western side of Sanders' Field, directly in front of Bartlett's brigade and extending for some dis-

tance beyond Wadsworth's left, was the Confederate division of Robert Rodes, along with Brigadier General John Jones's Virginia brigade of Johnson's division. Jones, who was formed just south of the turnpike with his left touching the road, was supported by Brigadier General Cullen Battle's Alabamans. To the right of Battle's brigade, extending Rodes's division to the south, were the commands of generals George Doles and Junius Daniel, respectively. The fact that Rodes's division overlapped the left of Wadsworth's line could prove particularly dangerous to the entire Federal Fifth Corps unless Crawford could quickly make the connection with Wadsworth and fill the half-mile gap that existed in Warren's lines.

As of 1:00 P.M., the only Union troops in position on the north side of the turnpike were the soldiers of Brigadier General Romeyn Ayres's brigade, which was holding Griffin's right. Opposing this lone Federal brigade and entrenched on the opposite side of Sanders' Field was Edward Johnson's entire division, minus Jones's brigade. Brigadier General George "Maryland" Steuart's brigade was deployed directly across from Ayres, while the brigades of James Walker and Leroy Stafford, on Steuart's left, extended the division to the north. Johnson's division thus overlapped the right of Ayres's brigade by several hundred yards, putting the right of Warren's line in the same peril as his left.[10]

Finally, General Ewell's Confederate Second Corps reserve was made up of the three brigades of Jubal Early's division, which were held in rear of the corps, straddling the turnpike. Harry Hays's Louisianans were formed on the north side of the road, while John B. Gordon's Georgia brigade occupied the south side. John Pegram's Virginians were deployed directly across the road, to the rear of Hays and Gordon.[11]

Meanwhile, returning to the Federal lines, while Crawford's men were converging on Wadsworth's left, the Sixth Corps division of Horatio Wright was marching down Culpeper Mine Road, from Germanna Road, on its way to support the right of Ayres's troops. As Warren's attack began, however, Wright's soldiers were engaged in a heavy skirmish with the 1st North Carolina Cavalry,

Officers of the Second Corps. Seated is Major General Winfield Scott Hancock. Standing are three of his division commanders. They are, left to right, Brigadier General Francis C. Barlow, Major General David Birney, and Brigadier General John Gibbon. *Courtesy National Archives.*

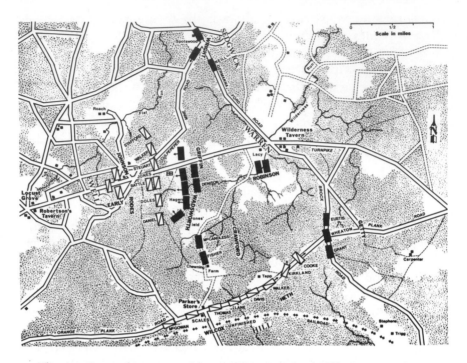

The situation at about 1 P.M., May 5. Warren's Federal Fifth Corps was just beginning its attack against Ewell's Confederates, who were entrenched on the western side of Sanders' Field. The advance of Sedgwick's Sixth Corps was moving into position on the left of Warren, with the exception of three brigades of Getty's division, which had, for the time being, secured the important Brock-Plank crossing against the advance units of A. P. Hill's Confederate Third Corps.

as well as sharpshooters from Walker's Stonewall Brigade. These Confederates slowed Wright's advance considerably, and it was nearly three o'clock before either Wright or Crawford were in position to support Warren's exposed flanks.

It is plain from the positions held by the opposing forces that most of the fighting on this portion of the field took place in and around Sanders' Field. This clearing (it has since grown over) which, as stated earlier, extended on both sides of the turnpike, was approximately 800 yards long (north to south) and 400 yards wide. A gully ran the length of the clearing, creating something of a natural hazard for troops trying to cross it while under fire.[12]

Sometime around 1:00 P.M., Warren gave the order to advance, and the fight was on. His 22,000 Federal enlisted men stood against

Lieutenant General Richard S. Ewell, C.S.A. *Courtesy USAMHI.*

This rare photograph shows Sanders' Field as it appeared shortly after the war. It was across this open ground and into the woods in the distance that Warren's Fifth Corps launched its savage assault against Ewell's Confederates during the afternoon of May 5. The turnpike can be seen as it runs westward toward Locust Grove, as can the gully, which cuts across the center of the picture. The white picket fence seen to the left of the turnpike encloses an old soldiers' cemetery, which was present at the time of the battle. *Courtesy USAMHI.*

The remains of Ewell's entrenchments, just south of the turnpike in what was Sanders' Field. *Photo by Ron Carlson.*

Ewell's 17,000 Confederates; however, not all of these men saw action during this phase of the battle, as some were to remain in reserve.[13]

As soon as the signal was given, Wadsworth's and Griffin's troops (who were by this time keyed up to the highest degree in anticipation of a clash) advanced simultaneously, with bayonets fixed. General Bartlett's brigade moved forward in two lines of battle. In the first line, from left to right, were the 18th Massachusetts, 83d Pennsylvania, and the 44th New York. In the second line were the regiments of the 118th Pennsylvania and the 20th Maine, the 20th on the right of the line with its right resting on the road. Deployed as skirmishers in advance of the entire brigade were the soldiers of the 1st Michigan.[14]

No sooner had Bartlett's men broken out of the woods and into the field than Jones's rebels opened up on them. With a "hurrah!" the Union boys charged across row after row of corn stubble, down into the gully and up the opposite side, coming to close quarters with the Confederates as soon as they had reached the woods on the far side of the clearing. General Bartlett rode up at the head of the second line, and as it cleared the woods he shouted "come on, boys, let us go in and help them."[15]

Lieutenant Holman S. Melcher, of the 20th Maine, remembered the scene:

> The bugles sounded the "charge" and advancing to the edge of the field, we saw the first line of battle about half way across it, receiving a terribly fatal fire from the enemy in the woods on the farther side. This field was less than a quarter mile across, had been planted with corn the year before, and was now dry and dusty. We could see the spurts of dust started up all over the field by the bullets of the enemy, as they spattered on it like the big drops of a coming shower you have so often seen along a dusty road.[16]

General Wadsworth's command advanced to the left of Griffin's men, with Cutler's Iron Brigade in direct support of Bartlett's left. The Iron Brigade, which was made up of western troops, was formed in two lines of battle. From left to right, the first line consisted of the 24th Michigan, the 19th Indiana, and the 2d and 7th Wisconsin. In the second line, from left to right, the 6th

Wisconsin was in support of the 2d Wisconsin and the 7th Indiana supported the 7th Wisconsin.[17]

If there was any semblance of a battle line when the Fifth Corps attack began, it was soon lost in the bushes and briars surrounding Sanders' Field. Most of the regiments lost sight of their colors, so the men fought in little groups, sticking together as best they could. In many places the brush was so thick that some units were forced to advance in single-file lines, with the man in front backing through the entanglement to make a path for the others. The only way a regiment could tell where it was headed in this wooded maze was with a compass, a tool many units lacked, or, if they had one, they found it did not work.

As Wadsworth's division pressed forward, the Iron Brigade lost direction and inclined to the right, losing its connection with Stone on the left and Bartlett on the right. As they moved to the northwest, Cutler's men charged across the field and into the rebel lines and when they hit, they hit hard. Jones's Confederate brigade was shattered after being hit simultaneously by Cutler on the right and Bartlett in the front. During the struggle, Private J. N. Opel, of the 7th Indiana, single-handedly captured the colors of the 50th Virginia, for which he was later awarded the Congressional Medal of Honor. While attempting to rally the pieces of his broken command, General Jones was killed, as was his aide, Captain Early, a nephew of General Jubal Early.

After Jones's command had crumbled, the Federals continued on and piled into Battle's brigade, in the rear of Jones, taking it completely by surprise and driving most of it off in total rout, along with the left of Doles's brigade. The crushed fragments of these three Confederate brigades (Jones, Doles, and Battle), fell back in confusion for nearly a mile and it was some time before they were of any further use in battle.[18]

The sound of gunfire during this fight was incredible, for it was of a higher pitch than usually heard during battle, due to the limited use of artillery. One veteran later commented that "the loudest and longest peals of thunder were no more to be compared to it in depth or volume than the rippling of a trout brook to the roaring of Niagra." General Humphreys stated simply that the noise "approached the sublime."[19]

Because of the extreme intensity of this musket fire, the dry tinder and dead leaves that blanketed the woods soon caught fire from the musket flashes. A stiff wind was blowing, and it fanned the little flames so that half of the Fifth Corps's front was soon ablaze. Many of the wounded who could not walk burned to death, and their screams could be heard even above the tremendous roar of battle. The strong scent of gunpowder, prominent in any battle, was soon mixed with the sick stench of burning flesh, giving this fight a gruesome characteristic unlike any engagement the army had previously experienced.

Frank Wilkenson wrote one of the best personal accounts of the fighting in Warren's front that afternoon. The battery to which this young private belonged had been put in reserve to the rear of the army, but Wilkenson, who had not yet experienced battle, was overcome by a spirit of adventure and soon found himself at the front:

> I stood behind a large oak tree, and peeped around its trunk. I heard bullets "spat" into this tree, and I suddenly realized that I was in danger. My heart thumped wildly for a minute; then my throat and mouth felt dry and queer. A dead sergeant lay at my feet, with a hole in his forehead just above his left eye. Out of this wound bits of brain oozed, and slid on a bloody trail into his eye, and thence over his cheek to the ground. I leaned over the body to feel of it. It was still warm. He could not have been dead for over five minutes. As I stooped over the dead man, bullets swept past me, and I became angry at the danger I had foolishly gotten into. I unbuckled the deadman's cartridge belt, and strapped it around me, and then I picked up his rifle. I remember standing behind the large oak tree, and dropping the ramrod into the rifle to see if it was loaded. It was not. So I loaded it, and before I fairly understood what had taken place, I was in the rear rank of the battle-line, which had surged back on the crest of a battle billow, bareheaded, and greatly excited, and blazing away at an indistinct, smoke-and-tree-obscured line of men clad in gray and slouch-hatted.[20]

As Rodes's division began to fall apart, only Daniel's brigade, along with the right of Doles's command, managed to hang on. General Daniel threw his Confederates in against Wadsworth's left and center brigades, which, as will be recalled, belonged to Rice and Stone. Unfortunately, Stone's men were hopelessly bogged down in a swamp with no support on either flank, as Rice had moved off to the northwest, just as Cutler had, exposing Stone's left to Confederate fire.

Just as Daniel was beginning his attack, up came General John B. Gordon's Georgians from Early's reserve division, shouting the spine-chilling rebel yell. Gordon thrust his troops head on into Stone's surprised Pennsylvanians, who were somehow able to pull themselves out of the morass and head for the rear. A member of the 121st Pennsylvania later wrote an enlightening, if not amusing, account of the predicament then faced by his brigade:

> The regiment had not progressed far through the swamp when, without seeing a single foe, a sheet of fire opened on the line—if line it could be called—already in great disorder from its endeavors to work through the mire and entangled bushes. Here the men were almost entirely at the mercy of the foe, who, no doubt, had been lying in wait for them for some time. The engagement at this point was of short duration, but quite lively while it lasted, and not at all satisfactory to our men, who could not do much execution while floundering about in the mud and water up to their middle. The obstacles in their way, however, were the means of saving the lives of many, as the aim of the enemy was merely at random, the balls passing harmlessly overhead. Neither combatant could see the other, and the only guide as to the locality of the opponent was the noise of the scrambling through the network of briers and floundering through the mud and water, as well as the irregular musketry fire on either side. It was evident before long that this locality was altogether too unhealthy; and when the order to retire was given, the scrambling to get out of that mud hole was amusing as well as ridiculous. The troops on the right had been withdrawn, and after extricating themselves from that champion mud hole of mud holes, it required considerable agility to catch up to the balance of the troops and regain their place in the division. During this stampede it very naturally followed that the men became somewhat confused and more or less scattered, many not being sure which way to turn. An amusing incident occurred right here, when Colonel Dana, of the 143d Penna. Vols., accosted Sergeant Dempsey, of Company "E", as related by the sergeant. The colonel, it seems, was making straight for the rebel lines, and, hailing Dempsey, asked, "What troops are those over there?" "The rebs," replied the sergeant, who had good reason to know. "Can't be," said the colonel, continuing on, no doubt to investigate. The sergeant replied: "All right, colonel, go over and you'll find out, for I've been there," and adds in his memorandum, "he

went, and I went down to the rear, you may bet. He went down to Dixie." [21]

Stone's rout proved disastrous for Wadsworth's entire division, as Gordon leaped into the gap vacated by the Pennsylvanians, split his command in two, and wheeled the halves onto the exposed flanks of Rice and Cutler with catastrophic effect. [22]

In the meantime, General Rodes had rallied the previously shaken brigades of Battle and Doles and, acting in concert with Gordon's attack, drove them into the front of Wadsworth's troops, routing the Iron Brigade for the first time in its history. Adjutant G. M. Woodward, of the 2d Wisconsin, who had stayed behind to watch the Confederates advance, heard someone behind him say: "Adjutant, what be I going to do with this flag?" Turning, Woodward saw the colorbearer standing in the woods, all alone, holding his flagstaff for all to see. Both immediately retreated along with the rest of the regiment, under a hail of bullets. [23]

Rice's brigade, which had not only been flanked on its right by Gordon but also on the left by Doles, was forced to follow the same course as the rest of the division and slowly fell back. Colonel J. W. Hoffman, commanding the 56th Pennsylvania, formed his men at the crest of a ridge in a bold attempt to delay the Confederate pursuit, but General Wadsworth, who had a remarkable capacity for keeping a clear head in the most trying situations, rode up to Hoffman and told him not to risk his regiment in such a futile effort. The 56th then withdrew to the Lacy farm, where the rest of the division was reforming. [24]

Having no support on either flank and heavily pressed in the middle by Rodes's rallied troops, Bartlett's brigade was compelled to retire, completing the withdrawal of Warren's forces on the south side of the turnpike. It was at about this time that a strange incident occurred that could have happened nowhere but in the Wilderness. During Bartlett's retreat, all of the troops had fallen back except Company F of the 20th Maine, commanded by Lieutenant Melcher. This small unit, which consisted of no more than eighteen men, had somehow gotten cut off from the rest of the regiment in the dense woods on the western side of Sanders' Field and thus did not receive the word to retire with the rest of the brigade. As the firing around the little group diminished, the men quickly discovered that there were no longer any rebels in their front; in fact, there were no other troops to be seen anywhere. To find out exactly what had happened, Melcher and a few other men worked their way through the brush to the turnpike, hoping to see other Federals on the road. Upon reaching the pike, however, the only troops in sight were a large body of Confederates moving eastward down the road toward the original Federal position, to the rear of Melcher's command. The situation, by now, was clear. Finding themselves in the rear of the enemy and cut off from any other Union troops, the company decided to fight its way back, rather than risk being captured and winding up in Libby Prison. Melcher shouted "Every man load his rifle and follow me." Then, after forming in the rear of the Confederates, who were busily engaged with the Federals in their front, Melcher's men fired into the rebel ranks and charged forward with fixed bayonets, shouting "surrender!" In the confusion that ensued, the Confederates thought they had been flanked by nothing less than a regiment and, miraculously, Company F reached the safety of the Union lines, suffering only two killed and six wounded, and capturing thirty-two prisoners to boot![25]

3. Ayres Advances North of the Turnpike

The fight on the north side of the turnpike was not going much better for the Fifth Corps than the one to the south of the road. Ayres's brigade advanced in two lines of battle, supported on its left by two guns under Lieutenant Shelton of Battery D, 1st New York Light Artillery. The 140th New York, its left touching the road, held the left of the first line, with the 2d, 11th, 12th, 15th, and 17th United States Infantry regiments extending to the right. From left to right in the second line were the regiments of the 146th New York and the 91st and 155th Pennsylvania.[26]

Shortly after 1:00 P.M. (about the time Bartlett and Cutler were attacking Jones), Ayres's first line emerged from the woods into the sunny glade. These men did not charge but marched in perfect formation, receiving a murderous fire from Steuart's Confederates, who were concealed in the woods on the opposite side of the field. Walker's and Stafford's brigades, which overlapped the right of Ayres's line, poured a fierce enfilade fire into the advancing troops. Although the Minié balls were flying fast and thick, Ayres's men did not waver but pressed on with colors held high through the

Ewell's breastworks at the edge of the woods on the western side of Sanders' Field. From a photograph taken soon after the war. *Courtesy USAMIII.*

leaden storm, as their comrades fell all about them. After marching across the field for what must have seemed an eternity, the men in blue at last reached the other side and plunged into the woods, greeting the rebels with swinging muskets and bayonets.

After the first line of battle had reached its destination, the second wave went in with a cheer. The 146th New York, also known as Garrard's Tiger Zouaves, clad in bright red uniforms, lunged across the field to the support of the 140th. One Zouave remembered: "Just as we reached the gully, a withering volley of musketry was poured into our line, followed a moment later by another. Many threw their arms wildly into the air as they fell backward, the death-rattle in their throats."[27]

Before long the effective flanking fire delivered by Walker and Stafford became too much for the Union troops to bear and all of Ayres's brigade except the 140th and 146th New York regiments was compelled to retreat to the eastern edge of the clearing. Somehow the New Yorkers held on, displaying tremendous feats of courage as the fighting around them became more intense.

In an effort to lend support to these troops, Shelton's guns fired their first and only round into the Confederate lines; however, in doing so they also hit the rear of the 140th as well as the front of the oncoming 146th, making it all the more difficult for those brave troops to hold their already precarious position. A soldier of the 146th later recalled that the artillery fire "obliqued across the front of our line, and some of us were so close that we could feel the strong wind of the discharges."[28]

Just as the 146th reached the rebel line, Steuart's men began to close in on the flanks of the New Yorkers and ultimately forced the Zouaves to retire to the limited protection offered by the gully. In the meantime, Lieutenant Shelton, finding that his artillery was dangerously far advanced, made an attempt to withdraw his pieces back to the safety of the Lacy farm, where the rest of the Fifth Corps artillery was parked. This effort, however, proved futile. A detachment of the 1st North Carolina had discovered Shelton's peril, went for the guns, and, after a bloody hand-to-hand struggle, captured them and the wounded Shelton.

At about this time the rallied brigades of Battle and Doles made their countercharge against Bartlett and Cutler. Some of Bartlett's men were apparently so severely routed that they made a dash for the rear and, without regard to anything in their path, overran the

North Carolinians who were just hoisting their colors on the captured cannon. The surprised Confederates jumped into the ravine, temporarily abandoning the guns, and continued the close fighting with the Zouaves.

As Bartlett's frightened troops ran to safety, up came Battle and Doles, following closely on the heels of the retreating Federals. When Battle's brigade broke into the field, some men of the 6th Alabama noticed the unmanned guns and immediately claimed them for their own. This act so infuriated the men of the 1st North Carolina that they jumped out of the ditch and announced that the guns were rightfully theirs. For a moment the Tarheels were more enraged at the Alabamans who were attempting to steal their capture than at their Yankee foes; however, just as the Confederates were rolling up their sleeves and about to go at each other, the argument was broken up by a Union counterattack. Ayres's main force, along with a portion of Sweitzer's brigade, which had crossed the road to serve as a rallying point for Ayres's outnumbered troops, moved forward to relieve the pressure on the hard-pressed New Yorkers. Advancing through the whispy clouds of battle smoke that were settling over the field, Ayres succeeded in forcing the Confederates back into the woods, thus allowing the two New York regiments to withdraw. An attempt was also made to recapture Shelton's guns, but the sharp firing of the rebels prevented the Federals from getting too near the pieces; as a result, the guns remained unclaimed until the night of May 6, when the Confederates were able to pull them into their lines.[29]

As if the bullets were not enemy enough for the troops fighting in Sanders' Field that afternoon, the dry grass and leaves caught fire, and before long several fires were sweeping across the clearing. An effort was made by men on both sides to reach the wounded, but in many cases it was hopeless, and the bodies of living and dead soldiers were consumed by the flames. The cartridge boxes that were strapped to the waists of the fallen men were eventually ignited as the fires closed in. One veteran remembered the horrible scene:

> The almost cheerful "Pop! Pop!" of the cartridges gave no hint of the dreadful horror their noise bespoke. Swept by the flames, the trees, bushes, and logs which Confederates had thrown up as breastworks now took fire and dense clouds of smoke rolled across the clearing, choking unfortunates who were exposed to it

and greatly hindering the work of the rescuers. The clearing now became a raging inferno in which many of the wounded perished. The bodies of the dead were blackened and burned beyond all possibility of recognition, a tragic conclusion to this day of horror.[30]

If anyone had said that afternoon that Warren's fight had not gone badly for the Federals, they would also have had to admit that neither had it gone well. According to Lieutenant Colonel Lyman of Meade's staff, "The pike was a sad spectacle indeed; it was really obstructed with trains and ambulances and with the wounded on foot; all had the same question, over and over again, 'How far to the 5th Corps' hospital?' "[31] There was, however, very little that Grant or Meade could have done to better the situation, for their hands were tied. Their presence on the front line would have been of no help to anyone, since they would have been unable to see what was happening; therefore, they remained at their headquarters, fed the troops into battle, and read the dispatches as they came in.

At 2:45 P.M., General Griffin, accompanied by an aide, rode up to Meade's headquarters and dismounted. He appeared to be very upset and demanded to know what had happened to Wright's division, which was supposed to have supported his right during the advance. He stated that he had driven Ewell back three-quarters of a mile but that he was forced to retreat because he had no help on either of his flanks.

General Rawlins, Grant's chief of staff, became very angry, considered Griffin's language mutinous, and demanded that he be placed under arrest. It seems that Grant was of the same mind and asked Meade: "Who is this General Gregg? You ought to arrest him!" Meade replied: "It's Griffin, not Gregg; and it's only his way of talking." Meade's response got Griffin off the hook, and, having aired his feelings, Griffin got back on his horse and returned to his command.[32]

By 3:00 P.M. Wright's division was finally moving in on the right of the Fifth Corps, allowing Warren to consolidate his entire command south of the turnpike on the open ground near the Lacy farm. Entrenching on the left was Crawford's division, which had at last rejoined the rest of the corps. Fisher's brigade was formed on the left of that division, with McCandless on the right.

Griffin's division was now aligned to Crawford's right; his

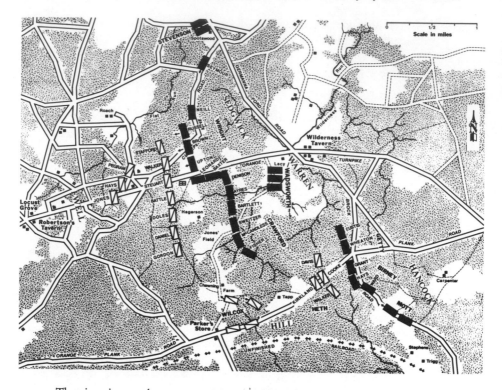

The situation at about 3 P.M., May 5. Although the fighting between Warren and Ewell had ended south of Orange Turnpike, Sedgwick was continuing the attack north of the road. The tense situation near the Brock-Plank
crossing continued to unfold as Hill deployed his Confederate Third Corps
and Hancock's Federal Second Corps continued to arrive in support of
Getty.

brigades were, from left to right, Sweitzer, Bartlett, and Ayres. To
the right of Griffin were Robinson's three brigades. Denison was
immediately to the right of Griffin. Leonard's and Baxter's
brigades were in a line perpendicular to the rest of Warren's command, in front of Denison and facing south, parallel to the turnpike.

For some unexplainable reason, none of Robinson's brigades
had been engaged that afternoon. Leonard and Baxter remained in
general reserve, and Denison, who had been formed and ready in
the rear of the Iron Brigade, never received the word to advance. If
these troops had been sent into action in time to follow up Bart-

lett's and Cutler's effective rout of Jones, Battle, and Doles, it is very likely that Warren would have punched an irreparable hole in Lee's army. For whatever reason, these troops were not sent in and a great opportunity was missed—such are the fortunes of war!

Meanwhile, as the rest of the Fifth Corps was busy throwing up dirt and logs to strengthen the new line of defense, Wadsworth's division, which had probably suffered the worst of the fighting that afternoon, was recuperating near the Lacy house from the effects of Gordon's counterattack, and was out of service for several hours.[33]

As the Fifth Corps was reforming, Ewell also took the time to perfect his lines. Edward Johnson's division remained in about the same order as before, except it had moved slightly to the right. Stafford and Walker remained north of the turnpike, but Steuart's brigade was now deployed directly across the road. This move was evidently made to allow the brigades of Pegram and Hays, of Early's division, to take position to the left of Johnson. Jones's still shaken troops remained in reserve on the turnpike and to the rear of the rest of the Confederate Second Corps.

Rodes's division was in line to Johnson's right, on the south side of the road; the brigades were, from left to right, Battle, Doles, and Daniel. Gordon's brigade of Early's division was now in formation on Daniel's right.[34]

Although heavy skirmishing continued on this front for several more hours, the fighting in Warren's sector was over for the day. As of 3:00 P.M., Wright was attacking all along his front, and, of more immediate concern, the threatening situation on Plank Road was quickly coming to a head.

CHAPTER FOUR

Carnage on Plank Road

1. Getty Makes a Second Assault

As of 2:00 P.M., it will be recalled, there was a general lull all along Hancock's and Getty's front, near the Brock-Plank intersection. The lull was fortunate, for Hancock's troops had not yet arrived but were, at that moment, pushing their way up Brock Road, which was jammed with the Second Corps' combat trains and artillery.

At noon General Humphreys sent a dispatch to Hancock, detailing instructions for him to launch a general attack down Plank Road:

> The enemy's infantry drove our regiment of cavalry from Parker's Store down the plank road, and are now moving down it in force. A. P. Hill's corps is part of it. How much not known. General Getty's division has been sent to drive them back, but he may not be able to do so. The major-general commanding directs that you move out the plank road toward Parker's Store, and, supporting Getty, drive the enemy beyond Parker's Store, and occupy that place and unite with Warren on the right of it.[1]

It appears that the courier who was bearing this dispatch had gotten lost enroute from Meade's headquarters to the Brock-Plank crossing, for General Hancock did not receive the message until 2:40 P.M., nearly two hours after he and his staff had reached the intersection. Judging by the time sent and the time received of other dispatches from Meade to Hancock, it should not have taken much more than an hour for the delivery of the above dispatch, which actually took over two and a half hours to reach Hancock. At any rate, when Hancock finally did receive the message at 2:40 P.M., another courier rode up with orders sent by Meade at 1:30 P.M., which basically reiterated the orders sent at noon. Upon

70

receipt of both dispatches, Hancock replied: "Your dispatches of 12 m. and 1:30 p.m. just received. I am forming my corps on Getty's left, and will order an advance as soon as prepared. The ground over which I must pass is very bad—a perfect thicket. I shall form two divisions with brigade front. General Getty says he has not heard of Warren's left, probably because he has not advanced far enough."[2]

In the meantime, much to the relief of everyone, the head of the Second Corps arrived at the crossing at about 2:00 P.M. Birney's heavily perspiring men formed in two lines of battle south of Plank Road and to the left of Colonel Grant's Vermont Brigade. Brigadier General Alexander Hays's brigade occupied the right of Birney's line, while Brigadier General J. H. H. Ward's brigade was formed on the left. By 4:00 P.M. Mott's division was moving in on Birney's left; Colonel Robert McAllister's brigade was on the right and Colonel William Brewster's Excelsior Brigade on the left. The regimental formation of Birney's and Mott's divisions is not known. As Hancock's troops arrived they were immediately set to work with pick, ax, and shovel, constructing log and earthen breastworks. (The remains of these trenches can still be seen today after nearly 120 years of exposure to the elements.)[3]

At 3:15 P.M. Meade instructed Humphreys to send the following orders to Hancock, instructing him to begin his attack immediately: "The commanding general directs that Getty attack at once, and that you support him with your whole corps, one division on his right and one division on his left, the others in reserve; or such other disposition as you may think proper, but the attack up the plank road must be made at once."[4]

These orders were delivered to Hancock at 4:05 P.M. by Lieutenant Colonel Lyman, who later described the scene at the crossing in a letter to his wife: "At the crossing of the dotted crossroad with the plank, sat Hancock, on his fine horse—the preux chevalier of this campaign—a glorious soldier, indeed! The musketry was crashing in the woods in our front, and stray balls—too many to be pleasant—were coming about. It's all very well for novels, but I don't like such places and go there only when ordered."[5]

In an attempt to carry out Meade's orders of 3:15 P.M. to the letter, Hancock made an effort to deploy his troops as suggested in the dispatch. At 4:05 P.M. he informed General Meade: "GEN-

Remains of Hancock's entrenchments just north of Plank Road. *Photo by Ron Carlson.*

ERAL: I have just received your order to attack one division on the right and one on the left of General Getty. I had previously made arrangements to attack with two divisions on his left, but as General Getty was going in, I have sent General Mott with him (on his left), and General Birney will go in on his right as soon as possible. He will soon be there."[6]

By 4:15 P.M. Getty's troops were advancing through the brush, formed in two lines of battle. Eustis's brigade was in formation on the far right of the division, north of Plank Road. Poised for the attack in Eustis's first line were, from left to right, the 10th Massachusetts and the 2d Rhode Island regiments. From left to right in the second line were the 7th and 37th Massachusetts.

Immediately to the left of Eustis was Wheaton's brigade, which was now entirely north of Plank Road, with its left touching the road. Wheaton's first line consisted of, left to right, the 102d and 139th Pennsylvania and the 62d New York. In the second line, in the same order, were the troops of the 98th and 93d Pennsylvania regiments.

L. A. Grant's Vermonters held the left of the division, just to the south of Plank Road. The Vermont Brigade's first line of attack was made up of, from left to right, the 3d and 4th regiments. In the second line, also from left to right, were the 6th and 2d regiments; the 5th Vermont was kept in reserve. Two guns of Battery F, 1st Pennsylvania Light Artillery, under the direction of Captain Bruce Ricketts, were in position at the crossroad, facing west down Plank Road, in support of Getty's advance.[7]

General Henry Heth's Confederate division was in line of battle in the woods, a couple of hundred yards west of Getty's men. General Joseph Davis's Mississippi brigade was formed on the north side of Plank Road, holding the left of Heth's line; General John Cooke's North Carolinians were deployed across the road, occupying Heth's center; General Henry Walker's brigade was in formation on the right of the division, just south of the road, and General William Kirkland's brigade was massed as a reserve to the rear of Cooke.[8]

At 4:00 P.M., by order of General Lee, Wilcox's division was marching north across the Chewning farm in order to connect with Ewell's right and thus fill the gap that existed between Hill and Ewell. A strange occurrence had taken place earlier in the day, which prompted Lee to order Wilcox to fill the gap. It seems that a

Confederate breastworks on the south side of Plank Road. From a photograph taken shortly after the war. *Courtesy USAMHI.*

regiment of Union soldiers had broken out of the woods and into the northern portion of the Tapp farm clearing and, upon doing so, spotted a group of Confederate officers in the center of the field. Lee, Stuart, and Hill were sitting under a tree in the clearing, casually conversing, and if the Federals had decided to rush them, they would have made the greatest capture of the war, for there were no Confederate troops in the immediate area to stop them.

Spotting the blue-clad troops emerging from the forest, Stuart jumped up in surprise, while Lee hurried off to inform one of his aides to ride back and tell Wilcox to get his division up on the double! Fortunately for the Confederates, the Union officer commanding the regiment turned his unit around and headed it back into the woods from whence it came, possibly in utter disbelief at what he had just seen sitting in the clearing. This was the closest Lee had come to being captured during the entire course of the war, and the Federals had missed it. It was the one golden opportunity which, more than any other, would have demoralized the ranks of the Army of Northern Virginia, and it had slipped through their fingers—a chance that did not present itself again.

Wilcox's brigades, however, were soon up, and, much to the relief of General Lee, the gap between Ewell and Hill was filled, at least for the time being. General James Lane's North Carolina troops, at the head of Wilcox's division, marched across the Chewning farm and made the connection with Ewell's corps, while the brigades of Edward Thomas, Alfred Scales, and Samuel McGowan extended the division to his right, stretching southward across the Chewning plateau to the northern boundary of Widow Tapp's farm.[9]

As Getty's bluecoats advanced, they encountered some of the thickest brush to be found in the Wilderness, and here the officers and men of the division first discovered the type of battle in which they had become engaged. General Stevens wrote of the terrain that was encountered by Getty's men that afternoon:

> This point is the very centre and type of the Wilderness. The scrubby woods and tangled thickets stretch away on every side, interminably to all appearance. The narrow roads offer the only means of going anywhere or of seeing anything. Once off, then low ridges and hollows succeed each other, without a single feature to serve as a landmark, and no one but an experienced woods-

man with a compass could keep his bearings and position or preserve his course.[10]

L. A. Grant's Vermonters went crashing into the woods and
encountered heavy resistance from the Confederate brigades of
Cooke and Walker after having advanced only a short distance. As
the 4th Vermont became engaged, the 3d, to its left, inclined to the
left and was greeted by a hail of lead. Although it was obvious that
they were in over their heads, these Green Mountain men continued to press forward, encouraged by the roar of Ricketts's guns,
which were just going into action. The first line of Grant's brigade
advanced to the crest of a ridge overlooking a swamp, and, having
walked directly into the rebels' line of fire, the men took cover
behind trees, stumps, and anything else that offered slight protection from the whizzing lead balls.

Minutes after the first line went in, the 6th and 2d regiments,
occupying the second line, moved to its support. The 2d Vermont
took a position alongside the 4th, while the 6th Vermont relieved
the thinned-out ranks of the 3d, which then retired to the rear,
where the 5th regiment was still waiting in reserve. Colonel Grant
recounts the fight in his report of operations:

> As soon as the first volleys were over, our men hugged the
> ground as closely as possible, and kept up a rapid fire; the enemy
> did the same. The rebels had the advantage of position, inasmuch
> as their line was partially protected by a slight swell of ground,
> while ours was on nearly level ground. The attempt was made to
> dislodge them from that position, but the moment our men rose to
> advance the rapid and constant fire of musketry cut them down
> with such slaughter that it was found impracticable to do more
> than maintain our then present position. The enemy could not
> advance on us for the same reason.[11]

It soon became apparent to General Getty that the Vermont
Brigade was desperately hard pressed, and he appealed to General
Birney for help. Hays's brigade of Birney's division was already
moving over to the far right of Getty's line, but Ward's brigade was
available and was ordered to form to the rear of Grant's brigade as
a support unit. Ward detailed three regiments to go to the immediate support of the Vermonters. The 141st Pennsylvania was
sent to the rescue of the 2d and 4th Vermont regiments, while the

40th New York and the 20th Indiana advanced to help the 5th Vermont. The remainder of Ward's brigade remained in formation on Brock Road, ready to go in wherever it was needed.[12] Colonel Grant continues his report:

> I went to Major Dudley, commanding the Fifth (Colonel Lewis having been previously wounded), and called his attention to the fact that the position of the enemy in his front was less protected than it was in front of the rest of the brigade, and asked him if he could, with the support of the two regiments in his rear, break the enemy's line. "I think we can," was the reply of the gallant major. I went to the commanders of those two regiments, and asked them to support the Fifth in its advance. The men rose and with a cheer answered, "We will." The order for the charge was given, and all advanced in good style, and the enemy partially gave way. The two rear regiments were thrown into some confusion, and soon halted and laid down, and Major Dudley, finding his regiment far in the advance, and exposed to a flank fire, wisely did the same. Our ammunition soon became well nigh exhausted, and a force from the Second Corps was sent in to relieve us. The regiments on the right were relieved first. As soon as the Second and Fourth were relieved and ordered to retire the enemy pressed forward and occupied the ground. So sudden was the enemy's advance that the staff officer who was sent to order back the Fifth fell into the hands of the enemy. The Fifth finding itself flanked judiciously retired. The brigade fell back to its former position on the Brock road. The Second Corps now held the front; darkness soon came on and the firing ceased.[13]

Grant's Vermonters suffered greater losses than any other Union brigade during the war. Within the next week, while engaged in the battles of the Wilderness and Spotsylvania Court House, Grant's brigade lost 1,645 of its 2,100 effective troops; it is said to have lost one thousand men in the Wilderness alone![14]

North of Plank Road, on Grant's right, Wheaton's brigade advanced in concert with that of Grant. No one can give a better account of the fighting on this front than General Wheaton himself:

> At 4 P.M., in conjunction with the rest of the division, the lines advanced, and notwithstanding the dense woods and underbrush, their alignments were well preserved. After an advance of about an eighth of a mile the skirmish line became warmly engaged, and a

short distance farther were involved in the line of battle, which at the same time received a terribly destructive fire, checking our advance, on a ridge about 50 yards from the enemy's line. The position, however, was held, the men keeping up a steady fire on the enemy, who occupied a crest not 50 yards in front. For nearly an hour the fighting was incessant, and the loss proportionately great, but the enemy was too strongly posted, and could not be dislodged. When the ammunition was exhausted by the troops in front, the first line was relieved from the second, which retained the advanced position until nearly 6 o'clock, when it was relieved by a portion of the Second Corps.[15]

Unfortunately, no in-depth account exists of the attack made by Eustis's brigade that afternoon. This much is known: its assault fell upon the front of Davis's Mississippi brigade but, to all appearances, it fared no better than Grant or Wheaton.

2. *The Second Corps Goes into Action*

Events along Hancock's front began to unfold rapidly at 5:00 P.M. Hays's brigade had at last made connection with the right of Getty's division and moved cautiously into the woods. Alexander Hays was the epitome of a brigade commander. Outwardly, he appeared to be a rough sort of man. He had a muscular build and sported a red beard; indeed, his appearance alone was enough to enforce any order he gave. Hays, however, was gentle-natured and it was not too difficult for his men to see through the coarse exterior and into his warm heart. He was a personal friend of both Grant and Hancock, having known them at West Point and served with them during the war with Mexico. Although Grant was Hays's superior, he respected the brigadier general's leadership qualities immensely. Grant later wrote of his comrade in arms: "With him it was 'Come, boys,' not 'Go.' "[16]

While riding along the front lines with his staff and seeing to the deployment of his brigade, Hays came across his old regiment, the 63d Pennsylvania, and stopped for a moment to offer a few brief words of encouragement to the men as they went into battle. Just as he began to speak, however, a bullet struck him in the skull, just above the cord of his hat. Hays reeled in his saddle, fell to the ground, and died a few hours thereafter.

Just that morning Hays had written a last letter to his wife and,

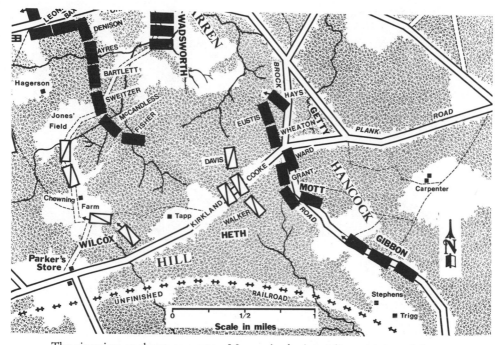

The situation at about 4:45 P.M., May 5, in the immediate vicinity of the Brock-Plank crossing. Hancock and Getty were now attacking all along their front against Heth's division of Hill's corps. Hays was attempting to deploy his brigade on the right of Getty, while Mott's division, in an effort to connect with Getty's left, lost direction and was broken. Meanwhile, Wilcox's division of Hill's corps was completing the connection with the right of Ewell's corps, thus filling the gap in Lee's army.

having read it, it is easy to believe that Hays had a premonition of his death. "This morning was beautiful," he wrote, "for

> "Lightly and brightly shone the sun,
> As if the morn was a jocund one."

Although we were anticipating a march at eight o'clock, it might have been an appropriate harbinger of the day of the regeneration of mankind; but it only brought to rememberance, through the throats of many bugles, that duty enjoined upon each one, perhaps, before the setting sun, to lay down a life for his country.[17]

The loss of Alexander Hays was a severe one for the Army of the Potomac. Both Grant and Hancock were said to have taken the

Brigadier General Alexander Hays, *Courtesy USAMHI.*

Remains of Hancock's entrenchments just west of Brock Road and north of Plank Road. The upright cannon marks the spot where Brigadier General Alexander Hays was killed May 5, 1864. *Photo by Ron Carlson.*

Monument to Brigadier General Alexander Hays, who was killed at this spot during the late afternoon of May 5, 1864. *Photo by Ron Carlson.*

news of his death quietly. Grant, however, did express the opinion that he was not at all surprised to hear that Hays had met his end at the head of his troops, saying: "It was just like him." Today a black, upright cannon marks the spot where this valiant Federal commander received his fatal wound.[18]

After Hays had fallen, the command of the brigade devolved upon the senior regimental commander (who this was is not certain), and the men continued to press forward on Getty's right. Sadly, there are only a few personal accounts of the fighting on Hays's front in existence today; however, the ones that are available are, at least, interesting. Color Sergeant D. G. Crotty, of the 3d Michigan Infantry, gave a brief description of his experiences that day: "The slaughter is fearful, men fall on every side, and my flag is receiving its share of bullets. Charge after charge is made on both sides. Sometimes we drive the enemy, and then they rally and drive us until both sides are almost exhausted, and night puts an end to our first day's conflict."[19]

Shortly after Getty's men had moved into the woods, Mott's division, on Getty's left, struck out through the forest. Brewster's Excelsior Brigade, formed in two lines of battle, occupied the left of Mott's line, with McAllister's brigade on the right, also formed in two lines. The division struggled through the thickets and quickly found itself under a galling fire from Walker's rebel brigade, which overlapped the left of Brewster's command. Shortly after 5:00 P.M. the entire division was routed. Colonel McAllister tells how it happened:

> An advance was ordered "by the right of companies to the front;" over the breastworks we went, but the dense thicket of underbrush made it impossible for the troops to keep their proper distance, so that when coming into line of battle, owing to pressure from the Sixth Corps on my right and the Excelsior Brigade on my left, there was not room to form line of battle in two ranks, which caused some little difficulty. We moved forward; the enemy's skirmishers opened on us, when I rode forward in front of line of battle and ordered the skirmish line to advance more rapidly. After moving a short distance the line of battle passed over the skirmish line and commenced firing. On receiving the enemy's fire, to my great astonishment, the line began to give away on the left. It is said first the Excelsior Brigade, then my left regiment—

First Massachusetts Volunteers—and regiment after regiment, like a rolling wave, fell back, and all efforts to rally them short of the breast-works were in vain.[20]

As soon as Mott's line crumbled, a staff officer from that division galloped up to Hancock to inform him of the disaster that had just taken place: "General Mott's division has broken, sir, and is coming back." Hancock was, of course, appalled at the event, and he immediately set off to restore order to the broken lines. Lyman recalled the scene:

> "tell him to stop them, sir!" roared Hancock in a voice like a trumpet. As he spoke, a crowd of troops came from the woods and fell back into the Brock Road. Hancock dashed among them "Halt here! Halt here. Form behind this rifle pit. Major Mitchell, go to Gibbon and tell him to come up on the doublequick!" It was a welcome sight to see Carroll's brigade coming along that Brock Road, he riding at their head as calm as a May morning, "Left face-prime-forward," and the line disappeared in the woods to waken the musketry with double violence. Carroll was soon brought back wounded.[21]

As related by Lyman, Gibbon's division was marching up the Brock Road as Hancock and his staff rode about Mott's line in an attempt to restore confidence to the shattered division. Colonel Samuel Sprigg Carroll's brigade led Gibbon's march that afternoon, followed by the brigades of brigadier generals Alexander Webb and Joshua Owen, respectively.

The bearded, red-haired Colonel Carroll, who hailed from a very distinguished family in the District of Columbia, was known to the officers of the army as "Brick" and had a knack for being in the right place at the right time. Upon arriving at Brock Road, General Hancock told Carroll to report with his entire command to General Birney, who had been given command of the right wing of Hancock's force. Birney ordered Carroll to put his brigade into action on the north side of Plank Road, to the rear of Wheaton's brigade. This movement was carried out by Carroll without hesitation. Meanwhile, Gibbon ordered Webb to aid Ward's reserve in staying the rout of Mott's troops, while Owen's troops were sent to the support of the Vermont Brigade.

Brock Road as it appears today, looking north from the Brock-Plank junction. *Photo by Ron Carlson.*

By 6:00 P.M., the Second Corps had relieved all of Getty's fought-out troops, which were then re-formed to the rear of Hancock's men. Carroll, at the head of his brigade, personally led his men in an assault against the Confederates in his front and succeeded in driving them back for nearly a quarter of a mile. Carroll, who was wounded in the attack, refused to leave the field, but after darkness set in he was persuaded to go to the rear and seek medical attention at the Second Corps hospital. He was, however, able to resume command the next morning.

Gibbon's division had arrived on the scene just in time to check the disaster that was about to befall Hancock's defenses on Brock Road. Not only had Mott's command fallen apart, but it was questionable how much longer Getty's weary soldiers could hang on. As Gibbon went into action, the woods along Brock Road were already boiling smoke from the intense musketry and the forest fires that had broken out in the dry brush. Many of the wounded were consumed by the flames, making the scene here every bit as grisly as the one taking place in Sanders' Field.

That afternoon the men in blue and gray fought as valiantly as at any other time during the war. There was no great panorama, as at Gettysburg, for the men could only catch occasional glimpses of the enemy they were fighting; moreover, the very fact that these men continued to fight virtually blindfolded and, for the most part, separated from their officers, was, in itself, a display of heroism. The fighting had been desperate but before the day was over it would worsen.

3. *Wilcox Threatens Hancock's Line*

Wilcox's Confederate division had not been in position on the Chewning farm heights for much more than an hour when, at about five o'clock, Lee ordered it to move out Plank Road and relieve Heth's exhausted troops. McGowan's brigade of South Carolinians was posted at the northern edge of Widow Tapp's field, on the far right of the division, when it received word to advance. Before the brigade marched off to face its uncertain future, however, the chaplain of the 1st South Carolina offered a brief prayer, and, for a moment, these hardened troops in gray stood silent, with hats off and heads bowed, while the roar of Heth's and Hancock's musketry resounded all around them and the smoke of battle drifted through their ranks. Then the order of "Attention!" rang out, and the regiment followed the rest of the brigade into action.[22]

Within half an hour after receiving the order to advance, the leading elements of Wilcox's division were swinging into line of battle on Plank Road. General McGowan deployed his South Carolinians directly across the road with their ranks extending a short distance to the right and left of the road. Scales's North Carolinians, who followed immediately behind McGowan's troops, filed off through the woods to the south of the road and formed their lines on McGowan's right.[23]

As soon as all was ready, McGowan's South Carolinians hurled themselves forward, passing Cooke's worn-out brigade and charging with full force into the Federal position in their front. Getty's troops, which had not yet been relieved by the Second Corps, bore the brunt of the attack. All reasoning suggests that these Union soldiers, who had fought about as hard as men could in the course of one day, should have been scattered in all directions by the onslaught of the fresh Confederate brigade; yet, remarkably, Getty's Federals had more to give and they unloaded their muskets into the ranks of the oncoming South Carolinians. General Stevens recounts McGowan's assault:

> At half-past five, after this bushwhacking combat had lasted an hour, numbers of the enemy were noticed jumping across the Plank Road, from side to side, about a hundred yards in front of our first line. Ricketts's section kept firing at these squads with cannister, but they always seemed to jump aside just in time to escape injury. At length the object of this performance was seen; namely, to draw the fire of our guns, when the enemy charged in force on both sides of the road. Our lines bent inward without breaking, and for an instant the assailants reached and planted a color at Ricketts's guns; but as the seasoned bow when strongly bent springs back with redoubled force, so the men of the white cross, who had momentarily given ground, with a cheer rushed forward upon the enemy and drove them headlong.
>
> It has been claimed that troops of the 2d corps retook these guns. Part of that corps was posted at the cross-roads in support, and may have moved up when the guns were endangered, but as an eye-witness, I know that the brave Vermonters and men of the

1st brigade next the Plank surged forward at the crisis without orders and drove the enemy from the guns, and that the presence of the 2d corps made no difference in the result.[24]

Although Stevens asserts that Getty's men recaptured Rickett's guns, the true identity of the troops who retook the pieces is one of the many unanswered questions of the battle. Hancock states in his report that Captain Butterfield of Carroll's staff, commanding detachments from the 14th Indiana and the 8th Ohio, repossessed the pieces. It would seem that a detailed description of the event such as Hancock gives could not be wrong; however, General Getty states in his report that portions of Grant's and Wheaton's brigades retook the guns. It is unfortunate that neither Carroll, Grant, nor Wheaton mention the incident in their official reports. At any rate, McGowan's attack was repulsed and the guns did not fall into Confederate hands. Ricketts, however, was forced to withdraw his pieces temporarily, but they were replaced by a section of Dow's 6th Maine battery.[25]

As soon as the Confederate assault had been successfully driven back, Lyman took a few moments to pen a message to Meade, which was sent by courier at 5:50 P.M., informing him of the condition of the Second Corps:

> GENERAL: We barely hold our own; on the right the pressure is heavy. General Hancock thinks he can hold the plank and Brock roads, in front of which he is, but can't advance.
>
> THEO. LYMAN,
Lieutenant-Colonel,
Volunteer Aide-de-Camp.
>
> Fresh troops would be most advisable.[26]

Having seen McGowan's attack from the Federal lines, let us return to the Confederates' ranks and view the assault from their position.

After McGowan's and Scales's brigades had gone into action, Wilcox's remaining two brigades (Thomas and Lane) went forward, relieving the remainder of Heth's division. Working his way across the Tapp farm, Thomas led his Georgians into the thicket north of Plank Road, replacing Davis's Mississippi brigade, which was just forming its thinned-out ranks for a last-ditch charge against the rapidly advancing Federal lines. The suicidal attack was, however, cancelled when Thomas arrived on the scene with his brigade and hurled it into the swarming blue line. (The Federals Thomas engaged were most likely the brigades of Carroll and Hays, as Getty's troops were by this time being relieved by the Second Corps.)

Meanwhile, after being informed by General Hill that Scales's brigade had run into trouble, General Lane led his North Carolinians to a position some one hundred yards south of the road, on McGowan's right, in an effort to re-establish the front line. Shouting the rebel yell, the North Carolinians stormed into the woods and down into a swamp, which they soon discovered was obstructed with dense brush, fallen trees, and Yankee Minié balls. As the North Carolinians advanced, they came upon a portion of Scales's brigade, which took position in the center of Lane's line. In a joint attack these Confederates drove the Yankees (probably the brigades of Webb and Owen) from their front, pursuing them across the swamp and up the ridge on the opposite side. General Lane continues the story:

> The enemy, reinforced, flanked us on the right, and on attempting to get in our rear, Colonel Barry broke back two of his companies and was soon afterwards forced to change the entire front of his regiment to meet the enemy in that direction. The enemy pressed this regiment so heavily that he was compelled to retire at dark.* While these movements were going on, on the right, the Seventh regiment, which was on the left and under the impression that McGowan was in front—none of us at that time were aware that McGowan had withdrawn under orders from General Wilcox—reserved its fire and pressed forward to within seventy-five yards of the enemy, who were massed in strong force on the high ground beyond the swamp. Here a terrible fire was opened upon it, and when it had become hotly engaged, the enemy, under cover of the darkness and dense smoke which had settled in the swamp, threw out a column on our left flank. When this column had gotten within a few paces of the Seventh, it demanded its surrender, and at the same time fired a destructive volley into it, which caused its left flank to fall back in considerable disorder. This exposed condition of my flanks induced me to order the balance of the brigade back to the high ground in

*The regiment referred to here is the 18th North Carolina, which occupied the right of Lane's line.

the rear of the swamp; which order was executed with difficulty on account of the darkness and the character of the ground. The Seventh, Eighteenth, Twenty-eighth, and the Thirty-third regiments, were all subsequently taken to the rear of Scales's brigade, which occupied a short breastwork that ran diagonally to the road on the right, where we found the Thirty-seventh regiment, to which point Colonel Barbour informs me it had been previously ordered.[27]

4. *Barlow and Wadsworth Converge on Hill*

Brigadier General Francis C. Barlow was, at twenty-nine years of age, one of the youngest generals in the Union army. Before the war he had been a lawyer, and he was a graduate of Harvard University. Desperately wounded in the first day's fighting at Gettysburg, Barlow was believed to be dying. When the Confederates captured the portion of the field on which Barlow lay, the Federals retreated and left the general to the care of the rebels; however, Confederate General John B. Gordon noticed the apparently mortally wounded Union officer lying on the ground, approached Barlow and asked if there was anything that he could do for him. Barlow requested that Gordon get word to Mrs. Barlow, who was working as a nurse in the Union lines. Gordon did so promptly, under a flag of truce, and Mrs. Barlow was soon able to nurse her husband back to health.[28]

Barlow's division was the last of the Second Corps commands to come up. The time of its arrival cannot be placed with any certainty, but it was probably on the scene no later than 6:00 P.M. General Hancock describes the position taken by Barlow's division that evening in his report of operations:

> Barlow's division, with the exception of Frank's brigade, which was stationed at the junction of the Brock road and the road leading to the Catharpin Furnaces, held the left of my line, and was thrown forward on some high, clear ground in front of the Brock road. This elevated ground commanded the country for some distance to the right and left covering the Fredericksburg and Orange Court-House Railroad in front. Owing to the dense forest which covered my front this was the only point where artillery could have an effective range, and I, therefore, directed that all of the batteries of my command, save Dow's (Six Maine) battery and

one section of Rickett's (F) company, First Pennsylvania Artillery, should be placed in position there, supported by Barlow's division, and forming the extreme left of the line of battle of the army.[29]

The railroad referred to by Hancock in his report was unfinished at the time of the battle, running roughly parallel to Plank Road from Orange Court House to Fredericksburg. The spot at which the line of the railroad crossed Brock Road was slightly over two miles from the Brock-Plank junction.

At about 8:00 P.M. Barlow ordered the brigade of Colonel Nelson A. Miles, accompanied by Colonel Thomas Smyth's Irish Brigade, to make an assault upon the Confederate brigades of Scales and Lane, on the far right of Hill's corps. Miles's men took position on the left as the Irish Brigade moved in on the right. Together these two units attacked westward, smashing into the front and right of Scales and Lane. The attack, however, was not delivered with the impetus that may have been expected.

At about nine o'clock it was clear that if Miles and Smyth were going to accomplish anything, they would have to have help; therefore, Barlow ordered Colonel John Brooke to send in the 64th and 66th New York regiments of his brigade. These reinforcements, however, were put in too late to be a deciding factor for, by the time their lines were formed, darkness had completely blanketed the field.[30]

There are very few personal accounts of Barlow's attack on the evening of May 5. The only report of operations that deals with this phase of the fighting in the *War of the Rebellion* series is the account given by Colonel Brooke. The remainder of the accounts of Barlow's attack can only be found in a few regimental histories. In one of the latter, a member of the 116th Pennsylvania, of the Irish Brigade, gives an account of his regiment's role in the fight:

> The crash of musketry filled the woods, the smoke lingered and clung to the trees and underbrush and obscured everything. Men fell on every side, but still the Regiment passed steadily on. One by one the boys fell—some to rise no more, others badly wounded—but not a groan or complaint, and a broad smile passed along the line when Sergeant John Cassidy, of Company E, finding fault because he was shot through the lungs, he had to walk off

without assistance, some one said to him: "Why, Cassidy, there's a man with all of his head blown off and he is not making half as much fuss as you are!"[31]

Sometime between four and five o'clock, General Wadsworth was ordered to move his Fifth Corps division southward, along with Baxter's brigade of Robinson's division, to attack the left of Hill's corps. By 6:00 P.M. Wadsworth's men, formed in two lines of battle, had left their position on the Lacy farm and were making their way through the woods toward the extreme left of Hill's battle line, about a half-mile northeast of the Tapp farm. Occupying the first line of Wadsworth's attack formation were, left to right, the brigades of Stone and Baxter. Cutler's Iron Brigade constituted Wadsworth's second line and Rice's brigade made up the reserve.

After advancing less than a mile, Wadsworth's cheering men plowed into the left and rear of Thomas's surprised Georgians who, being busily engaged with the Federals in their front, were not expecting an attack on their left. For a moment A. P. Hill found that he was in serious trouble for, just as Wadsworth hit the left of his corps, Barlow was pressing his right. Worse was that Hill had already thrown in all of his reserves. The only troops available to fend off Wadsworth's assault were the 125 men of the 5th Alabama, which had been detailed earlier to guard the prisoners. Spreading out into a thin line of attack, this meager force was miraculously able to put Wadsworth's troops in check. Shouting the characteristic rebel yell, which by then had been heard on many a field, the Alabamans hit Stone's and Baxter's line head on, breaking it and sending the pieces flying in all directions. The Iron Brigade, however, held fast, and was able to direct the fleeing troops back to the front at the point of a bayonet (a most effective instrument in stopping a rout). The brigade had been routed for the first time earlier in the day, and it was not about to bear such humiliation again, no matter what the price. By the time order was restored to the division it was dark, and any hopes of crushing Hill's left that day had vanished.[32]

Wadsworth's disheartened soldiers settled down for the night just a few yards from the Confederate lines. They were, in fact, so close that many of the men could hear what was being said in the rebel camps. The ever-present cries of the wounded persisted throughout the night, even though parties were sent from both armies to offer comfort to the suffering men. A soldier of the 6th Wisconsin, of the Iron Brigade, recalled: "At dark the firing died down to the skirmish line. We lay upon the ground surrounded by dead and dying rebel soldiers. The sufferings of these poor men, and their moans and cries were harrowing. We gave them water from our canteens and all aid that was within our power."[33]

CHAPTER FIVE

"He Won't Be Up—I Know Him Well!"

1. Sedgwick Battles North of the Pike

The Sixth Corps commander, amiable, fifty-year-old John Sedgwick, was probably the best-liked general in the army. While other officers had developed rivals as they vied for command, Sedgwick (or "Uncle John," as he was affectionately known to his troops) apparently had no enemies. He was as capable an officer as he was friendly, having served with distinction in the Mexican and Seminole wars. During the Battle of Antietam he was twice wounded while leading a division of the Second Corps into action. As the sun rose on May 5 no one could have imagined that Sedgwick had but four days left to live.[1]

Wright's division led the march of the Sixth Corps on the morning of May 5, and at about 11:00 A.M. it was ordered to move into position in the woods north of the turnpike and to connect with Warren's Fifth Corps. Brigadier General Thomas Neill's brigade of Getty's division, which had been left behind as the rest of Getty's men marched off toward Plank Road, also marched with Wright's division. Ricketts's division was left to guard the Germanna Ford and was massed at a point just south of the crossing.

It will be recalled that the advance of Wright's division was protested hotly by Confederate cavalry and sharpshooters, but the Federals were eventually able to brush this force aside, and the connection with the right of the Fifth Corps was finally made at 3:00 P.M. The division was then deployed with Colonel Emory Upton's brigade on the left (its left touching the road), Colonel Henry Brown's brigade in the center, and Brigadier General David Russell's brigade on the right. Neill's troops were held in reserve

93

Major General John Sedgwick. *Courtesy USAMHI.*

to the right and rear of Russell. The remaining brigade of Wright's division (Shaler's) was to the rear of the army, guarding the trains.[2]

As soon as a line of battle had been formed, Wright's troops advanced toward the Confederate position held by Edward Johnson's division, under a shower of shot and shell, which intensified with every step the Federals took. Emory Upton's brigade moved steadily forward, crossing Sanders' Field, which was still smouldering from the fire that had swept across it earlier in the day. The wreckage of the fighting that had taken place between Ayres's brigade and the Confederates a few hours before was present everywhere; so much so, in fact, that many of Upton's men stumbled over the charred remains of their compatriots, who had been so completely consumed by the flames that it must have been hard for the troops to imagine that the blackened masses had been living, breathing men just a short time before.[3]

Despite the horrors it encountered and the steady stream of lead that swarmed through the air, Upton's men continued to press on across the clearing. As the Federals neared the rebel breastworks in the woods on the opposite side of the field, a portion of the gray line leaped out of the trenches and stormed into the ranks of the 95th Pennsylvania, killing Lieutenant Colonel Edward Carroll. In retaliation, two or three companies of the regiment countercharged and succeeded in capturing about thirty prisoners.[4]

Meanwhile, Brown's New Jersey brigade, advancing through the woods north of Sanders' Field on Upton's right, walked into a ferocious fire from the rifles of Walker's Stonewall Brigade. During the attack the New Jersey men inclined slightly to the left, and, consequently, the left regiment, the 15th, became entangled with the right of Upton's command. To reduce the possibility of confusion, the Colonel of the 15th, W. H. Penrose, placed his regiment under Upton's command. According to Colonel Upton, the Jerseymen "behaved under all circumstances with a steadiness indicative of the highest state of discipline."[5]

The ground over which the Sixth Corps advanced was much too wooded to permit the use of artillery, and, as a result, the guns were put into park near Wilderness Tavern. Ewell, however, had several spots along his line where artillery could be employed, and he made good use of them. One battery was placed on the south side of the turnpike, west of Sanders' Field, while another was put into position at a point just north of the road.[6] The men of the

Confederate breastworks in the woods north of Orange Turnpike.
Courtesy USAMHI.

Sixth Corps were, unfortunately, well within range of Ewell's guns, which opened up on the Federals as they stumbled through the woods. For the most part the Confederate cannon did little damage, but occasionally a shot struck home. One particularly unnerving incident took place while General Sedgwick and his staff were visiting Brown's brigade. One of the staff, Thomas Hyde, recalls what happened:

> I had dismounted to fix my horse's bit, when a cannonball took off the head of a Jerseyman; the head struck me, and I was knocked down, covered with brains and blood. Even my mouth, probably gaping in wonder where that shell would strike, was filled, and everybody thought it was all over with me. I looked up and saw the general give me a sorrowful glance, two or three friends dismounted to pick me up, when I found I could get up myself, but I was not much use as a staff officer for fully fifteen minutes.[7]

Sometime during the afternoon, General Ewell ordered the brigades of Pegram and Hays, of Early's division, to move out of their reserve position and occupy the far left of the Confederate Second Corps. Hays was to go into position on the left of Stafford, while Pegram fell into place on the left of Hays. The exact time that these brigades reached their destination cannot be placed with any certainty, but it is safe to assume that Hays was in place by 4:00 P.M.[8]

Hays's Louisianans, supported by the 25th Virginia of Jones's brigade, rushed into the oncoming Union brigades of Russell and Neill, on the far right of Sedgwick's corps. The Confederates hit the right of Neill's command with great success but were driven back in a fierce countercharge made by the 49th New York and the 7th Maine. Meanwhile, Russell had deployed the 5th Wisconsin on his right as skirmishers, and as his brigade advanced, the 5th surrounded the 25th Virginia, capturing that regiment almost entirely. The Wisconsin men sent nearly 300 prisoners and a stand of colors to the rear.[9]

George T. Stevens, surgeon of the 77th New York of Neill's brigade, states that the opposing lines ran along slight ridges on opposite sides of a wooded marsh that was about 300 yards wide. Because of the dense timber, the Confederate lines were out of sight. Stevens describes the fighting that afternoon:

The rattle of musketry would swell into a continuous roar as the simultaneous discharge of 10,000 guns mingled in one grand concert, and then after a few minutes, became more interrupted, resembling the crash of some huge king of the forest when felled by the stroke of the woodsman's ax. Then would be heard the wild yells which always told of a rebel charge, and again the volleys would swell into one continuous roll of sound, which would presently be interrupted by the vigorous manly cheers of the northern soldiers, so different from the shrill yell of the rebels, and which indicated a repulse of their enemies.[10]

By 1:30 that afternoon General Willcox's division of the Ninth Corps (not to be confused with Cadmus Wilcox, of Hill's corps) had crossed the Rapidan and relieved Ricketts's division in guarding the ford. Ricketts then set off with his command to join the rest of the Sixth Corps. Truman Seymour's brigade was ordered to move in on Neill's right, while the remaining brigade of Ricketts's division, under William Morris, marched toward the Fifth Corps front to fill the gap left by Baxter's brigade, which had gone south with Wadsworth's attack column.[11]

By 5:00 P.M. Seymour was in position on Neill's right and had successfully driven back the Confederate skirmishers in his front. The way was now open for Seymour's men to flank the left of Ewell's corps, as there were no enemy troops in their immediate front to stop them; however, just as Seymour's troops began to move out, Pegram's Virginia brigade came flying through the woods, filling the unoccupied space on Ewell's left and stopping the Federals dead in their tracks.

General Seymour had just taken command of the brigade that morning, replacing Colonel Warren Keifer, and, as a result, both Seymour and Keifer submitted reports of the operations of the brigade during the campaign. These reports are, by far, the most detailed accounts given by any single brigade that relate directly to the battle.

According to the reports, Seymour's brigade was formed in two lines of battle. From left to right in the first line were the 6th Maryland and the 110th Ohio. In the second line, from left to right, were the 122d Ohio, 138th Pennsylvania, and the 26th Ohio.[12] Shortly after 5:00 P.M. the brigade advanced. Colonel Keifer, now commanding the 110th Ohio, was given general charge of the first line of battle. With orders to press forward and

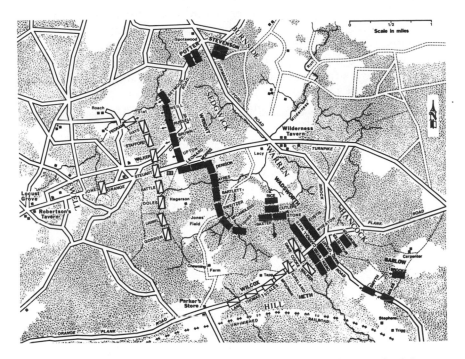

The situation at about 6 P.M., May 5. Sedgwick was battling north of the turnpike, while Hancock continued his attack near the Brock-Plank crossing. Wadsworth's division, meanwhile, had recovered from the severe shock it received during Warren's afternoon attack and, together with Baxter's brigade of Robinson's division, was converging on the left flank of Hill's Corps, while Barlow began to move in on Hill's right.

outflank the Confederate left, Keifer advanced. He recalls the action:

> The troops charged forward in gallant style, pressing the enemy back by 6 p.m. about one-half mile, when we came upon him upon a slope of a hill, intrenched behind logs, which had been hurriedly thrown together. During the advance the troops were twice halted, and a fire opened, killing and wounding a considerable number of the enemy. The front line being upon the extreme right of the army, and the troops upon its left (said to have been commanded by Brigadier-General Neill) failing to move forward in conjunction with it, I deemed it prudent to halt, without making an attack upon the enemy's line. After a short consultation

with Col. John W. Horn, I sent word to Brigadier-General Seymour that the advance line of the brigade was unsupported upon either flank, and that the enemy overlapped the right and left of the line, and was apparently in heavy force, rendering it impossible for the troops to attain success in a further attack. This word was sent by Lieutenant Gump, of General Seymour's staff. I soon after received an order to attack at once. Feeling sure that the word I sent had not been received, I delayed until a second order was received to attack. I accordingly made the attack without further delay. The attack was made about 7 p.m. The troops were in a thick and dense wilderness. The line was advanced to within 150 yards of the enemy's works, under a most terrible fire from the front and flanks. It was impossible to succeed; but the two regiments, notwithstanding, maintained their ground, and kept up a rapid fire for nearly three hours, and then retired under orders for a short distance only. I was wounded about 8:30 p.m., by a rifle-ball passing through both bones of the left fore-arm, but did not relinquish command until 9 p.m. [13]

The musketry died down to the skirmish line shortly after nine o'clock and the soldiers settled down to get what rest they could. The fight had been costly for both sides, and dead and wounded men littered the ground. During the afternoon, at the height of Brown's attack, the Confederates lost General Stafford, who fell mortally wounded by a Yankee bullet. He would linger on for six more days, only to succumb on May 11.

2. *Night of Loneliness and Compassion*

Throughout the night the ambulances creaked down the roads, bound for the corps hospitals, where they unloaded their suffering burdens to receive whatever medical attention was available. The soldiers had become good diagnosticians during the course of the war, and after being hit it only took them one glance at their wounds to predict their fate. In most cases, if they discovered that they had been shot in the arm or leg, they could breathe easily, but those who suffered stomach or chest wounds quietly lay back and tried to adjust their minds to the fact that they were going to die. Private Frank Wilkenson later recalled his experiences with wounded men during the battle:

Wounded soldiers, it mattered not how slight the wounds, generally hastened away from the battle lines. A wound entitled a man to go to the rear and to a hospital. Of course there were many exceptions to this rule, as there would necessarily be in battles where from twenty thousand to thirty thousand men were wounded. I frequently saw slightly wounded men who were marching with their colors. I personally saw but two men wounded who continued to fight. During the first day's fighting in the Wilderness I saw a youth of about twenty years skip and yell, stung by a bullet through the thigh. He turned to limp to the rear. After he had gone a few steps he stopped, then he kicked out his leg once or twice to see if it would work. Then he tore the clothing away from his leg so as to see the wound. He looked at it attentively for an instant, then kicked out his leg again, then turned and took his place in the ranks and resumed firing. There was considerable disorder in the line, and the soldiers moved to and fro— now a few feet to the right, now a few feet to the left. One of these movements brought me directly behind this wounded soldier. I could see plainly from that position, and I pushed into the gaping line and began firing. In a minute or two the wounded soldier dropped his rifle, and, clasping his left arm, exclaimed: "I am hit again!" He sat down behind the battle ranks and tore off the sleeve of his shirt. The wound was very slight—not much more than skin deep. He tied his handkerchief around it, picked up his rifle, and took position alongside of me. I said: "You are fighting in bad luck to-day. You had better get away from here." He turned his head to answer me. His head jerked, he staggered, then fell, then regained his feet. A tiny fountain of blood and teeth and bone and bits of tongue burst out of his mouth. He had been shot through the jaws; the lower one was broken and hung down. I looked directly into his open mouth, which was ragged and bloody and tongueless. He cast his rifle furiously on the ground and staggered off.[14]

The fact that he was alone and far from home certainly worsened the situation for any wounded soldier; however, if he was lucky, some fellow in his outfit would accompany him to the hospital to be of whatever service he could to his unfortunate comrade. This usually entailed writing a letter to the wounded man's family and, should that soldier die, seeing that his remains and personal possessions were sent home. Although the possibility that he might die was hard enough for any man to accept, the

These Federal soldiers were wounded during the Battle of the Wilderness and are seen here at the Marye House in Fredericksburg, which was being used as a hospital at that time. *Courtesy Library of Congress.*

thought of ending up in a nameless grave in the middle of nowhere was unbearable.

The moaning of the wounded caught between the lines that night was enough to disturb the most hardened veterans, and some of them risked death or capture to soothe these unfortunate men in whatever way they could. One Confederate, who was touched by the cries of the suffering warriors along Griffin's front, crawled on his hands and knees between the lines and, upon spotting a wounded Union lieutenant, asked if there was anything he could do to comfort him. The lieutenant replied: "I am very, very thirsty, and I am shot so that I cannot move." The Confederate crawled over to a brook and filled his canteen with water and, after offering some to the injured bluecoat, went off to see if he could be of help to others who had been shot, regardless of which side they fought on.[15]

Darkness brought a great relief for most of the soldiers. Sergeant E. B. Tyler, of the 14th Connecticut, recalls: "It is hard to tell about passing time in such a fight. A few hours some times seem long enough for a day and men often long for the night, not only to rest tired bodies, but to regain rest and quiet to mind and nerves wrought up to the highest degree of intensity."[16]

That night the army slept on its arms, and, as a matter of standard practice on the night after a fight, orders were given that no fires were to be built. Thus, to the dissatisfaction of the men, no coffee could be made, for the light emitted by the campfires might draw shots from enemy sharpshooters.[17]

As soon as the fighting died down, most of the men settled down to have some hardtack and salt pork and talk with their comrades about the day's battle. Often soldiers from separate commands, known as "newswalkers," would visit the various camps, and, after being invited by a group of men to sit down and light their pipes, they would exchange information about how the battle was going on different parts of the field. As a matter of pride these men were as accurate as possible in giving their information.[18]

Eventually things quieted down, the "newswalkers" returned to their regiments, and everyone tried to get whatever sleep would come to them. Many times, however, the men were too excited to sleep and would just lie on the ground and think of home. Private John W. Urban, of the 1st Pennsylvania, later wrote of that night:

Lieutenant General Ambrose Powell (A.P.) Hill, C.S.A.
Courtesy USAMHI.

Only those who have been in like situations can fully appreciate the feelings of a soldier on the night after an indecisive battle. Many of his comrades have fallen, and he knows that before the setting of another sun, many more will be added to the "bivouac of the dead." He cannot avoid thinking that the chances are many that he, too, may be among the number; and how lovingly he thinks of the dear ones at home, and hopes and prays that he may meet them again.[19]

3. Meade Confers with His Corps Commanders

A. P. Hill was sick. He looked pale and weak, and when darkness at last came to the Wilderness he welcomed the chance to sit down and rest. Pulling up a camp stool, he sat next to one of Poague's guns in Widow Tapp's field and stared into the small campfire before him. His front lines were a mess, but he decided to let his men rest as they were, for Longstreet was expected to relieve them before morning. Both Heth and Wilcox, however, were upset with the condition of their lines, and Heth took it upon himself to ask Hill to do something about it. He told his commander that his men could not even fire a shot without hitting each other, situated as they then were, and that if they were attacked in the morning, which they certainly would be, both his division and Wilcox's would be driven off by the Federals.

To Heth's request, Hill replied: "No, I will not have the men disturbed. Let them rest as they are. It is not intended that they shall fight tomorrow." He went on to explain that Longstreet would most assuredly be up long before day. General Heth went back to his command in a huff, but the state of his command was still gnawing at him, and, once again, he rode back to the Tapp farm to ask Hill if he could re-form his lines. The Confederate Third Corps commander was by this time growing tired of Heth's nagging, and he finally stated: "Damn it Heth, I don't want to hear any more about it; I don't want them disturbed." Heth could not bring himself to understand why Hill would not institute the simple defensive measure of rearranging his lines. He later said of the matter: "The only excuse I can make for Hill is that he was sick."[20]

Contrary to what Hill believed, Longstreet would not be up before daylight. He was in the vicinity of Richard's Shop, about ten miles from Parker's Store, resting his exhausted troops. Long-

Major General Ambrose Burnside. *Courtesy Library of Congress.*

street has long been criticized for not pressing his troops on to within supporting distance of Hill; however, the fact remains that had he done so his troops would probably have been of little use in battle on May 6. They had marched nearly thirty miles in two days and were dead tired. A soldier in Kershaw's brigade recalled the night of May 5 as the First Corps halted near Richard's Shop at 5:00 P.M.: "Men were too tired and worn out to pitch tents, and hearing the orders 'to be ready to move at midnight,' the troops stretched themselves upon the ground to get such comfort and rest as was possible. Promptly at midnight we began to move again, and such a march, and under such conditions, was never before experienced by the troops."[21]

Longstreet's First Corps was not the only Confederate reinforcement expected to arrive before daylight. General Richard Anderson's division of Hill's corps was in camp at Verdiersville and arrived on the field at about the same time as Longstreet. Also, Ramseur's brigade of Rode's division, along with six other regiments from Ewell's corps, marched onto the scene sometime during the night. Ramseur replaced Jones's brigade in general reserve. Finally, Robert Johnston's brigade of Rodes's division was marching from Hanover Junction and would be up by morning to go into position on the far left of Ewell's line of entrenchments.[22]

Just as the Confederates were making efforts to renew the fighting in the morning, so were the men of the Army of the Potomac. At about 10:00 P.M. General Meade called a conference of his corps commanders, at which time he told them to send their train guards, and anyone else who could carry a musket, into the front lines. (Ferrero's colored division and most of the army's engineers and reserve artillerymen were apparently the only exceptions.) Also, Burnside, whose corps was finally south of the Rapidan, was ordered to begin moving three of his divisions at 2:00 A.M. into position between Warren and Hancock. Burnside assured Meade that his men would indeed be on the march by two o'clock, but, as the meeting broke up and Burnside disappeared into the darkness, Major Duane, Meade's Chief of Engineers, remarked: "He won't be up—I know him well!" This, apparently, was also the feeling shared by the rest of the corps commanders.[23]

During the conference, Meade also informed his generals that General Grant had ordered a general attack to begin at 4:30 A.M. The generals, however, asked Meade if he could possibly persuade

Grant to postpone the attack until 6:00 A.M. Meade agreed that he would do this and so, on behalf of his officers, he sent the following message to General Grant at 10:30 P.M.:

> GENERAL: After conversing with my corps commanders, I am led to believe that it will be difficult, owing to the dense thicket in which their commands are located, the fatigued condition of the men rendering it difficult to rouse them early enough, and the necessity of some daylight, to properly put in re-enforcements. All these considerations induce me to suggest the attack should not be made till 6 o'clock instead of 4.30. I have ordered it for 4.30, but am of the opinion it will be more likely to be simultaneous if made at 6. Should you permit this change I will advise corps commanders. It appears to be the general opinion among prisoners that Longstreet was not in the action to-day, though expected, and that his position was to be on their right or our left. His force is supposed to be about 12,000. He probably will attack Hancock to-morrow. I have notified Hancock to look out for his left, but think it will be well to have Willcox up as soon as possible.[24]

When the courier delivered Meade's dispatch Grant had already turned in for the night; however, Lieutenant Colonel Rowley of Grant's staff relayed the message to the general-in-chief, promptly wrote Grant's reply, and sent it off to Meade. Meade was waiting at his tent, which was pitched on the eastern side of Germanna Road, just across from his headquarters on the knoll. The response read:

> GENERAL: I am directed by the lieutenant-general commanding to say that you may change the hour of attack to 5 o'clock, as he is afraid that if delayed until 6 o'clock the enemy will take the initiative, which he desires specially to avoid. General Burnside is directed to bring up General Willcox's division with his other troops if they can possibly be spared, and will probably bring them.[25]

So the first day's fighting ended in a draw. Both armies were in about the same position as they had been when the action began, neither had gained any decisive advantage in the tangled woodland, and both had reinforcements arriving on the field. The battle was far from over.

CHAPTER SIX

"Longstreet Slants through the Hauntedness!"

1. Hancock Crushes Hill's Defense

Early on the morning of May 6, the men of Grant's army arose from their beds on the hard ground and prepared their hasty breakfasts under the dark and starlit sky. The general-in-chief also arose before dawn, and he sat down to some black coffee and a sliced cucumber prepared in vinegar as he awaited the hour for the army to attack.[1]

During the early morning hours, changes had been made in both the Confederate and Union lines positioned near the turnpike. General Ewell had moved Gordon's Confederate brigade from its previous position on the far right to the far left of his corps, thus enabling it to rejoin the rest of Early's division. As Robert Johnston's brigade arrived from Hanover Junction, it was placed on Gordon's left.[2]

On the Federal side, the five-brigade front of Sedgwick's Sixth Corps (Upton, Brown, Russell, Neill, and Seymour), was moved slightly to the right in order to make room for Griffin's division of the Fifth Corps, which was now straddling the turnpike, extending for some distance to the right and left of that road. (Bartlett held the right of Griffin's division, with Sweitzer on the left and Ayres in reserve to the rear of Sweitzer.) Morris's brigade of Ricketts's division was sent back north of the turnpike and was formed as a reserve unit to the rear of Upton. Shaler's brigade of Wright's division, which had just arrived on the field, was held in reserve behind Neill's brigade. Crawford's division of the Fifth Corps was formed to the left of Griffin, while Robinson's command was in reserve near the Lacy house. Also, Colonel Howard Kitching's brigade of heavy artillery, now serving as infantry, had just arrived from Chancellorsville and was massed near Robinson's division.[3]

Much to Grant's chagrin, Lee gained the initiative that morning, for General Ewell's cannon boomed into action at 4:30 A.M., half an hour before the proposed Federal attack, showering the men of the Sixth Corps with iron and lead. Although it cannot be stated with certainty, Grant must have been upset with himself for having changed the hour of his attack; nevertheless, the rebels had gotten the jump on him, his right was threatened, and something had to be done about it.

It appears that Jubal Early's division, on Ewell's left, was the only command of the Confederate Second Corps to make a determined assault that morning. As soon as the signal was given, Early's rebels tore across the overgrown marsh that separated the opposing lines and slammed into the Federal brigades of Neill and Seymour; however, the sharp musketry of the bluecoats soon forced the rebels back to their original line of entrenchments. As Early's men retreated back across the marsh, the Federals turned the tables on them, and both Neill and Seymour led their commands forward in a violent counterattack. This retaliatory effort was, however, quickly repulsed, as the Federals discovered that the Confederates had strengthened their position during the night. Neill and Seymour ordered their brigades to fall back at once and, after that was done, instructed their men to dig in.[4] The skirmishing continued along this line for most of the day, but it was apparent to everyone that the major action was going to take place on Plank Road, where Hancock's men were already attacking. Surgeon George Stevens, of Neill's brigade, recalled: "At ten o'clock the roar of battle ceased, and from that time until five p.m., it was comparatively quiet in front of the Sixth Corps, but from the left where Hancock's corps and Getty's braves were nobly battling, the war of musketry was incessant."[5]

After returning to his command from the late-night conference of corps commanders, General Hancock set about making some changes in the formation of his troops. After being informed of the possibility of an attack by Longstreet on the left of his command, Hancock placed General Gibbon in charge of the left wing of the Second Corps, which at that time consisted of Barlow's division, supported by the forty-two guns of the corps artillery.

Miles's brigade was put into position on the left of Gibbon's

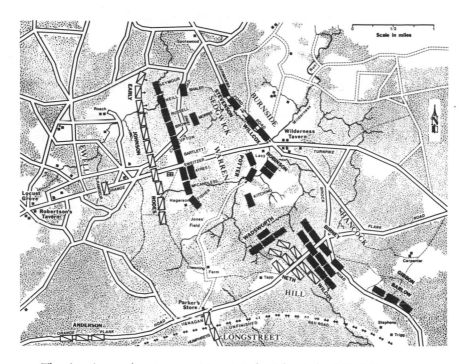

The situation at about 5 A.M., May 6. Sedgwick's Federal Sixth Corps was being attacked by the Confederates of Early's division, north of the turnpike. Hancock, meanwhile, had begun his assault down Plank Road, and Lee's right was already beginning to wither away. The vans of Longstreet's First Corps and Anderson's division of Hill's corps were, however, nearing Parker's Store and would soon be up to reinforce the threatened area. The advance of Burnside's Ninth Corps continued to move sluggishly toward the heights of the Chewning farm.

force, deployed across Brock Road, facing south, in order to meet an attack from that direction. To the right of Miles, curving northward along Brock Road, facing west, were the brigades of Frank, Brooke, and Smyth, in that order. The corps artillery was placed on the crest of a plateau to the rear of these troops, ready to swing into action and meet an attack from any direction.[6]

General Birney, who, of course, was still in command of Hancock's right wing, had his troops formed and ready to advance down Plank Road at an early hour. This force, which consisted of nine brigades and represented four divisions, totaled about 20,000 men, as opposed to A. P. Hill's 14,000 Confederates. However,

Wadsworth's 5,000 men were about to unite with Birney's, and, when this maneuver was completed, the Federal assault force on Plank Road would equal about 25,000 effective troops. (Although Gibbon had command of Barlow's division, the three brigades of his own division would be under the command of Birney during the attack.)[7]

Birney's first line, which was entirely south of Plank Road (thus allowing Wadsworth enough room to wheel his division into position on the north side of the road), consisted of, from left to right, the brigades of McAllister, Ward, and Hays. In the second line the brigades were, left to right, Brewster and Grant, south of the road; Wheaton, stretched across the road; and Eustis, entirely north of Plank Road. The third line was composed of the brigades of Owen and Carroll, formed on the left and right of the road, respectively. Webb's brigade was in reserve on Brock Road, ready to go in wherever needed.[8]

Wadsworth's troops were massed north of Plank Road, facing south, nervously awaiting the signal to descend upon the left of Hill's rebels. In Wadsworth's first line were, from left to right, the brigades of Cutler, Baxter, and Rice. Stone's brigade (now under the command of Colonel Edmund Dana), was in position to the rear of Baxter. Wadsworth's force was to move south and, after crushing Hill's left, make the connection with the right of Birney's command; it would then wheel to the right and advance with the rest of the assault force down Plank Road.[9]

Hill's Confederates, meanwhile, remained in about the same disorganized position that they had been in the previous evening, except Thomas's Georgians had been moved from the far left of the corps to the far right.[10]

Hancock, always on time, ordered Birney to advance his column at 5:00 A.M., and, without loss of a minute, the troops were on the move. These bold Federals attacked with an impetus that Hill's uneven lines could not withstand, and within a very few minutes the rebel brigades began to wither away. Ward's bluecoats piled into Scales's men and, after only a brief encounter, sent them off in wild disorder. At the height of this assault the 141st New York became viciously engaged with the rebels of the 13th North Carolina, but in the end this Confederate regiment was driven away, leaving its colors in the hands of the New Yorkers. As Scales's command broke, the brigades of Thomas and McGowan, on either side of it, found that they, too, had been flanked and were thus forced to retire.

Meanwhile, back at the Tapp farm, General Lee sat in anguish astride Traveller, watching his army, and possibly the Confederacy, fall to pieces. Plank Road was jammed with rebels who were both looking for a place to stand and running away, and to say that this scene saddened Lee would be a gross understatement. Finally, spotting McGowan's brigade running headlong for the rear, General Lee could take no more, and he rode up to the commander of that brigade and shouted: "My God, General McGowan, is this the splendid brigade of yours running like a flock of wild geese?" McGowan replied: "General, these men are not whipped. They only want a place to form, and they will fight as well as they ever did."[11]

The Union men pressed on, and seemingly no one could stop them. If they could reach Parker's Store, Lee's army would be cut in half and maybe, just maybe, the end of the war would be in sight. Near the Tapp farm the retreating Confederates continued to wander, willing to fight but lacking organization. Lee, of course, recognized that his army was in grave danger, and he sent Colonel Taylor of his staff to Parker's Store to prepare the trains for immediate evacuation. At the same time, he sent Colonel Venable to the rear to hasten the arrival of Longstreet, whose command had just reached Parker's Store.

Colonel Lyman, riding down from Federal army headquarters, approached a gleaming Hancock, who was sitting on his horse at the intersection, watching his men advance. Hancock turned to Lyman and said, joyfully: "We are driving them sir; tell General Meade we are driving them most beautifully." Lyman regretfully informed Hancock that, when he left Meade's headquarters, only one of Burnside's divisions was up. Upon hearing this, Hancock's face changed. "I knew it!" he shouted. "If he could attack now, we would smash A. P. Hill all to pieces!"[12] The fears harbored by the corps commanders at the meeting of the previous evening had been realized. Despite that, Hancock's attack was proving to be successful. At 5:40 A.M. Lyman sent the following dispatch to Meade: "GENERAL: General Hancock went in punctually, and is driving the enemy handsomely. Some prisoners. Nothing from Longstreet. Hancock has a rifle-pit on the left to be ready for him, and scouts out. Birney has joined with Wadsworth."[13]

View of the Tapp farm, looking southwest from Plank Road.
Photo by Ron Carlson.

As Lyman was writing the above dispatch, Hancock was penning his own message to Meade, which was also sent at 5:40 A.M.: "General: We have driven the enemy from their present position, and are keeping up the plank road, connected with Wadsworth, taking quite a number of prisoners. My attack is being made with three divisions on both sides of the plank road."[14]

As Wadsworth's command swooped down on Hill, it struck Kirkland's North Carolina brigade on the left flank, forcing it to fall back in considerable confusion; however, Wadsworth was unable to follow up his success, as his troops became entangled with those of Birney's command who were advancing down Plank Road. For a while Plank Road was a mass of confusion as officers tried desperately to separate their troops from those of other commands. In the end Getty was compelled to pull his division entirely south of the road in order to resume the advance, as was Colonel Carroll.[15]

The Plank Road mix-up halted the Federal movement on the north side of the thoroughfare just long enough to allow several Confederate brigades an opportunity to form a quick defensive line. Here, just east of the Tapp farm, the brigades of Cooke and Davis, along with a portion of Kirkland's command and a section of guns from a North Carolina battery, offered the first serious resistance to Hancock's attack; however, as soon as Wadsworth's men were reorganized, this rebel force was obliged to follow the same course as the rest of Hill's corps and thus withdrew from its advanced position, having bought a few minutes of precious time for Lee's endangered army.[16]

White-haired James S. Wadsworth, nearly sixty years old, was a wealthy native of the state of New York, who had volunteered to defend his country without pay—something that impressed his men very much. Unlike many other officers in the army, Wadsworth was not a West Point graduate; nevertheless, he handled his troops well in battle, for it was the valiant fighting of his division, inspired by his personal courage, that had saved the first day's fighting at Gettysburg from ending in a total rout of Meade's army.

After straightening out the mess on Plank Road, Wadsworth re-formed his division, forming the brigades en masse to reduce their exposure to Confederate artillery fire, which was beginning to pound his troops with deadly effect. Still occupying the woods north of the road and east of the Tapp farm, the division was now facing to the west, prepared to continue the advance. Cutler's Iron Brigade was in the lead, followed by the brigades of Stone (Dana), Baxter, and Rice, respectively.[17]

It was at about this time that Colonel Kitching's brigade of heavy artillery, which had just marched from the Lacy house on orders to join Wadsworth, moved into position on the right of the division. Also, while trying to re-form his troops, General Henry Baxter was wounded, and command of his brigade devolved upon Colonel Richard Coulter, who had previously led the 11th Pennsylvania.[18]

Hancock's force, meanwhile, continued to press Hill's rebels. The Federal assault column was, by this time, nearing the Tapp field and was beginning to feel the effects of Poague's twelve guns, which were lobbing shells into the woods from their emplacements on the western side of the glade. Hancock had no artillery fire whatever to support his attack line. Earlier, Dow's guns, in position at the intersection, had fired several rounds over the heads of the Federal troops as they moved down Plank Road, but the advance of these troops was so swift that their lines were quickly in range of their own battery; therefore, Dow was ordered to cease the shelling.[19]

The Confederates, who had been driven back for over a mile, were re-forming in rear of Poague's batteries when the blue line at last emerged from the woods and into the Tapp farm clearing. After waiting to the last possible moment for a few straggling rebels to clear the field, Poague's guns roared, belching canister as quickly as the pieces could be loaded.

(Of all the forms of artillery ammunition, canister was by far the deadliest. Essentially, the projectile was a tin can filled with iron balls packed in sawdust and was effective only at close range. As the piece fired, the can disintegrated and the balls were hurled forth, ripping through anything in their path.)

Just as Wadsworth's soldiers were preparing to charge the guns, canister tore through their ranks, and, when the smoke cleared, many were lying upon the ground at the edge of the woods, dead or dying of gruesome wounds. In order to escape further destruction, the division was led back into the protection of the forest to re-form its lines.

Meanwhile, south of the road, Federal skirmishers were breaking out of the woods and drawing a bead on the rebel gunners.

This was the advance of Hays's and Ward's brigades. The few Confederates left on the south side of the road could hold off this line of skirmishers without too much trouble, but when the main body arrived there would be nothing to stop it from totally rupturing Lee's army.

To meet this impending attack, Poague swung a couple of guns into action, and the Union advance in that sector momentarily ground to a halt. Color Sergeant Crotty never forgot the fighting he was involved in that morning at the front of Hays's brigade. He later wrote:

> The roar of musketry, the dying groans of the wounded, the hellish yells of the rebels, and the shouts and cheers of the Union men, mingle together, all making a noise and confusion that is hard to describe. Nothing is thought of but load and fire. The wounded must take care of themselves, and every man must stand and fight till either killed or wounded. The rebels fall in their line but those who fall have their places filled with a man in the rear. So they fall, one on another. Pretty soon those lines in the rear make breastworks of their dead comrades. We don't like this kind of fighting much, and forward on the charge in four or five lines deep. The rebels now give way and we chase them through the dense forest. We have to be very careful or we step on their dead and wounded, which lay around in thousands. We drive them nearly a mile, when they fall behind some works for shelter. We now halt, for their artillery begins to fire on us. We hear them forming their broken lines, and their officers lead them forward again. . . . About this time both armies . . . keep up a rattle of musketry like the boiling cauldron of hell, as it is represented to us by our good Chaplains. My beautiful flag that looked as bright as a dollar when we started, is fit now, after nearly two days' fighting, to send home, for it is completely riddled with bullets and torn by the brush.[20]

After a very short while, Wadsworth's men were re-formed and they again advanced for the attack. Simultaneously, to the south of the road, the brigades of McAllister, Hays, and Ward emerged from the woods. Confederate disaster was in sight. Lee had done all he could, but his troops were in such a state of disorder that there was little resistance to stop the oncoming Federals. Poague's artillery was still there, to be sure, but there was no way under the sky that his twelve guns alone could hold off Birney's 25,000 bluecoats if they had a mind to charge, which was exactly what

Although this photograph of the woods north of Plank Road was taken several years after the war, the grim effects of the battle are still present everywhere. The small saplings seen here were literally mowed down by the ferocious musketry that erupted on the afternoon of May 5, 1864. *Courtesy USAMHI.*

they were about to do. If they could just push the rebels back another half-mile it would be over, and Lee would be forced to retreat or risk destruction of his entire army.

Just when things looked most grim for the Army of Northern Virginia, a cheer went up from the rear of the Confederate lines, echoing through the woodland and striking a new hope in the hearts of the ragged Confederates. Longstreet—Lee's Old War Horse—had at last arrived.

> Watch and fast, march and fight—clutch your gun!
>   Day-fights and night-fights; sore is the stress;
> Look, through the pines what line comes on?
>   Longstreet slants through the hauntedness![21]

2. *"Go Back, General Lee! Go Back!"*

As Longstreet's First Corps arrived on the field at 6:00 A.M., General Joseph Kershaw directed his division off to the right (south) of Plank Road, while General Charles Field deployed his division north of the road, to the rear of Poague's artillery.[22]

Colonel John Henagan, commanding the leading brigade of Kershaw's division (the brigade of South Carolinians once led by Kershaw himself), ordered the 2d South Carolina to form on the north side of the road, to protect the artillery, for Field's troops were not yet in position. The remainder of the brigade filed off to the south of the road. In order to effectively cover the ground south of Plank Road until the rest of Kershaw's division was in place, Henagan was forced to stretch his brigade across a two-brigade front, covering twice the amount of ground he normally would. Moreover, there was a large gap between his two left regiments, i.e., the 2d South Carolina north of the road and the 3d just south of the road. This was done to allow room for Benjamin Humphreys's brigade of Mississippians to take position on his left.[23]

As the South Carolinians formed for battle, General Kershaw rode up and drew rein alongside the men, exclaiming: "Now, my old brigade, I expect you to do your duty." With that the brigade went into action. One soldier remembered: "Just in front of us, and not forty yards away, lay the enemy. The long line of blue could be seen under the ascending smoke of thousands of rifles; the red flashes of their guns seemed to blaze in our very faces."[24]

Lieutenant General James Longstreet, C.S.A. *Courtesy National Archives.*

Soon after the South Carolinians moved to the advance, the remainder of Hill's broken corps, which had not previously retreated, came flying back, crashing through the ranks of Henagan's brigade. The Federal troops of Hays, Ward, and McAllister were at their heels and were making a dash for the gap on the left of the brigade. Field was by this time going into position in the Tapp field, thus allowing the 2d South Carolina to rejoin the rest of the brigade, south of the road. With not a moment to spare, the 2d filled the gap in Henagan's lines and, with the aid of Humphreys's brigade, which had just arrived on the scene, and a portion of Jenkins's brigade of Field's division, successfully repulsed the Union attackers. Both sides suffered heavy losses in the fighting.[25]

As the front line of Birney's attack force, south of the road, charged the South Carolinians, General Getty's division, which was in Birney's second line, received a good deal of the rebel fire. It was during this action that a stray bullet struck General Getty in the shoulder, forcing him to leave the field and turn command of the division over to General Wheaton.[26]

Although Getty's troops were originally in the second line of battle, they soon found themselves in the front ranks. Apparently, some of the troops in their front had broken as a result of a charge made by Kershaw's division. Colonel Grant gives this account of the fighting in front of his brigade:

> During the advance, there being two and some of the time four lines in front, this brigade suffered only from stray bullets and shells which came to the rear. Soon, however, the advance was checked, and the enemy fought with great desperation. The tide of battle turned. Our front line was shattered and broken, and men came disorganized to the rear. This brigade at the time happened to occupy a slightly elevated or rolling position, where the enemy had, for his own use, thrown together two irregular lines of old logs and decayed timber. The regiments took position behind these lines of logs and rubbish, and awaited the progress of battle. In less than half an hour the four lines in our front were swept away, and heavy lines of the advancing enemy came upon us with great force. They were received with a bold front and galling fire, and their advance was completely checked and thrown back in confusion. Still determined, the enemy reformed his lines, and again advanced to the attack, and again went back. The attack was many times repeated, and as many times repulsed. The repulse, however, was complete only in front of this brigade.[27]

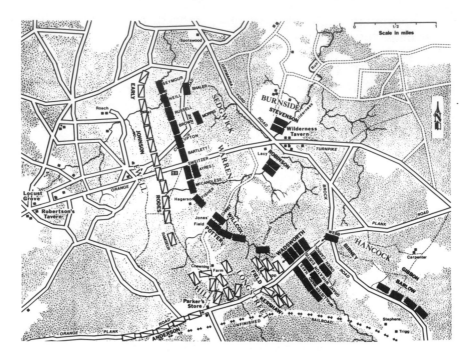

The situation in the vicinity of Plank Road at about 6:30 A.M., May 6. Hancock's assault had crushed Hill's corps and nearly succeeded in cutting Lee's army in two. Longstreet's First Corps, along with Anderson's division of Hill's corps, had just arrived on the scene, however, and were now moving to check the advance of Hancock's onrushing troops.

Colonel Grant indicates in the above that Birney's first line of battle was driven off at the onset of the Confederate counterattack on the south side of Plank Road. For the most part this was the case, as only McAllister's brigade appears to have held its ground, whereas the brigades of Ward and Hays were forced to retire. Moreover, General Getty states in his report that, although his division was able to hold the rebels in check for a considerable amount of time, it, too, was eventually compelled to fall back a short distance, abandoning the second line of battle. This, however, was no great cause for alarm, since the front-line troops were quickly replaced by the fresh brigades of Owen and Carroll, who immediately went into position on McAllister's right, thus restoring the front ranks.[28]

By this time (shortly after 6:00 A.M.), General Kershaw had completed the formation of his division, for the remainder of his brigades had arrived on the scene. Humphrey's brigade had filled the gap to the left of Henagan, while General Goode Bryan's Georgia brigade went into position on the right. Micah Jenkins's brigade of Field's division was massed in support of Bryan, while General Wofford's brigade of Kershaw's division formed to the rear as a reserve unit. Finally, General Richard Anderson's division of Hill's corps was pushing up Plank Road and temporarily went into position to the rear of Longstreet.[29]

While Kershaw was busy driving the Federals on the south side of the road back into the woods, Field was forming for the attack along the western edge of the Tapp farm. Wadsworth's Federals, who had just completed re-forming after their first repulse, were about to break out of the woods for a second time, and the Southerners had to do something quickly. Thus, in order to buy a few more precious minutes so that the newly arrived troops could be put into the proper attack formation, the advance of Field's division, General John Gregg's Texas Brigade, (which, incidentally, contained one regiment of Arkansans), was ordered to charge into Wadsworth's Yankees and give them the cold steel.

Just as the Texans were preparing for this charge, something happened: something that, above all else, displayed the admiration these ragged Confederates had for General Lee. Colonel C. S. Venable, who was on Lee's staff at the time, witnessed the event and tells it as he remembered:

> The Texans cheered lustily as their line of battle, coming up in splendid style, passed by Wilcox's disordered columns, and swept across our artillery pit and its adjacent breastwork. Much moved by the greeting of these brave men and their magnificent behavior, General Lee spurred his horse through an opening in the trenches and followed close on their line as it moved rapidly forward. The men did not perceive that he was going with them until they had advanced some distance in the charge; when they did, there came from the entire line, as it rushed on, the cry, "Go back, General Lee! Go back!" Some historians like to put this in less homely words, but the brave Texans did not pick their phrases. "We won't go on unless you go back!" A sergeant seized his bridle rein. The gallant General Gregg (who laid down his life on the 9th October, almost in General Lee's presence, in a desperate charge of his

This modern photograph of the Tapp farm was taken from the edge of the woods along its western border, where, on the morning of May 6, 1864, Poague's artillery recoiled as it poured canister into Hancock's advancing Federals. That same day Gregg's Texans swarmed across this field and into the woods in the distance as they launched their suicidal attack against Wadsworth's Federal division. *Photo by Ron Carlson.*

brigade on the enemy's lines in the rear of Fort Harrison), turning his horse towards General Lee remonstrated with him. Just then I called his attention to General Longstreet, whom he had been seeking, and who sat on his horse on a knoll to the right of the Texans, directing the attack of his divisions. He yielded with evident reluctance to the entreaties of his men and rode up to Longstreet's position.[30]

The Texans' attack was savage, and their ranks suffered horribly, as they had no support except for three pieces of artillery that were moved up Plank Road to rake the left of Wadsworth's advancing line. General Evander Law, of Longstreet's corps, recalled:

> The Federals . . . were advancing through the pines with apparently resistless force, when Gregg's 800 Texans . . . dashed directly upon them. There was a terrible crash, mingled with wild yelling which settled down into a steady roar of musketry. In less than ten minutes one-half of that devoted 800 were lying on the field dead or wounded; but they had delivered a staggering blow and broken the force of the Federal advance.[31]

Gregg's brigade held on as long as it could under the trying circumstances, but the 800 Texans, brave as they were, were no match for the nearly 5,000 Federals under Wadsworth's command. The Texans fell back, all the time firing into the advancing blue line, and General Gregg, like so many others, was brought back on a stretcher, having been wounded at the head of his men.[32]

As the Texans retreated under heavy pressure from the oncoming Union troops, General Henry Benning led his Georgians into the Federal ranks, following the same route taken by the Texans. The Georgians went in with a savage fury, fighting fiercely and inflicting heavy casualties on Wadsworth's men; however, although this gallant Confederate brigade battled tooth and nail, it was finally repulsed with as great a loss as was suffered by the Texas Brigade. Benning, like Gregg, was wounded at the front of his command.[33]

As the decimated ranks of the Texans and Georgians fell to the rear to re-form, the duty of repulsing Wadsworth's bruised but still advancing column fell upon the brigade of Alabamans under General Law, now commanded by Colonel W. F. Perry. Before we examine the details of this fight, however, let us return to the

Federal lines and look at the events that were taking place at Hancock's headquarters.

3. Burnside and Gibbon Falter

The portion of Plank Road in the rear of Hancock's battle line was by this time jammed with wounded soldiers making their way toward the Second Corps hospital. Although many of these men were able to walk under their own power, others, more seriously injured, were carried on the shoulders of their comrades or on litters. Upon arriving at the hospital, these men were classified by the seriousness of their wounds and treated accordingly. Chest and abdominal wounds, for instance, were given precedence over arm and leg wounds. Wounds requiring amputation, however, were quite serious as well as common, and anyone visiting one of the hospital sites would, as likely as not, encounter a gruesome stack of limbs outside the tents. Then, of course, there was the soldier for whom nothing could be done, except, perhaps, a shot of laudanum to ease his pain.

The wounded, however, were by no means the only ones making their way toward the rear of Hancock's line. Stragglers, skulkers, and outright cowards have infested every army throughout history, and the Army of the Potomac was in no way immune to this condition. The problem was, in fact, so bad that provost guards had to be stationed along Brock Road with orders to stop any man who could not show blood and return him to the front line.

For the most part, however, the army was made up of good men, who remained in the ranks even under the most grueling conditions. What exactly possessed a man to remain in the front line of battle, under fire, while his friends were falling all around him, has long been a subject of speculation. Captain A. M. Judson of the 83d Pennsylvania, who had the opportunity to observe many men under fire during the course of the war, believed that, on the whole, brawlers and fighters in civilian life did not usually have the stomach for fighting in battle. Warfare, according to Judson, required moral courage rather than physical courage, and he was convinced that "men of the most reliable principles in private life make the best and bravest soldiers in the field. Therefore you will always find that quarrelsome bullies, thieves, cheats, sneaks and liars, or to sum it all up in one word, unprincipled men in private life, are, without exception, cowards and poltroons in the army. A bad man may not fear his inferior in strength, but he dreads a death grapple with the King of Terrors."[34] This is not to say, however, that the "principled men" who remained fighting in the front ranks were unafraid, for quite the opposite is true. Sergeant E. B. Tyler, of the 14th Connecticut of Carroll's brigade, later recalled his feelings as he went into battle that morning:

> Sometimes our advance was very slow and every inch hotly contested and then again we progressed some distance in a short time, but all the while . . . fighting an almost . . . unseen enemy in thick woods. There is a feeling of uneasiness in the stoutest heart in facing danger that one cannot see and know. The mystery is doubly intensified by the sudden, silent dropping dead . . . of men on either hand that somehow does not seem to connect itself with the constant roar of musketry that is going on. The zip, zip of the bullets as they pass so closely to your head that you cannot help but think that had the rebel aim been varied never so little your career had been ended. Occasionally we captured a few prisoners, some of whom voluntarily deserted their lines and risking the gantlet of fire by both sides would come running into our lines, throwing up their hands and calling out to us not to shoot. They were evidently badly frightened, as well they might be, but we shouted encouragingly to them "Come on in, Johnny, come on in Johnny" and carefully held our fire until they were within our lines. Our shouts to them must have been heard in the rebel lines and perhaps encouraged others to take the risk.[35]

Now and then, as a matter of routine, some of the prisoners were escorted back to corps headquarters and questioned. It was from these individuals that General Hancock first learned of the arrival of Longstreet—not on his left, as had been feared, but directly in front of his lines. At 6:20 A.M. Lyman wrote Meade: "GENERAL: The left of our assault has struck Longstreet; 2 prisoners just in; sharp musketry. Longstreet is filing to the south of the plank road—our left; how far not yet developed. Gibbon and Barlow hold our left in reserve. Gibbon is just notified of Longstreet's presence by General Hancock. Our second line has advanced."[36]

By the time the above dispatch was sent off to General Meade, Hancock's advance had ground to a halt. The Second Corps commander was growing anxious, wondering why Burnside, who must surely be up by now, had not yet attacked Hill's left from the Chewning farm heights. At 6:30 A.M., unable to further stand the suspense, Hancock again asked Lyman to write Meade: "GENERAL: General Hancock requests that Burnside may go in as soon as possible. As General Birney reports, we about hold our own against Longstreet, and many regiments are tired and shattered."[37]

The reason why Burnside had not yet attacked was that, incredibly, he was not yet in position. The Ninth Corps was on the road at 2:00 A.M. as ordered; in fact, it began the march that morning at 1:00 A.M., as both Burnside and Potter testified in their official reports. Why then was the Ninth Corps not ready to attack from the Chewning farm at 5:00 A.M. as it should have been? It most certainly was not delayed by any force of the enemy's. Lieutenant Schaff, who had been detailed to meet Burnside on the turnpike and show him the way to Parker's Store Road, reports that the head of the Ninth Corps did not turn onto the pike until 5:30 A.M., and that General Burnside himself did not arrive at that point until after 6:00 A.M.! This is just another in the long line of examples of Burnside's inept leadership, which, by the way, should not reflect negatively on the abilities of the troops under his command, for under the proper leadership, these men could and later did perform their duty admirably.[38]

At 7:30 A.M., General Humphreys wrote Meade's reply to Lyman's dispatch of 6:30 A.M.: "Your dispatch is received informing the major-general commanding of the presence of Longstreet's force. I am directed to say that the only reserve force of the army (one division of the Ninth Corps) is here, and will be ordered to your support, should it become absolutely necessary. Call for it, therefore, only in case of the last necessity."[39]

The division of the Ninth Corps referred to in the dispatch is that of General Thomas Stevenson, which had just been placed in reserve at the old Wilderness Tavern, while the remaining divisions of the corps (those of Potter and Willcox) were heading for the Chewning farm.

Upon learning of the availability of the reserve division, Hancock immediately sent in an urgent request for it:

> Your dispatch just received, informing me that I can have a division from Burnside in case of absolute necessity. They are

pressing us on the road a good deal. If more force were here now I could use it; but I don't know whether I can get it in time or not. I am filling up the boxes of the men who are returning, and re-establishing my lines, closing up with right. Barlow is putting in a brigade on the enemy's right flank, and I will follow it up, if necessary, and have so directed. Am collecting the men near the plank road and issuing ammunition.[40]

After learning of Longstreet's arrival, General Hancock ordered Gibbon to throw in Barlow's fresh division and press the enemy's right. Hancock states in his report that this order was sent to Gibbon at 7:00 A.M. For some inexplicable reason, the left-wing commander only sent in Colonel Frank's brigade. Gibbon, however, who was one of the most dedicated officers in the army, insisted to his dying day that he never received Hancock's order to advance, although two staff officers state otherwise.[41] Whatever the case may be, only Frank's brigade was sent in and, apparently, these troops performed less than satisfactorily as they moved in on the left of Mott's division. Colonel McAllister, commanding the brigade in Mott's front line, recalls Frank's arrival in his report of operations:

> In a short time, Colonel Frank, of General Barlow's division, came with a few troops, and said that he wished to pass through my line to the front. I told him that I had skirmishers out and that I was advancing with the line of battle and did not wish him to go ahead of me, and that I understood that he was to protect my left, that I had orders to advance when this line advanced, and halt when it halted. He replied that he had orders "to find the enemy wherever he could find him, and whip him." Saying this he spurred his horse, faced his men to the left, and moved around my left flank, and advanced in my front, and soon engaged the enemy. But a very little firing took place until some of his men came back running, and in a few minutes a verbal message came for me to relieve him. This I declined to do, as my orders were to advance with this line. A few minutes more and all his troops came running back. I had my men stop them, and refused to let them through. Colonel Frank said to me, "I want to get ammunition." I asked him "where?" He replied "Away back in the rear." I informed him that mules loaded with ammunition had just come up on my right and if he would detail a few men I would send them with a sergeant and get the ammunition, which could be had in a few

minutes. At this moment the pickets became engaged and I opened my ranks and let Colonel Frank's command through, as I supposed, to get the ammunition. This is the last I saw of him or his command.[42]

Frank's troops probably broke due to a lack of leadership, for in his report Colonel McAllister came as close as he could to calling Frank a coward and a liar, without saying the words outright. The Army of the Potomac had its share of incompetents, as did the Army of Northern Virginia, but, fortunately, they were few in number. Indeed, a vast number of the officers in Grant's army, as has already been exhibited, displayed remarkable coolness while under fire at the heads of their commands. They had to do so, for they knew that their men would not do what they were unwilling to do themselves. The officers in both armies served as an inspiration to troops under fire. In fact, during the course of the Civil War, there were many instances in which the only thing that kept a desperately attacked unit from turning tail and running was the sight of its captain or colonel, calmly riding up and down the lines, while bullets flew all around him.

On Hancock's front, the perpetual rumble of musketry continued and many of the men began to exhaust their supply of cartridges. To counter this problem, mules, loaded with boxes of ammunition, were sent into the lines. A soldier of the 11th Massachusetts, of Mott's division, recalled the predicament that his outfit was in:

> The men reclined upon the ground, and returned the fire of the enemy until the forty rounds of cartridges were exhausted. There was a most earnest clamor for cartridges; and the boxes of the slain and wounded were opened and emptied, and a supply of those that were fitted for rifles, but unsuited to the caliber of the smooth-bore musket, was issued to the regiment in this distressing emergency. . . . The proper balls were brought up after a perilous delay, although some of these cartridges consisted of a solid cake of powder; and some exhibited a feeling of discontent because there were no buck-shot.[43]

By 7:00 A.M., army headquarters was seriously concerned as to how much ammunition was actually available to replenish the troops; so much so that General Meade issued the following circular to his corps commanders at that hour: "The question of ammunition is an important one. The major-general commanding directs that every effort be made to economize the ammunition, and the ammunition of the killed and wounded be collected and distributed to the men. Use the bayonet where possible."[44]

As it turned out, however, army headquarters soon discovered that there was no shortage of ammunition. There was, in fact, an abundance of it. How the misconception was created remains a mystery to this day, unless it was seeded by the seemingly endless roar of rifle fire alone.[45] The troops in the front lines were quickly expending the cartridges that had been issued to them, to be sure, but this was to be expected in a battle of this magnitude, and the problem was easily solved by sending for a fresh supply from the combat trains.

4. *The Alabamans Rout Wadsworth*

As noted previously, the fresh brigades of Owen and Carroll, from Gibbon's original division, relieved the hard-pressed troops in front of the Federal lines, south of Plank Road, where they successfully held off repeated charges of Kershaw's division, which continued to hammer away at the Union lines with relentless effort. It does appear, however, that during one of the Confederate assaults, Carroll's brigade was forced to give up a little ground. Sergeant Charles Blatchley of the 14th Connecticut recalls, almost comically, an experience he had while fighting at the head of the brigade: "I was awakened from my absorption in the business of saving my country by looking up, as I did occasionally, to see if the flag was still there, to find it gone. In another second I realized the fact that I was almost alone, and that the flag was rapidly making its way to the rear. I followed it."[46]

It was at about this point in the contest (seven o'clock) that Colonel W. F. Perry, commanding Law's Alabamans, relieved the Georgians of Benning's brigade, which had been all but destroyed in its assault on Wadsworth. Cutler's Iron Brigade, at the head of the Federal assault force north of Plank Road, was rapidly advancing through the woods but, as it reached the crest of a ridge on the eastern side of a ravine, the screaming gray line of Perry's command fell into position on the opposite side of the culvert and released a leaden storm into the Union ranks. The black-hatted Westerners of the Iron Brigade dropped to the ground and returned the fire from behind trees, logs, and stumps. The volleys continued on this front for some time, but neither side was able to gain any decided advantage over the other.

North of the ravine, however, Kitching's brigade of heavy artillery was advancing on the right of Wadsworth's division. As the bullets began to sweep through the ranks of the Alabamans from the left, Colonel Perry quickly perceived that he was flanked. He at once rode over to Colonel Oates, commanding the 15th Alabama on the far left of his line, and directed him to wheel his regiment to the left and whip Kitching's force. Oates carried out the maneuver without delay and met Kitching's force head-on. Unfortunately the artillerymen were wholly inexperienced in infantry warfare and, as a result, were by no means a match for the veterans of the 15th Alabama. Even though Kitching's command numbered close to 2,400 troops, they fired wildly and the great majority of their shots went over the heads of the Confederates, who remained cool and fired accurately. Within minutes Kitching's brigade was routed, and the frightened artillerymen took flight and were not stopped short of the Lacy farm. In the repulse of these troops the 15th, which numbered only 450 men, suffered only two killed and eleven wounded.[47]

In the meantime, Wadsworth's main line, pinned down on the eastern side of the ravine, continued to pour round after round into the two regiments on the right of Perry's brigade, to little effect. (These two regiments were, left to right, the 47th and 4th Alabama.) Although this Confederate force was unable to advance, the three regiments on the left of the brigade (left to right, the 15th, 44th, and 48th) were somehow able to press forward and cross the gully. This force, finding nothing in its front, inclined to the right and soon found itself on the right flank of the Federal division.[48]

Wadsworth's lines reeled as the Alabamans delivered an effective enfilade fire into its ranks, and, unable to change front quickly due to the density of the woods, all four brigades broke. The men of Cutler's and Dana's commands, who suffered heaviest in the attack, scattered and followed the path of Kitching's defeated brigade to the Lacy house. The two brigades that were in the rear of the division—Baxter (Coulter) and Rice—were pressed back through the woods but later re-formed on Brock Road. Meanwhile, generals Wadsworth and Rice were making monumental efforts to rally those troops who had not taken flight during the melee.[49]

Fortunately for the Federals, General Alexander Webb was riding up at the head of his brigade just as Wadsworth's command began to fall apart. He had been ordered by General Birney to deploy his troops on the north side of Plank Road and to move immediately to the support of Getty's men (probably Eustis's brigade), who were still believed to be on that side of the road. Webb advanced with his six regiments (the order not known, except that the 20th Massachusetts was on the left and the 19th Maine was on the right) without the protection of a skirmish line, for the only thing that Webb expected to find in his front was the rear of Getty's line. Getty, however, had by this time pulled Eustis to the south side of the road and was then occupying Birney's third line of battle.[50]

Webb pressed on through the brush but, to his sudden surprise, he discovered that he had stumbled smack into Perry's advancing Confederates, who were following up their victory over Wadsworth. To make matters worse for Webb, two brigades of Anderson's division were moving into the woods north of Plank Road and would soon be ready to attack. These were the brigades of generals Abner Perrin and Edward Perry (not to be confused with Colonel W. F. Perry, whose brigade will be referred to hereafter as Law's), which fell into line on the right and left of the Alabamans, respectively.[51]

The fighting here was desperate, but in the end Webb held his position. By this time it was about 8:30 A.M., and the musketry briefly died down as both sides took time to re-form their lines.[52]

CHAPTER SEVEN

A Specter Appears on Hancock's Left

1. The Pestered Corps Commander

At 8:00 A.M., General Hancock received a dispatch from army headquarters informing him that General Wadsworth's Fifth Corps division was now under his command. Wadsworth, of course, had previously received his instructions directly from General Warren's headquarters; however, since his division was now operating in the Second Corps's sector, it quickly became obvious to General Meade that, in order to minimize confusion, some other temporary arrangement would have to be made. The message Hancock received at eight o'clock also informed him that Burnside was in position at or near the Chewning farm: "General Wadsworth, with 5,000 on Birney's right is directed to take your orders. Two of Burnside's divisions have advanced nearly to Parker's Store, and are ordered to attack on their left, which will be your front. They ought to be engaged now, and will relieve you. Our only reserve is Burnside's third division, yet here, and I don't want to send it, if possible."[1]

General Hancock later stated in his report of operations that General Stevenson arrived at the Brock-Plank crossing with his reserve division of the Ninth Corps at about the same time that the above dispatch came in. This indicates that Meade must have changed his mind in regard to the reserve force and sent it to Hancock within minutes of sending the dispatch.[2]

General Burnside, as indicated in the above dispatch, had indeed arrived at the Chewning farm and was, at last, forming his divisions for the assault. Apparently, Willcox's division was on the left, covering the road to Parker's Store, while Potter moved forward with his division on the right, leading it westward across the Chewning plateau toward a patch of woods that extended over a portion of the farm. A. P. Hill had by this time re-formed his Confederate corps and deployed it across the previously unoccupied ground between Ewell's right and Plank Road. It was this force that Potter's division was then advancing on.[3]

The closer the Federals came to the rebel line that was posted in the woods, the more intense the musketry became, until it appeared that there was going to be a major action on the Chewning farm; however, just as the attack was beginning, General Potter received word to withdraw from his advanced position. Burnside describes the situation in his report:

> Just as preparations were being made to charge the enemy and drive them from the woods which intervened between this point and Parker's Store, an order was received from the lieutenant-general commanding to move all the available force of the corps to the left, with a view to attacking the enemy on the right of General Hancock. After consultation with Lieutenant-Colonel Comstock, who brought the order, it was thought best to move General Potter's command by the left flank through the woods until it reached a proper position for attack, and to leave General Willcox for the present to cover the Parker's Store road.[4]

Due to the difficulty of moving such a large body of troops through the dense brush, and due also to General Burnside's extreme slowness, it was midafternoon before the Ninth Corps was in position to attack the left of the Confederates on Plank Road.

Back at the Brock-Plank crossing, General Wadsworth responded to a message from Hancock, informing him that, by order of General Meade, Wadsworth was now to take orders from the Second Corps commander and was instructed to report to him at once. Hancock put Wadsworth in charge of all troops north of Plank Road and told him to launch an attack immediately.[5]

Accompanied by Colonel Carruth's brigade of Stevenson's division, Wadsworth rode back down Plank Road toward the front, his heart full of fire from the recent interview with Hancock. Hastily, he re-formed his lines on the north side of the road, and shortly thereafter the attack was renewed. Rice's brigade held the left of the line, its left resting on the road, while the brigades of Webb and Carruth (in that order) extended the line to the right.[6]

According to General Hancock, Wadsworth's assault was underway by 8:50 A.M. The fighting along his line raged furiously for about an hour as his troops battled with the brigades of Law, Perry, and Perrin, but neither side was able to do more than hold its own position. At 10:00 A.M., as the firing died down to the skirmishers, the opposing forces on the north side of the road were in about the same position as when the engagement had started.

While Wadsworth's attack was at its peak, Hancock was being bombarded with one dispatch after another, requiring him to handle several important matters simultaneously. At 9:10 A.M., Hancock's chief of staff, Lieutenant Colonel C. H. Morgan, galloped up to the Second Corps commander with a message from General Gibbon, stating that his pickets had spotted enemy infantry advancing up Brock Road toward his position on the left of the army. Rapid firing, coming from the direction of Todd's Tavern, could also be heard from Gibbon's position, underlining the fear that some Confederate force, perhaps Pickett's division of Longstreet's corps, was about to descend with violence upon the Federals' left flank.[7]

It must be kept in mind that the Federal high command was still unaware that Pickett's force was on detached duty near Petersburg and would not take part in this campaign. Moreover, prisoners had been taken from General Longstreet's other two divisions during the morning, but Pickett's force was still unaccounted for, thereby increasing the likelihood that it was his command that was marching up Brock Road.

At 9:15 A.M., Hancock sent an order to Birney, instructing him to send one brigade to the support of Gibbon. Birney responded to the order almost immediately by detaching Eustis's brigade of Getty's division, which was soon marching for Gibbon's front. Shortly thereafter, at 9:40 A.M., Colonel Leasure's brigade of Stevenson's newly arrived Ninth Corps division, was pulled out of reserve and sent to the aid of the left-wing commander. Finally, Brooke's brigade of Barlow's division (now under the command of Gibbon), accompanied by a section of artillery and a portion of Coulter's brigade, was sent from the far right of Gibbon's line to support Miles's brigade, which was deployed across Brock Road, on the left.[8]

While all of this was taking place, an order was received at Second Corps headquarters at 9:15 A.M., directing Hancock to attack simultaneously with Burnside: "The major-general commanding directs me to inform you that Colonel Comstock has gone out to General Burnside to point out to him where to attack the enemy on or near the plank road. He directs that you attack at the same time with Burnside."[9] By the time the dispatch was received, Hancock had already renewed his attack all along the line, making it impossible for him to attack in concert with Burnside. As soon as Meade learned of this, he recalled the order.[10]

In the meantime, a third development was presented to Hancock, which also called for his immediate attention. It appears that, after Wadsworth's division was smashed earlier in the day by the onslaught of Law's brigade and while the Iron Brigade was fleeing through the woods back toward the Lacy farm, General Cutler, commanding the brigade, spotted some Confederates advancing through the gap between Hancock's right and Warren's left. This potentially dangerous situation was at once reported to general headquarters and efforts were taken to correct it. At 9:45 A.M., Hancock received an order from Meade, instructing him to extend his right to make a connection with Warren. Hancock relayed the order to General Birney, and evidently some force was detached to fill the gap, although there is no record that indicates what command was assigned to this duty. There is, however, a verification that the connection with the Fifth Corps was made in a dispatch sent to army headquarters by Hancock at 10:30 A.M. The message is brief and simply states: "General Birney has made connection with the Fifth Corps."[11]

Hancock most certainly had his hands full. He was now in command of half the army—a trying situation at best for any officer. To make matters worse, he was being assaulted in front, there were reports of an unknown force advancing on his left, and he had to extend his lines in order to connect with the Fifth Corps. Although he was being badgered from nearly every conceivable angle, he effectively handled each problem as it was presented to him. Many another officer would have panicked in a like situation. Although it is widely accepted that Hancock was at his best while directing his troops in the defense of Cemetery Ridge, it cannot be denied that he was in at least comparable form in the Wilderness.

The firing along the Second Corps front had diminished considerably by ten o'clock, and the exhausted men in both armies welcomed the opportunity to get a little rest. They had been fighting for nearly two days and were drained mentally as well as physically. Their faces were blackened with gunpowder and their teeth ached from tearing open paper cartridges. Everyone operated in a daze—advance, fall back, load, reload. There was no time to think, only to act, for to think was to die. Everything could be reasoned out later, but for now they must fight to survive.

At 10:10 A.M., a courier delivered another dispatch to Second Corp headquarters. Although previous messages had gotten under Hancock's skin, this one brought a sigh of relief from the pestered corps commander. The message was from Gibbon, and it stated that the Confederates were not marching up Brock Road after all. The troops that had been spotted moving up the road turned out to be nothing more than a body of convalescents that had followed the Second Corps's line of march from Chancellorsville. Also, the sound of firing that was coming from the vicinity of Todd's Tavern was discovered to be a cavalry clash between Custer's Union horse soldiers and Rosser's Confederate troopers, from Wade Hampton's division.[12]

2. Cavalry Fight on Brock Road

During the night of May 5, Phil Sheridan's three cavalry divisions were disposed to cover the left and rear of the army. Wilson and Gregg were encamped near Todd's Tavern, while Torbert's division, minus Custer's brigade, was posted at Aldrich. General Custer's Michigan Brigade spent the night at Catherine Furnace.[13]

Shortly after 1:00 A.M., the strains of "Boots and Saddles" summoned the Michiganders to their mounts, and by 2:00 A.M. the brigade was riding down Furnace Road toward the intersection with Brock Road, under a clear and starlit sky. The brigade was to serve as a connecting link between Gregg's troopers and Hancock's left.[14]

George A. Custer was probably the most flamboyant officer in the Army of the Potomac (cavalrymen tended to lean in that direction in any case), but no one questioned his fighting ability. Although he was only twenty-four years old, he had already proven his capabilities on many a field. This was his first campaign under the newly arrived Sheridan, but the fiery cavalry commander took a liking to the dashing young Custer almost immediately. It was the beginning of a long friendship.

Custer reached the Furnace-Brock intersection well before daylight and remained in that position until about 8:30 A.M. At that time he received an order to move forward and harass the ghost division that was supposedly moving up Brock Road toward Hancock's left. Colonel Thomas Devin's brigade was to support Custer in the movement, but it had not yet arrived.[15]

Custer certainly must have known that there was no such Confederate force advancing up Brock Road, as his command had been posted along that road for some time when he received instructions to move against the mysterious force. Thus, any troops wishing to march up the road toward Hancock's left would first have had to encounter Custer.

Seeing no enemy troops anywhere near his position, Custer decided to make the connection between Hancock and Gregg and await any attack that might come. He posted his four regiments on the west side of Brock Road, in some woods that bordered the eastern edge of a field. This clearing, about 500 yards wide, was surrounded by woods and bisected by a ravine that ran diagonally from its southwest to its northeast corner.[16]

The brigade, facing west, was held on the right by the 1st and 6th Michigan Cavalry Regiments, formed in two lines, the 6th in the rear of the 1st. To the left of these units were the 5th and 7th cavalry regiments, probably in the order named. Pickets were posted well out in front of the brigade.

Anxiously, the troopers awaited the impending attack, standing in the woods at "in place, rest" in front of their mounts, clutching their seven-shot Spencer carbines. Custer himself, along with some of his staff and escort, was out inspecting the picket line. No one can better describe what happened next than the commander of the 6th Michigan, Major (later Colonel) J. H. Kidd:

> Suddenly, the signal came. A picket shot was heard, then another, and another. Thicker and faster the spattering tones were borne to our ears from the woods in front. Then, it was the "rebel yell;" at first faint, but swelling in volume as it approached. A brigade of cavalry, led by the intrepid Rosser, was charging full tilt toward our position. He did not stop to skirmish with the pickets but, charging headlong, drove them pell-mell into the reserves, closely following, with intent to stampede the whole command.[17]

Major General Philip H. Sheridan. *Courtesy USAMHI.*

As the Confederates drew near, Custer, who welcomed a fight with as much enthusiasm as Hancock, rode furiously back to his main line. Reaching the brigade, he ordered the band, which was posted in rear of the command, to strike up an inspiring tune. Turning to the rest of the troopers, he bellowed: "Forward, by divisions!" With that the mounted lines began to move. Major Kidd continues:

> As the band struck up the inspiriting strains of "Yankee Doodle," the First Michigan broke by subdivisions from the right, the Sixth following in line, regimental front and the two regiments charged with a yell through the thick underbrush out into the open ground just as the confederate troopers emerged from the woods on the opposite side. Both commands kept on in full career, the First and Sixth inextricably intermingled, until they reached the edge of the ravine, when they stopped, the confederates surprised by the sudden appearance and audacity of the Michigan men and their gallant leader; Custer well content with checking Rosser's vicious advance. Some of the foremost of either side kept on and crossed sabers in the middle of the ravine. Among these was Lieutenant Cortez P. Pendill, of the Sixth Michigan, who was severely wounded among the very foremost. One squadron of the confederates, possibly a small regiment, charging in column of fours, went past our right flank, and then, like the French army that marched up a hill and then marched down again, turned and charged back, without attempting to turn their head of column towards the place where Custer was standing at bay, with his Michiganders clustered thick about him. Pretty soon the confederates ran a battery into the field and opened on us with shell. Every attempt to break Custer's line, however, ended in failure, the Spencer carbines proving too much of an obstacle to be overcome.[18]

After the successful repulse of several Confederate charges, Custer rode up to Major Kidd and directed him to lead the 6th Michigan through the woods at the northern end of the clearing (the right of the brigade) and flank the left of Rosser's force.

The bugler of the 6th sounded the "Rally" and the scattered troopers assembled on the regimental colors. As the blue horsemen began to work their way around the Confederate left, they were surprised at the sight of a dismounted line of gray troopers in their front, obviously intent on carrying out the same maneuver that had been assigned to the 6th. This rebel line, however, extended for some distance to the right of Major Kidd's command, and, shortly after the shooting began, the Federals realized that their right flank was in danger. The Yankee carbines spoke with authority and the tremendous firepower of these weapons succeeded in halting the advancing Confederates in front of the regiment. There was, however, little that could be done to protect the right, and Major Kidd at once dispatched an officer to ride to General Custer for help.[19]

Pulling his frothing horse to a halt in front of the brigade commander, the officer told Custer of the 6th's predicament. Fortunately, Devin's brigade had just arrived and the 17th Pennsylvania, of that command, and the 5th Michigan of Custer's own brigade, were ordered to ride to the support of the 6th with all haste.[20]

The reinforcements arrived none too soon, for the Confederates were heavily pressing the right of the 6th, which seemed about to break at any moment. The two regiments, under the command of Colonel Russell Alger of the 5th Michigan, wheeled into position on the right of Major Kidd's command and drove everything before them. The Confederates gave way in disorder and fled from the field.[21]

Custer had won a signal victory over Rosser's brigade, which had been supported by a couple of regiments from Fitz Lee's division. This victory ended any chance the Confederate cavalry may have had of striking the left of Hancock's command. At noon Custer sent the following dispatch to General Torbert, who forwarded it to Sheridan, who in turn sent it to Meade:

I was attacked by Fitz. Lee's division near the intersection of the Furnace and Brock roads. After an obstinate fight I drove him in disorder from the field, compelling him to leave a considerable number of dead and wounded on the field. My loss will be about 20 in all. General Rosser's assistant adjutant-general was killed. I have prisoners from Young's and Rosser's brigades. Colonel Devin, with his command, arrived in the nick of time and rendered good service. Gregg also let me have two guns. The enemy retired rapidly to my left, and are now in front of Gregg.[22]

3. *Longstreet Forms for a Flank Attack*

The lull at 10:00 A.M. marked an end to the first half of the day's fighting. As was now evident, this battle would not be won or lost by any general's tactics; rather, it would be decided by the sheer ability of the men in the ranks to stand up to the enemy's violent musketry.

The very fact that the Confederate lines were almost entirely out of sight made Hancock nervous. He thrived on the ability to ride up and down the lines, in plain sight of his men as well as the enemy, as he had on other fields; but here the Wilderness prevented it and made him restless. Grant, however, calmly accepted the fact that there was simply nothing he could do but issue orders. He spent this day much as he had the previous one, sitting with his back against a tree, whittling sticks and smoking the ever-present cigar.

Earlier in the day an incident occurred that strongly illustrated Grant's character in battle. Horace Porter recalled what happened:

> Warren's troops were driven back on a portion of his line in front of general headquarters, stragglers were making their way to the rear, the enemy's shells were beginning to fall on the knoll where General Grant was seated on the stump of a tree, and it looked for a while as if the tide of battle would sweep over that point of the field. He rose slowly to his feet, and stood for a time watching the scene, and mingling the smoke of his cigar with the smoke of battle, without making any comments. His horse was in charge of an orderly just behind the hill, but he evidently had no thought of mounting. An officer ventured to remark to him, "General, wouldn't it be prudent to move headquarters to the other side of the Germanna road till the result of the present attack is known?" The general replied very quietly, between the puffs of his cigar, "It strikes me it would be better to order up some artillery and defend the present location." Thereupon a battery was brought up, and every preparation made for defense. The enemy, however, was checked before he reached the knoll.[23]

During the brief respite, the opposing forces were making use of the time to strengthen their breastworks and re-form their lines. Warren and Sedgwick, whose commands had only been engaged in minor skirmishing throughout the morning, were issued orders at

10:35 A.M. to send as many troops as possible over to the left of the army, to support Hancock in his attack. The following dispatch is the one received by General Warren:

> The major-general commanding directs that under existing circumstances your attack and that of General Sedgwick be suspended. You will at once throw up defensive works to enable you to hold your position with the fewest possible number of men, and report at once what number of men you will have disposable for an attack upon Hancock's right. General Sedgwick has the same instructions. You will confer with him respecting the line you are both to hold.[24]

Inexplicably, the orders sent to Warren and Sedgwick were never carried out, for Hancock received no other troops until 2:10 P.M., when the remainder of Robinson's Fifth Corps division reported to him. This force most certainly did not indicate the major shift of troops by both the Fifth and Sixth Corps that was called for in the above dispatch. The only conclusion that can be reached is that General Meade must have abrogated the orders sometime during the morning, although no record of this exists. In the meantime, the Confederates were making some dispositions of their own.

Realizing that the chances for success of a frontal assault were slim in this impenetrable forest, General Longstreet sent Lee's chief of engineers, General M. L. Smith, on a reconnaissance mission around the left of Birney's force, to scout out a route for a flank march in that direction. After completing this assignment, Smith reported back to Longstreet at 10:00 A.M. and informed the First Corps commander of the presence of an open, unfinished railroad bed that ran in an east-west direction about a mile south of Plank Road, running roughly parallel to the road. Smith went on to explain that this railroad bed would allow for the easy formation of an attack force on Birney's left; moreover, there seemed to be no Federals in the area, and the movement of such a force would be masked by the foliage on either side of the bed. General Smith also told Longstreet that it was his opinion that it would even be possible to get some troops on Brock Road, on Hancock's extreme left, and to launch an assault from there.[25]

After Smith had finished his optimistic report, Longstreet directed him to take a small party and trace a route around the extreme Federal left. For the present, however, "Old Pete" was more directly concerned with a flank attack on Birney's force, west of Brock Road, which at that time was the greatest threat to his position.[26]

As Smith headed south on his second reconnaissance, General Longstreet called on one of his most trusted staff officers, Colonel G. Moxley Sorrel, and told him:

> Colonel, there is a fine chance of a great attack by our right. If you will get into those woods, some brigades will be found much scattered from the fight. Collect them and take charge. Form a good line and then move, your right pushed forward and turning as much as possible to the left. Hit hard when you start, but don't start until you have everything ready. I shall be waiting for your gun fire, and be on hand with fresh troops for further advance.[27]

The brigades Longstreet referred to in his instructions to Sorrel were those belonging to generals William Wofford, G. T. Anderson, and William Mahone, from the divisions of Kershaw, R. Anderson, and Field, respectively. Each of these brigade commanders was extremely capable of carrying out the difficult maneuver, especially Mahone, whom Colonel W. F. Perry later described as "a dangerous man."[28] Their commands were not, however, in a disorganized state from the day's fight, for they had been held in reserve, to the rear of Kershaw's main line of battle. Colonel Sorrel wasted no time in forming the brigades for the attack and it was probably not much later than 10:30 A.M. when he led the troops off through the woods toward the line of the railroad bed and along its cleared pathway into position on Birney's left flank.[29]

A small note should be made here about the unfinished railroad that was, and still is, one of the interesting features of the battlefield. It was completed shortly after the war and operated as the Piedmont, Fredericksburg, and Potomac Railroad. It has since been abandoned, however, and is once again in the same state as it was in 1864.[30]

The cleared ridge of the railroad bed had been available to either army as a route for a flank march against the other; however, the Federals, who surely knew it was there, never grasped its strategic importance—that is, not until Colonel McAllister discovered it while reconnoitering during the lull, at about 10:00 A.M. McAllister remembered:

> All now became quiet, the pickets ceased firing, and my men laid down. I took an orderly with me and went through the picketline to reconnoiter. By crawling along from tree to tree in front I discovered a ravine; parallel with it lay a number of very large trees; behind these trees and in the ravine were the enemy's pickets; a short distance in rear of the enemy's pickets was a railroad cut, and on the left across a ravine was an embankment; there was the position of the enemy. After taking a careful survey of it, I came back and sent an aide to report the fact to General Mott, commanding the division.[31]

By the time Mott learned of the railroad cut, however, it was too late. By 11:00 A.M. Sorrel was already in position and ready to press the attack. His brigades were arranged facing northward (from left to right, Wofford, Mahone, and Anderson). Also, Davis's brigade of Mississippians, from Heth's division, had joined the march at the last minute and was deployed in the rear of Mahone.[32]

Finally, when everything was ready, the long gray line rolled forward. The specter that had haunted Hancock's left throughout the morning had at last materialized into flesh and blood and was about to break his entire assault line.

CHAPTER EIGHT

"You Rolled Me Up Like a Wet Blanket . . ."

1. Birney's Left is Swept Away

It will be recalled that the portion of Birney's command that was stationed south of Plank Road was formed in three lines of battle. The first line consisted of, from left to right, the brigades of McAllister, Owen, and Carroll. The units of Brewster, Ward, and Hays were massed from left to right in the second line. Colonel Grant's Vermont Brigade constituted the third line, as Wheaton's brigade, formerly on Grant's immediate right, had moved to the north side of the road and taken position to the rear of General Wadsworth's command.[1]

Colonel McAllister had no sooner returned from his reconnaissance than, at about 11:00 A.M., the storm broke on the left of his brigade. His troops were the first to feel the effects of Sorrel's flanking force, which took the Federals so completely by surprise that there was little time for the officers to effect a proper change of front to meet the attack. McAllister, however, was on his horse within seconds of realizing what was taking place, riding about his men and desperately urging them to rally. At about this time he ordered Colonel Sewell, commanding the 5th New Jersey on the far left of the brigade, to "change front on the right company, right regiment." This movement was carried out with all due haste, but the resistance it offered was minor, for the rest of the brigade was beginning to crumble. Colonel McAllister gives this account in his report:

> The line was soon formed, facing the enemy, when General Mott and staff came up and was informed of the difficulty. At this time some troops (but did not know what they were) were engag-

147

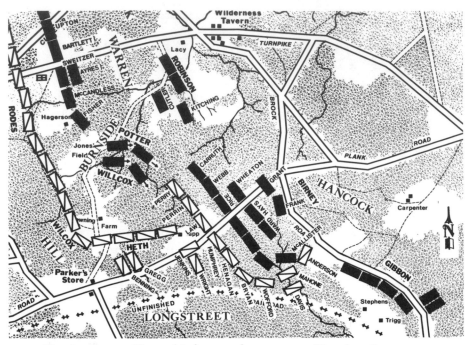

The situation on Hancock's front at about 11 A.M., May 6, as Longstreet began his flank attack against the Federal left.

ing the enemy in my front; a few moments more they gave way and I received the fire of the enemy. Held the enemy in front and delivered volley after volley into their ranks, but soon I discovered that they had flanked my left and were receiving a fire in my front, on my left flank, and rear. Here my horse was mortally wounded by two or three rifle-balls, but still able to move slowly. At this time my line broke in confusion, and I could not rally them short of the breast-works. Sick myself, and unable to walk, I urged my wounded horse slowly along before the enemy's advancing line and reached the breastworks in safety. There changed horses and reformed my brigade.[2]

As McAllister's men withdrew, their dead were left behind as if to mark the position the brigade once held. Some of the wounded were also abandoned by the Federals, as the rebel lines swiftly advanced. The fortunate ones ended up in a rebel prison, while others perished in the flames, for the Wilderness was once again ignited by the musket flashes that touched off the dry leaves that covered the ground.[3]

After routing Mott's division, Sorrel's gray band continued to systematically roll up Birney's column. Grant's Vermont Brigade was next in line, and as the right of the Confederate flank force struck its left and rear, the Green Mountain men found their position untenable. Colonel Grant also made efforts to organize some sort of resistance, but to no avail, as he recalls:

> Foiled in every attempt at this point, the enemy massed forces, about one-fourth of a mile to our left, and made a vigorous attack. Our lines at that point suddenly gave way and came in confusion past our rear. I immediately ordered two regiments to face to the left, but before the order could be executed the enemy rushed through the breach and opened fire in our rear, and at the same time made another attack in front. Perceiving that it was worse than useless to attempt further resistance there, I ordered the regiments to rally behind the breast-works on the Brock road, at which point we had been ordered to rally in case of disaster. Our entire lines at this part of the army went back in disorder. All organization and control seemed to have been lost. But out of that disorder the Vermont Brigade quietly and deliberately took its position in front of the works on the Brock road, and awaited the enemy's advance.[4]

The rout experienced by the commands of McAllister and Grant was typical of the fate of the remaining brigades on the south side of Plank Road. As soon as Longstreet heard the firing in the direction of Sorrel's force, indicating that the flank attack was underway, he ordered the divisions of Field and Kershaw to advance and strike the front of Birney's lines with everything they had. Defending two fronts proved to be an impossible task for Birney's men, and they were compelled to fall back to the trenches on Brock Road, which was soon awash with thousands of disorganized Federals. Some of these men were earnestly looking for a place to stand and fight, while others made every effort to get as far away from the fight as possible. In the meantime, General Hancock and his staff were riding back and forth along the breastworks, attempting to form a new line of defense. Theodore Lyman gives an interesting account of the scene on Brock Road at this time:

At a little after eleven Mott's left gave way. . . . The musketry now drew nearer to us, stragglers began to come back, and, in a little while, a crowd of men emerged from the thicket in full retreat. They were not running, nor pale, nor scared, nor had they thrown away their guns; but were just in the condition described by the Prince de Joinville, after Gaines Mill. They had fought all they meant to fight for the present, and there was an end of it! If there is anything that will make your heart sink and take all the backbone out of you, it is to see men in this condition! I drew my sword and rode in among them, trying to stop them at a little rifle-pit that ran along the road. I would get one squad to stop, but, as I turned to another, the first would quickly walk off. There was a German color-bearer, a stupid, scared man (who gave him the colors, the Lord only knows!) who said, "Jeneral Stavenzon, he telled me for to carry ze colors up ze road." To which I replied I would run him through the body if he didn't plant them on the rifle-pit. And so he did, but I guess he didn't stick.[5]

By 11:30 A.M. it was evident that Birney's entire column was in real danger and that his line would have to be abandoned. At that time Lyman quickly penned the following dispatch to Meade: "GENERAL: The rebels have broken through Barlow's right, and are now pushing us back along the plank road. General Gibbon has been sent for to close the gap. Sharp firing along the plank road."[6]

The only point at which the Union troops offered any stiff resistance was on Plank Road, where Wadsworth's men had successfully repulsed the vicious onslaught of Field's division. As noon approached, however, the volume of musketry began to increase steadily as Sorrel's four brigades neared the left of Wadsworth's line—Birney's only remaining stronghold west of the Brock Road defenses. There was a great crashing in the woods south of Plank Road as Sorrel's men battled their way through the thickets, brushing aside whatever token resistance remained between them and Plank Road. Shortly thereafter, the Minié balls began to rip through Wadsworth's ranks from the left side of the road, and he was compelled to make a quick change of front.

In order to complete this maneuver, however, Wadsworth had to stall for time. Turning to Colonel Macy, commanding the 20th Massachusetts, Wadsworth ordered him to drive his troops into the line of Confederates that was advancing swiftly down Plank

Road. It was a suicidal attack if ever there was one, and Wadsworth knew it; but if he could keep the Confederates in his front occupied long enough, he just might be able to handle the ones converging on his left. Realizing that he could not send the 20th on such a hopeless mission while he remained behind, Wadsworth spurred his horse in the direction of the enemy and leaped the breastworks that had been constructed across the road; the 20th, of course, followed closely behind him.[7]

Somehow, during the advance, Wadsworth lost control of his horse, which was apparently frightened by a bursting shell, and it made a dash to within twenty feet of the Confederate line. Lieutenant Earl Rogers, the general's aide-de-camp, was able to grab the horse's reins and get it started back in the right direction, but it was too late. As the two riders started back toward the Federal position, several of the rebels spotted the two officers and let loose a volley that found its mark. One bullet killed Rogers's mount and another crashed into the back of Wadsworth's skull, splattering Rogers with brains and blood. The general fell from his horse, unconscious and mortally wounded. Rogers, however, believed that Wadsworth had been killed instantaneously, and, mounting the general's horse, he rode to Fifth Corps headquarters, where he reported the incident at 12:45 P.M.[8]

Wadsworth, of course, fell into the hands of the Confederates, who took the Union general to the rear and cared for him. Apparently Colonel Sorrel was on hand to witness the incident, as he later wrote: "Every care was given to General Wadsworth by our surgeon. Before they could get to him, however, some of his valuables—watch, sword, glasses, etc.—had disappeared among the troops. One of the men came up with, 'Here, Colonel, here's his map.' It was a good general map of Virginia, and of use afterwards."[9] (Wadsworth never regained consciousness, and he died two days later.)

At about the same time that Wadsworth fell, the 20th Massachusetts was receiving a withering fire from the contesting Confederates in their front. Colonel Macy was wounded in the early stages of the fracas, and command of the regiment thus devolved upon Major Henry L. Abbott, one of the most highly esteemed officers in the army.

Young Abbott, who hailed from Lowell, Massachusetts, enlisted as a private in May, 1861, at the age of nineteen. Soon after,

Brigadier General James S. Wadsworth, who was mortally wounded at the height of Longstreet's flank attack, May 6, 1864. He died three days later. *Courtesy USAMHI.*

This photograph, taken shortly after the war, shows the location on Plank Road where Brigadier General James Wadsworth was mortally wounded. Note the tree in the center of the picture that was shattered by artillery fire. *Courtesy USAMHI.*

Major Henry L. Abbott, 20th Massachusetts, who was killed May 6, 1864.
Courtesy USAMHI.

however, he received a commission as a second lieutenant in the 20th Massachusetts, largely through the efforts of his father, Judge Josiah G. Abbott. Abbott's abilities, however, soon demonstrated that he was worthy of the rank. He won distinction in every action in which he was engaged, and his star rose rapidly in the Army of the Potomac. He was wounded in the arm at Glendale, during the Peninsular campaign, and his direction of Company I during the Federal occupation of Fredericksburg on December 11, 1862, is legendary. Captain Oliver Wendell Holmes, Jr., who knew Abbott well, perhaps summed him up best when he stated succinctly: "In action he was sublime."[10]

Although the 20th was up against a major advance of Field's division, this valiant band of Bay Staters held on, without support, under a horrendous fire from the rebels. As soon as the regiment began to waver, Abbott ordered his men to lie down, but yet, courageously, he remained erect and walked slowly back and forth before his troops to keep their lines steady. As the bullets flew over the heads of these soldiers with ever-increasing fury, one of them struck the noble Abbott, and he fell to the ground, mortally wounded. Some of the men picked him up and tenderly carried him to the rear. Captain Magnitsky, of the regiment, later told Lieutenant Schaff, with tears streaming down his face: "My God Schaff . . . I was proud of him as back and forth he slowly walked before us."[11]

Another regiment of Webb's brigade, the 19th Maine, also performed heroically in an attempt to check the rebel attack. The 19th, formerly on the right of the brigade, had gone to the rear to get a fresh supply of ammunition. After the men had filled their cartridge boxes, Colonel Seldon Connor, commanding, led the regiment back to the front; however, hearing musketry coming from the woods to the left of Plank Road, Colonel Connor sensed trouble, and, instead of returning to his former position, he wisely marched his regiment straight up the road. The 19th arrived on the scene just as Sorrel's graycoats broke out of the woods and was able to form a line quickly enough to meet the threat. The valiant resistance offered by these troops enabled the remainder of Wadsworth's force to fall back to the Brock Road defenses with fewer casualties than might have been otherwise.[12]

After the 19th withdrew, the woods west of Brock Road were completely void of Union troops, except for the dead and

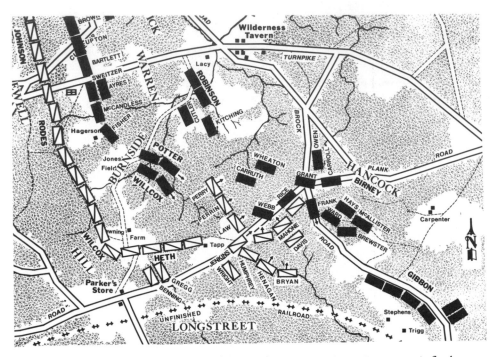

The situation on Hancock's front at about noon, May 6. Longstreet's flank attack was at its peak. Hancock's troops were falling back toward Brock Road, where Hancock and his officers were trying desperately to re-form the Federal lines.

wounded who littered the ground. Longstreet's flank movement had proven a success; however, as far as "Lee's Old War Horse" was concerned, the attack was not yet over.

2. *History Repeats Itself*

Wishing to make his victory complete, General Longstreet continued to press the divisions of Field and Kershaw forward in order to strike Hancock's disorganized Federals before they had an opportunity to rally. Accompanied by his staff and generals Kershaw and Jenkins, Longstreet rode down Plank Road at the head of his line of battle. At about this time, General Smith returned from his second reconnaissance and, after reining in alongside the First Corps commander, he reported that he had traced out the route for a flank march around Hancock's extreme left, as previously or-

Orange Plank Road, looking east. The marker at the left of the road marks the spot where Lieutenant General James Longstreet was seriously wounded at the height of his flank attack against Hancock, May 6, 1864. *Photo by Ron Carlson.*

dered. Again pleased with Smith's work, Longstreet told him to gather Sorrel's brigades and lead them into position. With that, Smith rode off to collect his troops, and Longstreet and staff continued their march.[13]

There was a general feeling of optimism among the Confederate officers as they rode down Plank Road that May morning. They had just experienced one victory and were preparing to follow it up with another, greater one. General Micah Jenkins, a promising young officer who would have had a bright future ahead of him if the Confederacy had survived, spoke jubilantly to Longstreet: "I am happy; I have felt despair of the cause for some months, but am relieved, and feel assured that we will put the enemy back across the Rapidan before night."[14] Little did anyone realize that those words were Jenkins's last, but fate has a way of stepping in when least expected.

No sooner had Jenkins finished speaking than a volley erupted from the woods on the right, and a swarm of leaden missiles swept through the band of officers. Before anyone quite realized what had happened, Jenkins was lying on the ground with a bullet in his head—not yet dead, but mortally wounded. Two staff officers were killed instantly, and General Longstreet was seriously wounded. He later remembered:

> At the moment that Jenkins fell I received a severe shock from a minie ball passing through my throat and right shoulder. The blow lifted me from the saddle, and my right arm dropped to my side. But I settled back to my seat, and started to ride on, when in a minute the flow of blood admonished me that my work for the day was done. As I turned to ride back, members of the staff, seeing me about to fall, dismounted and lifted me to the ground.[15]

General Kershaw made a quick survey of the situation and discovered that it had been their own troops that had fired upon them. Jenkins's brigade, however, did not realize this and was preparing to return the fire. Kershaw then calmly raised his hand and shouted, "F-R-I-E-N-D-S!" Upon hearing this, Jenkins's men lowered their weapons and threw themselves to the ground to avoid any further fire, but none came.[16]

Apparently, the Confederate soldiers of Sorrel's command had been as disorganized by victory as the Federals had been in defeat. As the flanking brigades approached Plank Road, the 12th Virginia, of Mahone's command, had gotten a little ahead of the other regiments and had crossed to the north side of the road. After discovering that they were the only troops in the area, the 12th made an about-face so it could recross the road and rejoin the rest of the brigade. By this time, however, Mahone's main line had reached the road and, spotting some troops emerging from the woods on the opposite side of the road, mistook the 12th for an advance of the enemy. Leveling their guns, the confused Confederates let loose a volley into the ranks of the 12th, and, unfortunately, Longstreet and staff had just ridden directly into the line of fire.[17]

At first it appeared that "Old Peter" was dying. He had lost an extreme amount of blood and was very pale. As his litter was taken to the rear, his hat was placed over his face, and, to the men standing alongside the road, it seemed certain that their general was no more. Longstreet heard one soldier remark: "He is dead, and they are telling us he is only wounded." After hearing several other statements to this effect, Longstreet raised his hat into the air with his left hand to dispel the rumors. This action brought about wild cheers from his men, and, according to Longstreet, this eased his pains somewhat.[18]

It has often been said that history repeats itself, and what happened in the Wilderness during the afternoon of May 6, 1864, seems to verify that belief. Exactly one year and four days earlier, Stonewall Jackson had delivered his famous flank attack on Hooker's army at Chancellorsville, less than five miles away from the sight of Longstreet's attack. Even more amazing is the fact that both Jackson and Longstreet were wounded at the height of their respective assaults by their own men! Unfortunately for the Confederacy, however, Jackson never recovered from his wounds.

Jackson's flank attack of May 2, 1863, has long been heralded as one of the most brilliant maneuvers of the war, while Longstreet's assault, so similar to Jackson's, has largely been ignored. Had Longstreet died of his wounds, however, this would not have been the case, for the South seems to sanctify its dead heroes by placing them upon pedestals far above the ones they occupied during life.

After the war, Longstreet's affiliation with the Republican party caused some of his former comrades (John B. Gordon and Fitzhugh Lee to name two) to turn against him and place the entire blame for the Confederate defeat at Gettysburg on his shoulders—an assertion that, by the way, has no basis in fact. In an effort to clear his name, Longstreet wrote *From Manassas to Appomattox*, in which he not only gave a good account of his experiences but also bitterly rebuked those who slandered his name. He died, however, without seeing justice done. Only recently has Longstreet begun to receive the credit he so fully earned.[19]

After Longstreet was wounded, General Field, the senior officer present, took command of the First Corps. Shortly afterward, however, General R. H. Anderson came up, and, since he was senior in rank to Field, the responsibilities of command fell to him. Longstreet's lines, however, were in such a state at the time he was wounded that no one but he could have properly directed the further advance of his troops. Therefore, when General Lee arrived on the scene, he ordered the movement abandoned and the lines re-formed.[20]

Field later stated his belief that, had the advance not been suspended, Grant would have been driven back across the river before night. This, of course, is speculation; however, Grant was not Hooker, nor was he in any way like him. He had not given up an inch of ground during any of his previous battles (except at Belmont, his first engagement during the war, which was, in fact, only a minor skirmish); moreover, there were other moves open to him short of recrossing the Rapidan—namely, withdrawing to Chancellorsville.[21]

In any case, Longstreet's flank attack was over, and, although it had not driven Grant back across the river, it had proven successful, for Hancock was forced to pull his troops back to the Brock Road defenses, thus abandoning over a half-mile of ground. Brock Road was Hancock's last line of defense and, as stated earlier, if he lost it, the Army of the Potomac would indeed have been in trouble. In a meeting with Longstreet after the war, Hancock remarked: "You rolled me up like a wet blanket, and it was some hours before I could reorganize for battle."[22]

3. Burnside's Feeble Attack

At about 1:00 P.M., after Longstreet's plan for another flank attack was terminated by General Lee, the roar of gunfire descended to a sporadic crackling while the antagonists again reformed their lines. In an effort to clear the woods in his front of enemy troops, General Hancock directed Colonel Daniel Leasure to march his brigade across the front of the Union lines, from the far left to the far right of his command. Leasure executed the maneuver with precision, but found only a few Confederate pickets in the brush. Hancock had also ordered General Gibbon to close up on the left, while he engaged the majority of his troops in strengthening the log and earth works along Brock Road. It seemed a certainty that the rebels would follow up their success, and, when they did, Hancock wished to be ready.[23]

In the meantime, Burnside continued advancing at a snail's pace toward the left of the Confederate position on Plank Road, even though Comstock had been sent by army headquarters to prod his movement. At 10:00 A.M. Burnside was still nearly a mile from his ultimate point of attack, as was conveyed in Comstock's dispatch to Grant at that hour: "Burnside has gained 1½ miles to his left to connect with Wadsworth, and now moves at once toward Hancock's firing, with Potter's division deployed, supported by a brigade. I should think Hancock's firing a mile away."[24]

Grant's headquarters received the message at 10:50 A.M., and, after waiting nearly an hour longer but hearing nothing further from Comstock that would indicate the Ninth Corps had attacked, General Grant directed his chief-of-staff, General Rawlins, to urge Burnside to attack at once. In compliance with this directive, Rawlins sent the following order to Burnside at 11:45 A.M.: "Push in with all vigor so as to drive the enemy from General Hancock's front, and get in on the Orange and Fredericksburg plank road at the earliest possible moment. Hancock has been expecting you for the last three hours, and has been making his attack and dispositions with a view to your assistance."[25]

At 1:30 P.M., Burnside's troops were at last in a position from which an attack could be launched, and, shortly before two o'clock, his lines went forward. Colonel Griffin's brigade spearheaded the attack and was supported directly by Colonel Zenas Bliss's brigade. Colonel Benjamin Christ's brigade of Willcox's division remained in reserve, while Hartranft's unit was moving in on the right.[26] General Potter gave this account of the advance in his official report:

> On arriving near the new position, I reformed as quickly as possible and moved to the attack, being entirely unable to see

anything from the thickness of the wood. The enemy were posted on the opposite side of a swampy ravine and were entrenched. After sharp firing at pretty close range we charged the enemy and got into their rifle-pits in some places, but were unable to maintain our footing and fell back. The charge was twice renewed, but although we gained considerable ground we did not succeed in getting possession of the enemy's line.[27]

The first attack made by Potter struck the left of Edward Perry's Florida brigade, which quickly melted away. As the Floridians retreated, the Federals piled into the left of Law's brigade, catching it totally off guard and driving it off in complete and unglorious rout. (It was the first and last such humiliation ever inflicted on Law's illustrious brigade during the entire course of the war.)[28]

As Griffin's brigade struck the Confederates, the first attack wave buckled, but, as related by a veteran of the 6th New Hampshire in one of the few personal accounts of this attack, the second wave met with better success: "Our men wavered for a moment when they saw the front line thus broken, but Colonel Pearson, seizing one of the flags, rushed in front of the line, and shouted, 'Come on, Sixth New Hampshire! Forward!' The boys gave a cheer and rushed on, firing as they went. The rebels were surprised by this gallant charge and tried to fall back, but we were too quick for them."[29] The 6th advanced with great success for nearly a half-mile before it realized that the rest of the brigade had withdrawn and, finding itself alone, was forced to retire, but not before capturing 106 men and 7 officers from the broken brigades of Law and Perry.[30]

The willingness of the New Hampshire men to continue the advance indicates something other than heroism, for it shows that the temporary victory gained by Potter's assault had cleared an avenue of approach to Plank Road and the Confederate rear—that is, if Burnside cared to press his advantage. The troops were available, to be sure, but for some unknown reason Griffin's brigade was withdrawn rather than reinforced. What could have been accomplished had a stronger head been in charge of the attack is anyone's guess.

As it was, however, the time used by Burnside in re-forming his lines was similarly used by the Confederates, and, by the time the Ninth Corps's assault was renewed, the rebels were fully prepared to meet it. Law's brigade had rallied and was by then strongly entrenched, facing northward, with the commands of Perrin and Perry supporting its left and right, respectively. Also, Perrin had made the connection with the right of Hill's corps, and, for the first time during the battle, the Army of Northern Virginia had an uninterrupted line of battle.[31]

Hartranft's brigade arrived on the right of the Ninth Corps at the close of the fighting and, with the impetuous drive of fresh troops, succeeded in capturing a section of the enemy's works. This attack, however, went largely unsupported, for the majority of Burnside's troops withdrew, and, consequently, Hartranft was obliged to follow the same course. By 3:00 P.M. the attack was over, having accomplished nothing, and silence once again overcame the Wilderness.[32]

CHAPTER NINE

"We Fairly Howled Them Down"

1. A Final Assault on Brock Road

By 2:15 P.M., after Burnside's attack had begun, Hancock had completed the re-formation of his lines along Brock Road. His men had worked feverishly with axes and shovels under the warm sun to improve their defenses, but, now that the work was finished, the troops sat down to rest. No one could guess what would happen next.[1]

General Robinson had reported to Hancock at 2:10 P.M. with the remaining two brigades of his Fifth Corps division (Leonard and Denison), thus giving Hancock command of a total of twenty brigades, entrenched two and three lines deep. For all purposes, his position was as secure, if not more so, than the line he had held on Cemetery Ridge at Gettysburg. Besides three lines of earthworks, an abatis of sharpened logs had been constructed in the woods about 100 paces in front of the first row of trenches.[2]

It is difficult to state with certainty the formation of Hancock's lines at this point during the battle, as the sources are contradictory. As closely as can be ascertained, however, the brigades were formed thus from left to right: Miles, Brooke, Frank, Webb, and Smyth of Gibbon's provisional command; Brewster and McAllister, of Mott's division, formed in two lines, Brewster in front; and Ward and Hays, from Birney's division, also formed in two lines, their right resting on Plank Road. North of the road was Colonel Grant's Vermont Brigade, its left touching the road, supported by Carruth's brigade of Stevenson's division. The brigades of Carroll and Rice, belonging to the divisions of Gibbon and Wadsworth, respectively, were held in reserve in rear of Carruth. Continuing to the right of Grant were the commands of Wheaton and Owen, from the divisions of Getty and Gibbon. Robinson's brigades were formed in three lines on Owen's right; however, their order is uncertain. On Robinson's right were the brigades of Eustis and Leasure, belonging to Getty and Stevenson, respectively.[3]

It will be recalled that the majority of the Second Corps artillery was on the left of Hancock's line, one of the few open areas along Brock Road that would allow for their placement. There were, however, at least two other clearings along his line where batteries could be placed. One of these openings was located directly in the rear of Mott's division, where four guns from Captain Dow's 6th Maine Light Artillery and six guns from Captain Edgell's 1st New Hampshire Light Artillery were set and ready for service. These guns, as we shall see shortly, had their chance for action before the end of the day, as did the remaining two guns of Dow's battery, which were in position at the Brock-Plank crossing, under the command of the very able Lieutenant Rogers.[4]

Lee's line of attack remains equally uncertain, but it is believed to have been deployed as follows, from left to right: Wofford, supported by Jenkins, north of Plank Road; Mahone, supported by Humphreys, formed across the road; Henagan, backed by G. T. Anderson, just south of the road; and Davis, supported by Bryan, with Wright's brigade holding the extreme right of the line.[5]

As Hancock's men continued to rest, a dispatch was delivered at Second Corps headquarters at 3:00 P.M., in which Meade instructed Hancock to have his troops ready for an advance at six o'clock that evening: "I have been expecting to hear from Lyman as to the morale of your command. Should Burnside not require any assistance and the enemy leave you undisturbed, I would let the men rest till 6 p.m., at which time a vigorous attack made by you, in conjunction with Burnside, will, I think, overthrow the enemy. I wish this done."[6]

The only flaw in Meade's planning was that Lee was not about to leave Hancock undisturbed—not after Longstreet's earlier success—and, even as Hancock read the dispatch, the Confederate commander was preparing for one last, desperate attack on Brock Road.

Meanwhile, as things remained quiet, Lyman had received permission to go back to the Second Corps hospital and visit the dying Major Abbott. Lyman later wrote:

Two miles back, in an open farm surrounded by woods, they had pitched the hospital tents. I will not trouble you with what I saw there, as I passed among the dead and dying. Abbot [sic] lay on a stretcher, quietly breathing his last—his eyes were fixed and the ashen color of death was on his face. Nearby lay his colonel, Macy, shot in the foot. I raised Macy (Colonel of the 20th Massachusetts, wounded in the same action with Abbot) and helped him to the side of Abbot, and we stood there till he died. It was a pitiful spectacle, but a common one that day. I left in haste, after arranging for sending the remains home, for the sudden sound of heavy firing told of some new attack. The Rebels (unquenchable fellows they are!) seeing that Burnside had halted, once more swung round and charged furiously on Hancock to his very rifle-pits.[7]

By 4:15 P.M. everything was ready, and Lee's nine-brigade strike force went forward with an élan that suggested, perhaps, that this attack would deliver just the blow that was needed to break Grant's army and send it flying out of the Wilderness.

The first hint the Federals had of an impending attack was a loud crashing in the woods in their front. Then, from the ascending sound of musketry, Minié balls began to whistle through the trees, snapping twigs and leveling small trees, but not yet reaching Hancock's lines, as the Confederates were still too deeply in the forest. Federal buglers stationed on the breastworks recalled the skirmish line, which fell back in a hurry and joined the rest of the troops waiting anxiously behind the log works, their hearts pumping wildly as the call rang out to "Fix bayonets."

Suddenly, a wild, demonic yelling sprang from the throats of their yet unseen foe, and, to the Federals who were waiting to receive the attack, it must have seemed as if the very gates of Hell had sprung open. The long gray line could now be seen through the trees about a hundred yards away as the rebels were halted at the abatis, and, upon the command "Fire!" the Union troops poured volley after volley into their ranks. Dow's and Edgell's guns burst into action, hurling shell and spherical case into the attackers, causing their lines to sway.

At about this time, the fire that had been burning in the woods since midmorning ignited the log works in Mott's front line, and a stiff wind, blowing eastward, fanned the flames and blew the searing heat and billowing clouds of black smoke into the faces of

Mott's men. Private Warren Goss recalled: "The fire swept on and reached our second line of intrenchments. . . . The men formed at some places eight and ten ranks deep, the rear men loading the muskets for the front ranks, and thus undauntedly kept up the fight while the logs in front of them were in flames. Finally, blistered, blinded, and suffocating, they gave way."[8]

The Confederates certainly recognized an opportunity when they saw one, and, as the flames forced Mott's men back, they charged forward, reached the burning breastworks, and planted their colors on them. These were the troops from Henagan's South Carolina brigade, supported by Anderson's Georgians—two of the toughest outfits in Lee's army. It would take more than a few flames to spoil their victory.[9]

Dow's gunners were by now working their pieces furiously in an attempt to stave off the Confederate onslaught, but their effort was beginning to seem fruitless. Every time the belching cannon knocked down a stand of colors, some bold rebel picked them up and carried them on until killed or wounded. It is difficult to imagine that the Federals could not have been moved by the bravery and sheer audacity of their devoted foes. Captain Dow later mentioned in his report that his guns knocked one particular flag down five times.[10]

While Dow was busily engaged in repelling the attack on his immediate front, someone called his attention to a column of advancing Confederates further to his right, where the right of Mott's division had once stood. Noting the impending danger, Dow swung a couple of his pieces around to meet the attack and opened fire on the charging gray line with double-shotted canister, crossing his fire with Rogers's section of guns at the crossroads. The iron balls ripped through the Confederates with horrendous effect, but did not prevent them from reaching Brock Road. The tide of battle had turned full circle, and now Grant was in the same fix that Lee had been in earlier in the day when Hancock's advance had reached the Tapp farm. Obviously, Dow's guns would not be able to hold the determined Confederates off for long. Infantry was needed to drive them back into the woods and fill the gap left by Mott's division, and, if some did not arrive soon, the damage inflicted on Hancock's position would be irreparable.[11]

After receiving word that Mott's division had taken flight, General Hancock called on the brigades of Carroll and Brooke to

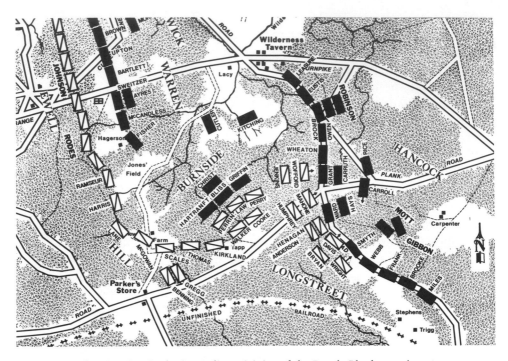

The situation in the immediate vicinity of the Brock-Plank crossing at 4:45 P.M., May 6. The Confederates of Longstreet's First Corps, with elements of Hill's Third Corps, attempted one last grand assault against the Federals of Hancock's Second Corps, which had been re-formed behind the breast-works along Brock Road. Mott's division had given way as the Confederates under Davis and Henagan poured into the gap. Carroll's Federal brigade was, however, marching toward the threatened area and would succeed in checking the break in Hancock's line.

plug the hole, while he and his staff attempted to rally the broken division. If there was such a thing as shock troops in the Union army, the title would certainly have applied to the men of Carroll's brigade; there were none better. When the Louisiana Tigers had broken through the Federal lines on Cemetery Hill after the second day's fighting at Gettysburg, it was Carroll's men who repaired the break. It was only logical, then, that Hancock should call on this intrepid command to execute the task that was then presented to him.

Marching at the double-quick, Carroll's cheering men reached the break with not a moment to spare and plunged into the Confederate lines. After a brief moment of hand-to-hand conflict, the rebels were driven into a total rout, and the disaster that had come within a hair's breadth of the Army of the Potomac was averted.[12]

An hour after the Confederate attack began, it was over, and Lee's men withdrew dejectedly to collect their dead and wounded who had fallen in the track of the storm. The victory that had been within their reach was gone, and any further hope of capturing Brock Road, they realized, had vanished. At 5:25 P.M. General Hancock wrote to Meade, informing him of his successful repulse of the Confederate attack:

> At 4:15 p.m. the enemy made a very determined assault upon my lines, covering a great part of the front. The attack was strongest from the left up to the plank road. The enemy was finally and completely repulsed at 5 o'clock. The ammunition being almost exhausted, and the hour for Burnside's attack not having arrived, I did not advance, but threw skirmishers out in pursuit. I wish now to know whether to make the assault you mentioned. I find some slight prospect of an attack farther up the Brock road, but it may be only skirmishers, but still I do not like to leave my position to make an advance with this uncertainty. The enemy's attack was continuous along my line and exceedingly vigorous. Toward the close one brigade of the enemy (Anderson's brigade) took my first line of rifle-pits from a portion of the Excelsior Brigade, but it was finally retaken by Colonel Carroll. The attack and the repulse was of the handsomest kind. Please send me your orders.[13]

Five minutes after sending this dispatch to army headquarters, Hancock was prompted to follow it up with another, specifically requesting that his planned attack of 6:00 P.M. be cancelled. The dispatch, sent at 5:30 P.M., reads as follows:

> GENERAL: Owing to the fact that I cannot supply my command with ammunition, my wagons being so far to the rear, having been sent farther back on account of the enemy's assault this morning, I do not think it advisable to attack this evening, as the troops I would select are the ones whose ammunition is exhausted, and I would have no time to prepare a formidable attack, the troops are so mixed up, owing to the occurences of to-day. Still, if I get the order, I will send some in on my right. The enemy give a little evidence of another attack farther to my right, where I find considerable want of order, which I would wish to correct. Therefore, my opinion is adverse, but I await your order.[14]

Brigadier General John B. Gordon, C.S.A. *Courtesy National Archives.*

Hancock's message was received by army headquarters at 5:45 P.M., and Meade, noting the late hour and the condition of Hancock's command, cancelled the orders for the assault, probably realizing that the chances for a successful attack, made so late in the day by exhausted troops, were slim. Hancock received the news at 6:10 P.M., in a dispatch that stated simply: "Your dispatch is received. The major-general commanding directs that you do not attack to-day. Remain as you are for the present."[15]

After two days of constant fighting, the men of Hancock's command had battled to a standstill with the Confederate troops in their front. Victory, as well as defeat, had been near for both sides, but now the fighting on this front was over; the troops had had enough. The Confederates in front of Sedgwick, however, had not yet given up their hope for success, and, even as the shadows lengthened and dusk descended, they were forming for another attack.

2. *Gordon Launches an Evening Attack*

As the firing began to slacken along Sedgwick's front after the repulse of the Confederate's dawn attack, the Federal troops of his Sixth Corps, as well as the Confederates of Ewell's Second Corps, went to work to strengthen their defenses. Others, however, were out to make more productive use of the time, namely, Confederate brigade commander John B. Gordon.

At about 8:00 A.M., Gordon sent a scouting party around the extreme right of the Federal army to ascertain the prospects of a flanking movement in that direction; a reconnaissance very similar, one might note, to the one made by General Smith around the Union left, later that morning.[16] The information gained by this small scouting force was so favorable that Gordon must have been beside himself with delight. First of all, it was noticed that Ewell's line overlapped the right of Sedgwick's corps by nearly a two-brigade front, thus eliminating the need to march a large body of troops a long distance through the woods in order to reach the point of attack. Second, the woods extended for nearly 400 yards to the north of the Federal line, where they ended at an open field, providing cover for the formation of a flank attack. Third, and perhaps most importantly, the scouting party was able to reconnoiter as far as Germanna Ford Road, on the right and to the rear of the Federal Sixth Corps, without anyone discovering its presence. Apparently, the only Union troops in the area (other than Sedgwick's men) were a handful of cavalry and one regiment of infantry, which had been posted to guard the river crossing.[17]

All of the elements for a successful flank attack were present, and at about 9:00 A.M. Gordon rode off to division headquarters to report his discovery to General Early. Upon arriving there, however, Gordon was informed that Early was not present, as he was out inspecting Johnston's brigade on the far left of the Confederate line. Due to the importance of the matter, Gordon chose not to await Early's return but to ride on to Second Corps headquarters, where, shortly after 9:00 A.M., he reported to General Ewell.

Ewell seems to have been impressed with Gordon's findings from the start, but, before giving him the official go-ahead, he wished first to confer with General Early. After his return from the Confederate left, Early was informed of Gordon's proposed attack, but he quickly made it known that he was strongly opposed to such a venture. In the first place, it was believed that Burnside's command was still within supporting distance of Sedgwick's corps and that, if Sedgwick was attacked, Burnside would be able to march to his assistance at once. (Burnside, of course, had already left the area and was at that time moving down Parker's Store Road.) Further, Early's trains were parked near Locust Grove, and, if Gordon's attack failed, the way to a Confederate disaster was open.[18]

Due to Early's objection to the movement, Ewell determined to make a personal examination of the attack area before rendering a final judgment on the matter. He later related that his reconnaissance "was made as soon as other duties permitted, but in consequence of this delay and other unavoidable causes the movement was not begun until nearly sunset."[19] After finally examining the situation, Ewell ordered the attack, for by then it was known that Burnside was not within supporting distance of the Sixth Corps, but was instead in position in the center of the Federal army.

After receiving the attack order from Ewell, Gordon swung his Georgia brigade around to the far left of the Confederate line and faced it southward, on a direct collision course with Shaler's brigade, on Sedgwick's right. Johnston's North Carolinians were formed behind Gordon's command in order to give depth and power to the attack. The rest of the troops stationed north of the

turnpike were to lend support to Gordon by making a simultaneous frontal assault on Sedgwick's line.[20]

Shortly before 7:00 P.M., Gordon ordered his brigade forward
upon the unsuspecting troops of the Sixth Corps in a mirror image
of Longstreet's earlier assault. As Gordon plunged into Shaler's
right, Johnston made a side step to the left and smashed into the
rear of the Federal brigade. Shaler's command was shattered before
anyone realized exactly what had happened, and those that had not
fled at the beginning of the onslaught were either captured or
killed.[21]

After Shaler's brigade dissolved, the right of Seymour's brigade
was exposed and became the next target for the Confederates,
who, sensing victory, crashed into his troops and completely overran the brigade. General Seymour later wrote:

> Just before sunset the enemy made an attack by throwing a
> brigade around the right and directly into the rear of my line,
> which was rolled up with great rapidity. Portions of the command
> faced to the rear and held their position for a short time, but were
> compelled to give way. The One hundred and thirty-eighth Penn-
> sylvania was promptly moved to check the enemy's advance, but
> yielding to the temporary panic, also fell to the rear. Near the
> termination of this attack, while riding toward the enemy to ascer-
> tain his force and position, I was taken prisoner.[22]

Colonel Bidwell, commanding Neill's brigade on Seymour's
left, was next to receive the attack, and, although his front line was
actively engaged in repelling Ewell's vicious frontal assault, the
forewarning sound of battle on his right and rear allowed him
enough time to change his second line from front to rear in order
to meet the impending onslaught.[23] No sooner had Bidwell re-
formed his second line than Gordon's Georgians came on, preceded by the fleeing fragments of Shaler's and Seymour's brigades.
Occupying a portion of Bidwell's new line was the 61st Pennsylvania, and, as the frightened Union men broke through its ranks, the
regimental commander, Colonel George Smith, ordered his men to
halt the flow of panic-stricken troops in any way possible: "shoot
them, bayonet them stop them any way you can," shouted the
Colonel. It is doubtful, however, that anyone actually carried out
his orders to the letter. In any case, some of the stampeding Federals were re-formed behind the new line of defense, although the

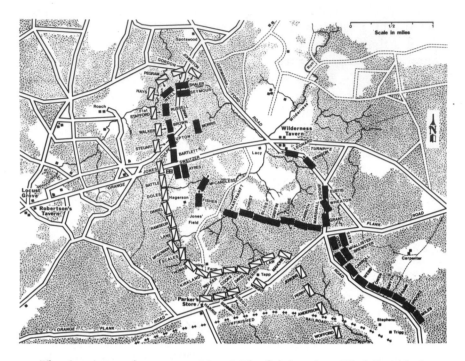

The situation at about 7 P.M., May 6. The fighting along Plank Road had ended. North of the turnpike, however, Gordon had launched a successful flank attack against the right of Sedgwick's Sixth Corps. A portion of the brigades of Upton and Morris had been sent to check the rout of Shaler and Seymour, while Crawford's division moved to reinforce that sector. Wadsworth's shattered division, which was regrouping near the Lacy house, has been omitted from this map. Also not shown are the Confederate brigades of Humphrey, Henagan, and Bryan, which were formed, respectively, to the right of Wofford, on the extreme Confederate right.

majority of them were not stopped until they had reached the turnpike.[24]

Meanwhile, elements from the brigades of Emory Upton and William Morris, on the left of Sedgwick's line, were ordered to march to the right, check Gordon's advance, and restore order to that sector of the field. General Morris detached three of his best regiments for this duty—the 10th Vermont, 14th New Jersey, and 106th New York. As these troops were being deployed, General Sedgwick rode up with several of his staff, and, under his watchful eye, the three regiments swung to the right and marched into the fight with a howl that resounded high above the crash of musketry—hoping to unnerve the rebels before they met them in battle. The chaplain of the 10th Vermont later recalled: "We fairly howled them down."[25]

Rapidly moving to Morris's support were two regiments from Upton's brigade, the 121st New York and the 95th Pennsylvania, under the command of Lieutenant Colonel James Duffy. As this force marched toward the threatened area, its line became disorganized due to the density of the woods and, when an enfilading fire ripped through its ranks from the left, the troops broke.

Fortunately, Colonel Upton had decided to leave his main line under the command of Colonel W. H. Penrose and to follow Duffy's men into battle. By the time Upton caught up with Duffy's force, many of its members had taken flight, but the aggressive young Colonel succeeded in rallying about half of the force and advanced with it shortly thereafter. Upton had not progressed very far, however, when he encountered hundreds of officers and men who were falling back. These troops were neither frightened nor running, but were simply returning to their lines, and all had the same message: there were no longer any rebels in their front or on their right—Gordon had withdrawn.[26]

Upon receiving this news, Upton led his men back and formed them in a line of trenches to the right of Morris's detached command. Gordon's flank attack had at last run itself out, but not before routing three brigades, killing about 400 Yankees, and capturing hundreds of others—among them, brigadier generals Shaler and Seymour.[27] Shaler wrote an absorbing account of his fate in his personal diary:

> By extraordinary efforts on the part of Sedgwick and other officers, the panic was stopped at the road (at the right flank of Neill's brigade) and a line formed to advance against the enemy. I had contributed my efforts, and galloping to the right to collect what scattering men might have taken to the road to the rear, and to see to the more perfect organization of that part of the line, found myself in an instant surrounded by a dozen or more butternuts each having his gun pointed in the direction of my innocent carcass—a summons to surrender and dismount was answered precisely as a good soldier would obey any lawful order of his superior. To my extreme disgust and mortification I found myself a prisoner of war and captured by a dozen or more straggling vagabonds, who with half the number of my fellows, I could have

driven from the woods and captured with ease. My sword was jerked from me by a nasty nosed ruffian, but in a moment after when the danger of my situation was over, an officer stepped from behind a tree and received it. My horse, my splendid stallion, was to share my fate. By a circuitous route I was taken to the rear and turned over to Capt. Page, inspector of Gordon's brigade of Georgia troops who treated me kindly, especially after I had given him my gold belt, which according to the value placed upon their money was worth 330 dollars. For this act of forced kindness I was permitted to ride 2½ miles on an old nag which could be sold in N.Y. for 20 shillings. Here at Locust Grove, I met Genl. Seymour who was captured a few minutes before. We were very kindly treated by Col. Seward, Insp. Gen. of Ewell's Corps and furnished with a comfortable bed and breakfast.[28]

Sedgwick's quick handling of the situation had certainly prevented the panic from spreading further than it did. Not only was he responsible for sending Upton and Morris to stabilize the right, but he personally set about to restore order to the broken troops. "Halt! For God's sake, Boys, rally!" shouted Sedgwick as he rode among the scattering troops, waving his sword: "Don't disgrace yourselves and your General this way!"[29]

While Sedgwick was engaged in this activity, the rebels continued to pour through the gaps in the Federal lines, and, suddenly, from out of nowhere, a Confederate officer appeared before the Sixth Corps commander, pointed a revolver in his face and shouted: "Surrender, you Yankee Son of a Bitch!" Someone shot the Confederate, however, and the matter ended there. It is, in a way, unfortunate that Sedgwick was not captured, for if he had been, he would not have been killed at Spotsylvania Court House.[30]

The manner in which Federal army headquarters received the news of Gordon's attack is one of extreme interest and, before concluding the account of the action, we should examine the events that took place there.

By the time Gordon's assault reached its peak, darkness had completely blanketed the field, and, when the rebels came screaming out of the black unknown, it was enough to frighten any man. Some of Sedgwick's staff officers, attempting to deliver a dispatch to the right of the line, encountered some of the fugitives on Germanna Road, and from these men the officers heard not only that the right of the corps had been crushed but also that both Sedgwick and Wright had probably been captured. Turning rein at once, the officers spurred their mounts in the direction of army headquarters, where they arrived shortly thereafter. Dismounting, the excited men found General Humphreys and explained to him the state of affairs on the Sixth Corps front.

Humphreys was not certain what to believe, but he immediately sent for General Meade, who came over directly with General Grant. Upon hearing that many of Sedgwick's men had taken flight at the onset of a Confederate attack, Meade's temper hit the roof, and, turning to one of the staff officers, he roared: "Do you mean to tell me that the Sixth Corps is to do no more fighting this campaign?"[31]

Even Grant seemed perturbed at the turn of events, and, when one officer remarked that Lee would probably cut them off from the river and roll up the entire army, Grant responded tersely by saying that he was sick and tired of hearing what Lee was going to do. "Some of you always seem to think he is suddenly going to turn a double somersault and land in our rear and on both flanks at the same time."[32]

In order to make sure that the Confederates did not reach the turnpike, Meade called on Crawford's division of Pennsylvania Reserves and sent them in to check the rebel advance. By the time these troops reached Sedgwick's lines, however, the fight had ended, and the Confederates, firing sporadically, disappeared into the darkness from which they had come. That night Sedgwick withdrew his right, uncovering Flat Run Road, thus abandoning Germanna Ford. If the army was to retreat, it would now have to do so by way of Ely's and United States fords.[33]

After Gordon's attack had been repulsed and the day's commotion had ended, Grant and his staff settled down to enjoy a few minutes of peace and quiet before retiring for the night. The day had been exceedingly long, Grant was tired, and he needed a cigar. His servant, Bill, had given him two dozen at the beginning of the day, and the General had stuffed them into the pockets of his frock coat. Now, however, as he reached for one, he discovered that the pockets were empty. Incredibly, during the course of the day, Grant had smoked all twenty-four of them—a record he never again equalled. Finally, bidding his staff good night, Grant walked over to his tent, pulled down the flap, and went to sleep. The second day of fighting in the Wilderness was at an end.[34]

3. *"Keep Moving On"*

As the first rays of the sun began to pierce through the forest on May 7, they revealed a smoldering Wilderness, strewn with the wreckage of two days of intense fighting. During the course of the night both armies had re-formed their lines into totally defensive formations, closing all the gaps that had formerly existed between units, and, in the case of the Army of the Potomac, all detached troops were returned to their original commands. Meade's corps now stood, from left to right: Second, Ninth, Fifth, and Sixth. Lee's three corps were arranged, left to right: Second, Third, and First.[35]

Entrenchments had also been improved during the night, and, as the sun began to top the trees, the tired men of both armies stood behind them, waiting apprehensively for their enemy to attack. Experience had taught them that if an attack was going to come, it would more than likely happen at daylight. Finally, dawn arrived, but nowhere was there any sign of an impending assault. Both forces had sent in their last reserve; they had used up every bit of energy and now resigned themselves to sit back and lick their wounds. Skirmishing continued throughout the day as the armies felt each other's lines, but the only real action that took place was a very brief clash of cavalry at Todd's Tavern, where Sheridan's and Stuart's horsemen vied for possession of the Catharpin-Brock crossing. The details of this engagement are sketchy, at best, but in the end the Federal troopers drove off the Confederate cavalry-men.[36]

The battle was over, and, tactically, it was a draw. Both armies remained on the field and both were still very formidable forces. In short, neither had compelled the other to retreat. Lee, who was barely able to hold his own on May 5, had tried two flank maneuvers as well as a massive frontal assault, and, although he had forced the Federals to give up some ground, he had not achieved the desired result; that is, Grant was not forced back over the Rapidan, and the Army of the Potomac remained a very real threat.

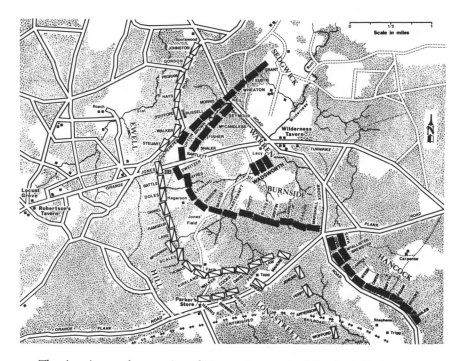

The situation on the morning of May 7. As a result of Gordon's flank attack the night before, Meade had refused his right flank, north of Orange Turnpike, and abandoned Germanna Ford. For the most part, the brigades had returned to their respective divisions, and the four infantry corps of the army were once again straightened out.

Just as Lee had not accomplished his desired purpose, neither had Grant—although he had come very close to cutting the Army of Northern Virginia in half on the morning of May 6, when Hancock's men reached the Tapp farm. Longstreet's timely arrival, however, relieved the situation for the Confederates and put that army out of danger.

It can now be seen clearly that, as things stood on the morning of May 7, only the movement of one of the two armies could determine the final outcome of the battle. Because Lee was fighting on the defensive, protecting the advances to Richmond, he left the first move up to Grant.

In the meantime, the relative inactivity, even if only temporary, gave the troops an opportunity to get some much needed rest.

Some of the men slept, and here and there some could be seen playing cards or writing letters, but for the first time they were able to reflect on what had happened over the past two days and what their future as an army might be. It was the perfect time for rumors to spread (something that plagued the Federal army horribly), and one in particular had Grant's men worried—was the army going back across the Rapidan? It was the course taken the previous May after the defeat at Chancellorsville, and, as it seemed then, they had certainly gained no victory in the Wilderness. So who was to say that Grant was any different from Hooker? After all, he was new to this army and the rank and file had yet to learn his ways.

General Wilson was, in fact, so disturbed by rumors of retreat that he decided to go and see his old friend Grant and find out the true situation once and for all. Grant, who was sitting before the door of his tent, saw Wilson dismount and, noting the anxious look on his face, immediately knew the purpose of the visit. As Wilson approached, Grant remarked: "It's all right, Wilson; the Army of the Potomac will go forward to-night."[37]

At 6:30 A.M. Grant wrote Meade and gave him the official word to move south by the left flank:

> GENERAL: Make all preparations during the day for a night march, to take position at Spotsylvania Court-House with one army corps; at Todd's Tavern with one, and another near the intersection of Piney Branch and Spotsylvania Railroad with the road from Alsop's to Old Court-House. If this move should be made, the trains should be thrown forward early in the morning to the Ny River. I think it would be advisable in making this change to leave Hancock where he is until Warren passes him. He could then follow and become the right of the new line. Burnside will move on the plank road to the intersection of it with the Orange and Fredericksburg plank road, then follow Sedgwick to his place of destination. All vehicles should be got out of hearing of the enemy before the troops move, and then move off quietly. It is more than probable the enemy will concentrate for a heavy attack on Hancock this afternoon. In case they do we must be prepared to resist them and follow up any success we may gain with our whole force. Such a result would necessarily modify these instructions. All the hospitals should be moved to-day to Chancellorsville.[38]

After receiving the above orders, Meade notified his corps commanders, and arrangements were made to get the trains moving. The central idea, of course, was to withdraw quietly and be well under way before the Confederates realized what was taking place. If Grant could gain possession of Spotsylvania before Lee did, the Confederate army would be cut off from its capital, and the door to Richmond would be open.

Lee was, most certainly, wondering throughout the day what Grant's next move would be. Since the Federals had abandoned Germanna Ford, they were cut off from their line of supplies and, as a result, could not remain in their present position for very much longer; therefore, reasoned Lee, Grant had to move and move soon. Although there was, as yet, no solid evidence to support his belief, Lee determined that the most likely destination for the Army of the Potomac would be Spotsylvania Court House. There the Federals could not only establish a new supply line with the coast via an overland route from Fredericksburg, but also, if they moved quickly enough, they could interpose their army between his troops and Richmond. It was with this knowledge, and this knowledge alone, that Lee ordered General Pendleton to cut a road through the woods on the right of the army to the Shady Grove Church Road, which led directly to Spotsylvania. If it could be completed in time, the route would give the Confederates a slight edge on the Federals.[39]

Meanwhile, accompanied by Sorrel and Gordon, Lee boarded Traveller and struck out to survey the ground over which Gordon had launched his flank attack the night before. Speaking more candidly than usual, the Confederate commander told his two subordinates of his guess for the probable route of the Union army. "Grant is not going to retreat," Lee said, confidently. "He will move his army to Spotsylvania." Gordon, impressed at this bit of information, asked Lee if he had received some sort of intelligence that would indicate a movement in that direction. "Not at all, not at all," replied Lee, "but that is the next point at which the armies will meet; Spotsylvania is now General Grant's best strategic point."[40]

Shortly after the Confederate leader returned to his headquarters at the Tapp farm, news came in of Stuart's clash with Sheridan's cavalry at Todd's Tavern. The movement of the Union cavalry to the right, together with reports that Federal artillery was seen moving in the same direction, gave Lee the solid evidence he had been seeking. The race for Spotsylvania Court House was on, and a new campaign had begun.

Losses over the past two days had been staggering. Out of over 100,000 Union troops involved, 2,246 were dead, 12,037 were wounded, and 3,383 were missing in action, resulting in a total Federal loss of 17,666. Confederate losses remain unknown, but reports placed the number of rebel casualties at a minimum of 7,500.[41] Although these men had not suffered in vain, the fact was of little comfort to the more than 25,000 homes, North and South, that were grieving as a result of this engagement.

That night the roads leading south were packed with creaking wagons, tired men, and horses, as the Army of the Potomac and the Army of Northern Virginia marched out of the Wilderness forever. Once again the woodland was silent, except for the peaceful rustling of the trees in the winds and the rippling of Wilderness Run. Hell had visited the forest for two days, but now it was gone. And although the Wilderness was scarred forever by war, it would never again be the host of such violence.

Grant was heading south and had thus converted a drawn battle into what became, at the very least, a moral victory for the North. Although the troops never forgot what had happened on those two days in May, the Army of the Potomac continued its march toward Richmond, just as if it had never encountered Lee in the Wilderness, thereby proving to the nation once and for all that the war in the eastern theater would not continue the attack and retreat tactics that had been demonstrated over the past three years. Grant had fulfilled his military creed to "keep moving on."

APPENDIX A

ORDER OF BATTLE, ARMY OF THE POTOMAC

HEADQUARTERS, ARMIES IN THE FIELD
Lt. Gen. Ulysses S. Grant
Escort: B, F, and K, 5th U.S. Cavalry

COMMANDER, ARMY OF THE POTOMAC
Maj. Gen. George G. Meade

PROVOST GUARD
Brig. Gen. Marsena R. Patrick

1st Massachusetts Cavalry, C and D
80th New York Infantry (20th Militia)
3d Pennsylvania Cavalry
68th Pennsylvania Infantry
114th Pennsylvania Infantry

VOLUNTEER ENGINEER BRIGADE*
Brig. Gen. Henry W. Benham

15th New York
50th New York

BATTALION U.S. ENGINEERS
Capt. George H. Mendell

GUARDS AND ORDERLIES
Independent Company Oneida (New York) Cavalry

II CORPS—Maj. Gen. Winfield S. Hancock
Escort: 1st Vermont Cavalry

First Division, Brig. Gen. Francis C. Barlow

FIRST BRIGADE	SECOND BRIGADE
Col. Nelson A. Miles	Col. Thomas A. Smyth
26th Michigan	28th Massachusetts
61st New York	63d New York

*With the exception of eleven companies of the 50th New York, this command, with its commander, was at the Engineer Depot, Washington, D.C.

183

81st Pennsylvania
140th Pennsylvania
183d Pennsylvania

69th New York
88th New York
116th Pennsylvania

THIRD BRIGADE
Col. Paul Frank

FOURTH BRIGADE
Col. John R. Brooke

39th New York
52d New York*
57th New York
111th New York
125th New York
126th New York

2d Delaware
64th New York
66th New York
53d Pennsylvania
145th Pennsylvania
148th Pennsylvania

SECOND DIVISION
Brig. Gen. John Gibbon

PROVOST GUARD
2d Company Minnesota Sharpshooters

FIRST BRIGADE
Brig. Gen. Alexander S. Webb

SECOND BRIGADE
Brig. Gen. Joshua T. Owen

19th Maine
1st Company Andrew
(Massachusetts
Sharpshooters)
15th Massachusetts
19th Massachusetts
20th Massachusetts
7th Michigan
42d New York
59th New York
82d New York (2d Militia)

152d New York
69th Pennsylvania
71st Pennsylvania
72d Pennsylvania
106th Pennsylvania

THIRD BRIGADE
Col. Samuel S. Carroll

14th Connecticut
1st Delaware
14th Indiana
12th New Jersey

*Detachment 7th New York attached.

10th New York Battalion
108th New York
4th Ohio
8th Ohio
7th West Virginia

THIRD DIVISION
Maj. Gen. David B. Birney

FIRST BRIGADE
Brig. Gen. J. H. Hobart Ward

20th Indiana
3d Maine
40th New York
86th New York
124th New York
99th Pennsylvania
110th Pennsylvania
141st Pennsylvania
2d U.S. Sharpshooters

SECOND BRIGADE
Brig. Gen. Alexander Hays

4th Maine
17th Maine
3d Michigan
5th Michigan
93d New York
57th Pennsylvania
63d Pennsylvania
105th Pennsylvania
1st U.S. Sharpshooters

FOURTH DIVISION
Brig. Gen. Gershom Mott

FIRST BRIGADE
Col. Robert McAllister

1st Massachusetts
16th Massachusetts
5th New Jersey
6th New Jersey
7th New Jersey
8th New Jersey
11th New Jersey
26th Pennsylvania
115th Pennsylvania

SECOND BRIGADE
Col. William R. Brewster

11th Massachusetts
70th New York
71st New York
72d New York
73d New York
74th New York
120th New York
84th Pennsylvania

ARTILLERY BRIGADE
Col. John C. Tidball

Maine Light, 6th Battery (F)
Massachusetts Light, 10th Battery
New Hampshire Light, 1st Battery
1st New York Light, Battery G

4th New York Heavy, 3d Battalion
1st Pennsylvania Light, Battery F
1st Rhode Island Light, Battery A
1st Rhode Island Light, Battery B
4th United States, Battery K
5th United States, Batteries C and I

V CORPS—Maj. Gen. Gouverneur K. Warren

PROVOST GUARD
12th New York Battalion

FIRST DIVISION
Brig. Gen. Charles Griffin

FIRST BRIGADE
Brig. Gen. Romeyn B. Ayres

140th New York
146th New York
91st Pennsylvania
155th Pennsylvania
2d   United States, Companies B, C, F, H, I, and K
11th United States, Companies B, C, D, E, F, and G, First Battalion
12th United States, Companies A, B, C, D, and G, First Battalion
12th United States, Companies A, C, D, F, and H, Second Battalion
14th United States, First Battalion
17th United States, Companies A, C, D, G, and H, First Battalion
17th United States, Companies A, B, and C, Second Battalion

SECOND BRIGADE	THIRD BRIGADE
Col. Jacob B. Sweitzer	Brig. Gen. Joseph J. Bartlett
9th Massachusetts	20th Maine
22d Massachusetts*	18th Massachusetts
32d Massachusetts	1st Michigan
4th Michigan	16th Michigan
62d Pennsylvania	44th New York
	83d Pennsylvania
	118th Pennsylvania

*2d Company Massachusetts Sharpshooters attached.

SECOND DIVISION
Brig. Gen. John C. Robinson

FIRST BRIGADE
Col. Samuel H. Leonard

16th Maine
13th Massachusetts
39th Massachusetts
104th New York

SECOND BRIGADE
Brig. Gen. Henry Baxter

12th Massachusetts
83d New York (9th Militia)
97th New York
11th Pennsylvania
88th Pennsylvania
90th Pennsylvania

THIRD BRIGADE
Col. Andrew W. Denison

1st Maryland
4th Maryland
7th Maryland
8th Maryland

THIRD DIVISION
Brig. Gen. Samuel W. Crawford

FIRST BRIGADE
Col. William McCandless

1st Pennsylvania Reserves
2d Pennsylvania Reserves
6th Pennsylvania Reserves
7th Pennsylvania Reserves
11th Pennsylvania Reserves
13th Pennsylvania Reserves
(1st Rifles)

THIRD BRIGADE
Col. Joseph W. Fisher

5th Pennsylvania Reserves
8th Pennsylvania Reserves
10th Pennsylvania Reserves
12th Pennsylvania Reserves

FOURTH DIVISION
Brig. Gen. James S. Wadsworth

FIRST BRIGADE
Brig. Gen. Lysander Cutler

7th Indiana
19th Indiana
24th Michigan

SECOND BRIGADE
Brig. Gen. James C. Rice

76th New York
84th New York (14th Militia)
95th New York

1st New York Battalion   147th New York
       Sharpshooters   56th Pennsylvania
2d   Wisconsin
6th Wisconsin
7th Wisconsin

THIRD BRIGADE
Col. Roy Stone

121st Pennsylvania
142d   Pennsylvania
143d   Pennsylvania
149th Pennsylvania
150th Pennsylvania

ARTILLERY BRIGADE
Col. Charles S. Wainwright

Massachusetts Light, Battery C
Massachusetts Light, Battery E
1st New York Light, Battery D
1st New York Light, Batteries E and L
1st New York Light, Battery H
4th New York Heavy, Second Battalion
1st Pennsylvania Light, Battery B
4th United States, Battery B
5th United States, Battery D

VI CORPS—Maj. Gen. John Sedgwick
Escort: 8th Pennsylvania Cavalry, Company A

FIRST DIVISION
Brig. Gen. Horatio G. Wright

FIRST BRIGADE   SECOND BRIGADE
Col. Henry W. Brown   Col. Emory Upton

1st   New Jersey   5th   Maine
2d   New Jersey   121st New York
3d   New Jersey   95th Pennsylvania
4th   New Jersey   96th Pennsylvania
10th New Jersey
15th New Jersey

THIRD BRIGADE
Brig. Gen. David A. Russell

6th Maine
49th Pennsylvania
119th Pennsylvania
5th Wisconsin

FOURTH BRIGADE
Brig. Gen. Alexander Shaler

65th New York
67th New York
122d New York
82d Pennsylvania (detachment)

SECOND DIVISION
Brig. Gen. George W. Getty

FIRST BRIGADE
Brig. Gen. Frank Wheaton

62d New York
93d Pennsylvania
98th Pennsylvania
102d Pennsylvania
139th Pennsylvania

SECOND BRIGADE
Col. Lewis A. Grant

2d Vermont
3d Vermont
4th Vermont
5th Vermont
6th Vermont

THIRD BRIGADE
Brig. Gen. Thomas H. Neill

7th Maine
43d New York
49th New York
77th New York
61st Pennsylvania

FOURTH BRIGADE
Brig. Gen. Henry L. Eustis

7th Massachusetts
10th Massachusetts
37th Massachusetts
2d Rhode Island

THIRD DIVISION
Brig. Gen. James B. Ricketts

FIRST BRIGADE
Brig. Gen. William H. Morris

14th New Jersey
106th New York
151st New York
87th Pennsylvania
10th Vermont

SECOND BRIGADE
Brig. Gen. Truman Seymour

6th Maryland
110th Ohio
122d Ohio
126th Ohio
67th Pennsylvania (detachment)
138th Pennsylvania

ARTILLERY BRIGADE
Col. Charles H. Tompkins

Maine Light, 4th Battery (D)
Massachusetts Light, 1st Battery (A)

New York Light, 1st Battery
New York Light, 3d Battery
4th New York Heavy, First Battalion
1st Rhode Island Light, Battery C
1st Rhode Island Light, Battery E
1st Rhode Island Light, Battery G
5th United States, Battery M

IX CORPS—Maj. Gen. Ambrose E. Burnside*

PROVOST GUARD
8th U.S. Infantry

FIRST DIVISION
Brig. Gen. Thomas G. Stevenson

FIRST BRIGADE	SECOND BRIGADE
Col. Sumner Carruth	Col. Daniel Leasure
35th Massachusetts	3d Maryland
56th Massachusetts	21st Massachusetts
57th Massachusetts	100th Pennsylvania
59th Massachusetts	
4th United States	
10th United States	

ARTILLERY
Maine Light, 2d Battery (B)
Massachusetts Light, 14th Battery

SECOND DIVISION
Brig. Gen. Robert B. Potter

FIRST BRIGADE	SECOND BRIGADE
Col. Zenas R. Bliss	Col. Simon G. Griffin
36th Massachusetts	31st Maine
58th Massachusetts	32d Maine
51st New York	6th New Hampshire
45th Pennsylvania	9th New Hampshire
48th Pennsylvania	11th New Hampshire
7th Rhode Island	17th Vermont

*This corps was under the direct orders of Lt. Gen. Grant until May 24, 1864, when it was assigned to the Army of the Potomac.

ARTILLERY
Massachusetts Light, 11th Battery
New York Light, 19th Battery

THIRD DIVISION
Brig. Gen. Orlando B. Willcox

FIRST BRIGADE	SECOND BRIGADE
Col. John F. Hartranft	Col. Benjamin C. Christ

2d Michigan	1st Michigan Sharpshooters
8th Michigan	20th Michigan
17th Michigan	79th New York
27th Michigan*	60th Ohio**
109th New York	50th Pennsylvania
51st Pennsylvania	

ARTILLERY
Maine Light, 7th Battery (G)
New York Light, 34th Battery

FOURTH DIVISION*
Brig. Gen. Edward Ferrero

FIRST BRIGADE	SECOND BRIGADE
Col. Joshua K. Sigfried	Col. Henry G. Thomas

27th U.S. Colored Troops	30th Connecticut (colored) detachment
30th U.S. Colored Troops	
39th U.S. Colored Troops	19th U.S. Colored Troops
43d U.S. Colored Troops	23d U.S. Colored Troops

ARTILLERY
Pennsylvania Light, Battery D
Vermont Light, 3d Battery

CAVALRY
3d New Jersey
22d New York
2d Ohio
13th Pennsylvania

*1st and 2d Companies Michigan Sharpshooters attached.
**9th and 10th Companies Ohio Sharpshooters attached.
*This division was not available for battle during the Wilderness Campaign, but was restricted to guard detail.

RESERVE ARTILLERY
Capt. John Edwards, Jr.

New York Light, 27th Battery
1st Rhode Island Light, Battery D
1st Rhode Island Light, Battery H
2d United States, Battery E
3d United States, Battery G
3d United States, Batteries L and M

PROVISIONAL BRIGADE
Col. Elisha G. Marshall

24th New York Cavalry (dismounted)
14th New York Heavy Artillery
2d Pennsylvania Provisional—Heavy Artillery

CAVALRY CORPS
Maj. Gen. Philip H. Sheridan
Escort: 6th United States

FIRST DIVISION
Brig. Gen. Alfred T. A. Torbert

FIRST BRIGADE	SECOND BRIGADE
Brig. Gen. George A. Custer	Col. Thomas C. Devin
1st Michigan	4th New York*
5th Michigan	6th New York
6th Michigan	9th New York
7th Michigan	17th Pennsylvania

RESERVE BRIGADE
Brig. Gen. Wesley Merritt

19th New York (1st Dragoons)
6th Pennsylvania
1st United States
2d United States
5th United States**

*Detached, guarding trains.
**Companies B, F, and K detached as an escort to Lt. Gen. U. S. Grant.

SECOND DIVISION
Brig. Gen. David McM. Gregg

FIRST BRIGADE
Brig. Gen. Henry E. Davies, Jr.

1st Massachusetts
1st New Jersey
6th Ohio
1st Pennsylvania

SECOND BRIGADE
Col. J. Irvin Gregg

1st Maine
10th New York
2d Pennsylvania
4th Pennsylvania
8th Pennsylvania
16th Pennsylvania

THIRD DIVISION
Brig. Gen. James H. Wilson
Escort: 8th Illinois (detachment)

FIRST BRIGADE
Col. Timothy Bryan, Jr.

1st Connecticut
2d New York
5th New York
18th Pennsylvania

SECOND BRIGADE
Col. George H. Chapman

3d Indiana
8th New York
1st Vermont

ARTILLERY
Brig. Gen. Henry J. Hunt

ARTILLERY RESERVE
Col. Henry S. Burton

FIRST BRIGADE
Col. J. Howard Kitching

6th New York Heavy
15th New York Heavy

SECOND BRIGADE
Maj. John A. Tompkins

Maine Light, 5th Battery (E)
1st New Jersey Light, Battery A
1st New Jersey Light, Battery B
New York Light, 5th Battery
New York Light, 12th Battery
1st New York Light, Battery B

THIRD BRIGADE
Maj. Robert H. Fitzhugh

Massachusetts Light, 9th Battery
New York Light, 15th Battery
1st New York Light, Battery C
New York Light, 11th Battery
1st Ohio Light, Battery H
5th United States, Battery E

HORSE ARTILLERY

FIRST BRIGADE*
Capt. James M. Robertson

New York Light, 6th Battery

2d United States, Batteries B and L
2d United States, Battery D
3d United States, Battery M
4th United States, Battery A
4th United States, Batteries C and E

SECOND BRIGADE
Capt. Dunbar R. Ransom

1st United States, Batteries E and G
1st United States, Batteries H and I
1st United States, Battery K
2d United States, Battery A
2d United States, Battery G
3d United States, Batteries C, F, and K

ARMY OF NORTHERN VIRGINIA—GEN. ROBERT E. LEE
I CORPS—Lt. Gen. James Longstreet

KERSHAW'S DIVISION
Brig. Gen. Joseph B. Kershaw

KERSHAW'S BRIGADE
Col. John W. Henagan

2d South Carolina
3d South Carolina
7th South Carolina
8th South Carolina
15th South Carolina
3d South Carolina—Battalion

HUMPHREYS'S BRIGADE
Brig. Gen. Benjamin G. Humphreys

13th Mississippi
17th Mississippi
18th Mississippi
21st Mississippi

*Detached with Cavalry Corps.

WOFFORD'S BRIGADE
Brig. Gen. William T. Wofford

16th Georgia
18th Georgia
24th Georgia
Cobb's (Georgia) Legion
Phillips (Georgia) Legion
3d Georgia Battalion
—Sharpshooters

BRYAN'S BRIGADE
Brig. Gen. Goode Bryan

10th Georgia
50th Georgia
51st Georgia
53d Georgia

FIELD'S DIVISION
Maj. Gen. Charles W. Field

JENKINS'S BRIGADE
Brig. Gen. Micah Jenkins

1st South Carolina
2d South Carolina
5th South Carolina
6th South Carolina
Palmetto (South Carolina)
—Sharpshooters

ANDERSON'S BRIGADE
Brig. Gen. George T. Anderson

7th Georgia
8th Georgia
9th Georgia
11th Georgia
59th Georgia

LAW'S BRIGADE
Brig. Gen. E. McIver Law

4th Alabama
15th Alabama
44th Alabama
47th Alabama
48th Alabama

GREGG'S BRIGADE
Brig. Gen. John Gregg

3d Arkansas
1st Texas
4th Texas
5th Texas

BENNING'S BRIGADE
Brig. Gen. Henry L. Benning

2d Georgia
15th Georgia
17th Georgia
20th Georgia

ARTILLERY
Brig. Gen. E. Porter Alexander

HUGER'S BATTALION
Lt. Col. Frank Huger

Fickling's (South Carolina)
  Battery
Moody's (Louisiana) Battery
Parker's (Virginia) Battery
Smith's, J. D. (Virginia) Battery
Taylor's (Virginia) Battery
Woolfolk's (Virginia) Battery

HASKELL'S BATTALION
Maj. John C. Haskell

Flanner's (North Carolina)
  Battery
Garden's (South Carolina) Battery
Lamkin's (Virginia) Battery
Ramsay's (North Carolina)
  Battery

CABELL'S BATTALION
Col. Henry C. Cabell

Callaway's (Georgia) Battery
Carlton's (Georgia) Battery
McCarthy's (Virginia) Battery
Manly's (North Carolina) Battery

II CORPS—Lt. Gen. Richard S. Ewell

EARLY'S DIVISION
Maj. Gen. Jubal A. Early

HAYS'S BRIGADE
Brig. Gen. Harry T. Hays

5th Louisiana
6th Louisiana
7th Louisiana
8th Louisiana
9th Louisiana

PEGRAM'S BRIGADE
Brig. Gen. John Pegram

13th Virginia
31st Virginia
49th Virginia
52d Virginia
58th Virginia

GORDON'S BRIGADE
Brig. Gen. John B. Gordon

13th Georgia
26th Georgia
31st Georgia
38th Georgia
60th Georgia
61st Georgia

JOHNSON'S DIVISION
Maj. Gen. Edward Johnson

STONEWALL BRIGADE
Brig. Gen. James A. Walker

2d Virginia
4th Virginia
5th Virginia
27th Virginia
33d Virginia

STEUART'S BRIGADE
Brig. Gen. George H. Steuart

1st North Carolina
3d North Carolina
10th Virginia
23d Virginia
37th Virginia

JONES'S BRIGADE
Brig. Gen. John M. Jones

21st Virginia
25th Virginia
42d Virginia
44th Virginia
48th Virginia
50th Virginia

STAFFORD'S BRIGADE
Brig. Gen. Leroy A. Stafford

1st Louisiana
2d Louisiana
10th Louisiana
14th Louisiana
15th Louisiana

RODES'S DIVISION
Maj. Gen. Robert E. Rodes

DANIEL'S BRIGADE
Brig. Gen. Junius Daniel

32d North Carolina
43d North Carolina
45th North Carolina
53d North Carolina
2d North Carolina Battalion

RAMSEUR'S BRIGADE
Brig. Gen. Stephen D. Ramseur

2d North Carolina
4th North Carolina
14th North Carolina
30th North Carolina

DOLES'S BRIGADE
Brig. Gen. George Doles

4th Georgia
12th Georgia
44th Georgia

BATTLE'S BRIGADE
Brig. Gen. Cullen A. Battle

3d Alabama
5th Alabama
6th Alabama
12th Alabama
26th Alabama

JOHNSTON'S BRIGADE
Brig. Gen. Robert D. Johnston

5th North Carolina
12th North Carolina
20th North Carolina
23d North Carolina

ARTILLERY
Brig. Gen. Armistead L. Long

HARDAWAY'S BATTALION*
Lt. Col. Robert A. Hardaway

Dance's (Virginia) Battery
Graham's (Virginia) Battery
Griffin's, C. B. (Virginia) Battery
Jones's (Virginia) Battery
Smith's, B. H. (Virginia) Battery

NELSON'S BATTALION*
Lt. Col. William A. Nelson

Kirkpatrick's (Virginia) Battery
Massie's (Virginia) Battery
Milledge's (Georgia) Battery

BRAXTON'S BATTALION*
Lt. Col. Carter M. Braxton

Carpenter's (Virginia) Battery
Cooper's (Virginia) Battery
Hardwicke's (Virginia) Battery

CUTSHAW'S BATTALION**
Maj. Wilfred E. Cutshaw

Carrington's (Virginia) Battery
Garber's, A. W. (Virginia) Battery
Tanner's (Virginia) Battery

PAGE'S BATTALION**
Maj. Richard C. M. Page

Carter's, W. P. (Virginia) Battery
Fry's (Virginia) Battery
Page's (Virginia) Battery
Reese's (Alabama) Battery

III CORPS—Lt. Gen. Ambrose P. Hill

ANDERSON'S DIVISION
Maj. Gen. Richard H. Anderson

PERRIN'S BRIGADE
Brig. Gen. Abner Perrin

8th Alabama
9th Alabama

MAHONE'S BRIGADE
Brig. Gen. William Mahone

6th Virginia
12th Virginia

*Under the special direction of Col. J. Thompson Brown.
**Under the special direction of Col. Thomas H. Carter.

10th Alabama
11th Alabama
14th Alabama

16th Virginia
41st Virginia
61st Virginia

HARRIS'S BRIGADE
Brig. Gen. Nathaniel Harris

WRIGHT'S BRIGADE
Brig. Gen. Ambrose R. Wright

12th Mississippi
16th Mississippi
19th Mississippi
48th Mississippi

3d Georgia
22d Georgia
48th Georgia
2d Georgia Battalion

PERRY'S BRIGADE
Brig. Gen. Edward A. Perry

2d Florida
5th Florida
8th Florida

HETH'S DIVISION
Maj. Gen. Henry Heth

DAVIS'S BRIGADE
Brig. Gen. Joseph R. Davis

KIRKLAND'S BRIGADE
Brig. Gen. William W. Kirkland

2d Mississippi
11th Mississippi
42d Mississippi
55th North Carolina

11th North Carolina
26th North Carolina
44th North Carolina
47th North Carolina
52d North Carolina

COOKE'S BRIGADE
Brig. Gen. John R. Cooke

WALKER'S BRIGADE
Brig. Gen. Henry H. Walker

15th North Carolina
27th North Carolina
46th North Carolina
48th North Carolina

40th Virginia
47th Virginia
55th Virginia
22d Virginia Battalion

ARCHER'S BRIGADE
Brig. Gen. James J. Archer

13th Alabama
1st Tennessee (Provisional Army)
7th Tennessee
14th Tennessee

WILCOX'S DIVISION
Maj. Gen. Cadmus M. Wilcox

LANE'S BRIGADE
Brig. Gen. James H. Lane

7th North Carolina
18th North Carolina
28th North Carolina
33d North Carolina
37th North Carolina

McGOWAN'S BRIGADE
Brig. Gen. Samuel McGowan

1st South Carolina (Provisional Army)
12th South Carolina
13th South Carolina
14th South Carolina
1st South Carolina (Orr's Rifles)

SCALES'S BRIGADE
Brig. Gen. Alfred M. Scales

13th North Carolina
16th North Carolina
22d North Carolina
34th North Carolina
38th North Carolina

THOMAS'S BRIGADE
Brig. Gen. Edward L. Thomas

14th Georgia
35th Georgia
45th Georgia
49th Georgia

ARTILLERY
Col. R. Lindsay Walker

POAGUE'S BATTALION
Lt. Col. William T. Poague

Richard's (Mississippi) Battery
Utterback's (Virginia) Battery
William's (North Carolina) Battery
Wyatt's (Virginia) Battery

McINTOSH'S BATTALION
Lt. Col. David G. McIntosh

Clutter's (Virginia) Battery
Donald's (Virginia) Battery
Hurt's (Alabama) Battery
Price's (Virginia) Battery

PEGRAM'S BATTALION
Lt. Col. William J. Pegram

Brander's (Virginia) Battery
Cayce's (Virginia) Battery
Ellett's (Virginia) Battery
Marye's (Virginia) Battery
Zimmerman's (South Carolina) Battery

CUTTS'S BATTALION
Col. Allen S. Cutts

Patterson's (Georgia) Battery
Ross's (Georgia) Battery
Wingfield's (Georgia) Battery

RICHARDSON'S BATTALION
Lt. Col. Charles Richardson

Grandy's (Virginia) Battery
Landry's (Louisiana) Battery
Moore's (Virginia) Battery
Penick's (Virginia) Battery

CAVALRY CORPS—Maj. Gen. James E. B. Stuart

HAMPTON'S DIVISION
Maj. Gen. Wade Hampton

YOUNG'S BRIGADE
Brig. Gen. Pierce M. B. Young

7th Georgia
Cobb's (Georgia) Legion
Phillips's (Georgia) Legion
20th Georgia Battalion
Jefferson Davis (Mississippi)
Legion

ROSSER'S BRIGADE
Brig. Gen. Thomas L. Rosser

7th Virginia
11th Virginia
12th Virginia
35th Virginia Battalion

BUTLER'S BRIGADE
Brig. Gen Matthew C. Butler

4th South Carolina
5th South Carolina
6th South Carolina

FITZHUGH LEE'S DIVISION
Maj. Gen. Fitzhugh Lee

LOMAX'S BRIGADE
Brig. Gen. Lunsford Lomax

5th Virginia
6th Virginia
15th Virginia

WICKHAM'S BRIGADE
Brig. Gen. Williams C. Wickham

1st Virginia
2d Virginia
3d Virginia
4th Virginia

WILLIAM H. F. LEE'S DIVISION
Maj. Gen. William H. F. Lee

CHAMBLISS'S BRIGADE	GORDON'S BRIGADE
Brig. Gen. John R. Chambliss	Brig. Gen. James B. Gordon
9th Virginia	1st North Carolina
10th Virginia	2d North Carolina
13th Virginia	5th North Carolina

HORSE ARTILLERY
Maj. R. Preston Chew

BREATHED'S BATTALION
Maj. James Breathed

Hart's (South Carolina) Battery
Johnston's (Virginia) Battery
McGregor's (Virginia) Battery
Shoemaker's (Virginia) Battery
Thomson's (Virginia) Battery

APPENDIX B

Order for Movement, Army of the Potomac, May 2, 1864

Orders   Headquarters, Army of the Potomac
May 2, 1864.

1. The army will move on Wednesday, the 4th of May, 1864.
2. On the day previous, Tuesday, the 3d of May, Major-General Sheridan, commanding Cavalry Corps, will move Gregg's cavalry division to the vicinity of Richardsville. It will be accompanied by one-half the canvas pontoon train, the engineer troops with which will repair the road to Ely's Ford as far as practicable without exposing their work to the observation of the enemy. Guards will be placed on all the occupied houses on or in the vicinity of the route of the cavalry and in advance toward the Rapidan, so as to prevent any communication with the enemy by the inhabitants. The same precaution will be taken at the same time in

front of the First and Third Cavalry Divisions, and wherever it may be considered necessary. At 2 a.m. of the 4th May, Gregg's division will move to Ely's Ford, cross the Rapidan as soon as the canvas pontoon bridge is laid, if the river is not fordable, and as soon as the infantry of the Second Corps is up, will move to the vicinity of Piney Branch Church, or in that section, throwing reconnaissances well out on the Pamunkey road, toward Spotsylvania Court-House, Hamilton's Crossing, and Fredericksburg. The roads past Piney Branch Church, Todd's Tavern, &c., will be kept clear for the passage of the infantry the following day. The cavalry division will remain in this position to cover the passage of the army trains, and will move with them and cover their left flank. At midnight of the 3d of May, the Third Cavalry Division, with one-half the canvas pontoon bridge train, which will join it after dark, will move to Germanna Ford, taking the plank road, and cross the Rapidan as soon as the bridge is laid, if the river is not fordable, and hold the crossing until the infantry of the Fifth Corps is up. It will then move to Parker's Store, on the Orange Court-House plank road, or that vicinity, sending out strong reconnaissances on the Orange pike and plank roads and the Catharpin and Pamunkey roads, until they feel the enemy, and at least as far as Robertson's Tavern, the New Hope Church, and Almond's or Robertson's. All intelligence concerning the enemy will be communicated with promptitude to headquarters and to the corps and division commanders of the nearest infantry troops.

3. Major-General Warren, commanding Fifth Corps, will send two divisions at midnight of the 3d instant, by way of Stevensburg and the plank road, to the crossing at Germanna Ford. So much of the bridge train of the Fifth Corps as may be necessary to bridge the Rapidan at Germanna Ford, with such artillery as may be required, will accompany these divisions, which will be followed by the remainder of the corps at such hour that the column will cross the Rapidan without delay. Such disposition of the troops and artillery as may be found necessary to cover the bridge will be made by the corps commander, who, after crossing, will move to the vicinity of the Old Wilderness Tavern, on the Orange Court-House pike. The corps will move the following day past the head of Catharpin Run, crossing the Orange Court-House plank road at Parker's Store.

4. Major-General Sedgwick, commanding Sixth Corps, will move at 4 a.m. of the 4th instant, by way of Stevensburg and the Germanna plank road to Germanna Ford, following the Fifth Corps, and, after crossing the Rapidan, will bivouac on the heights beyond. The canvas pontoon train will be taken up as soon as the troops of the Sixth Corps have

crossed, and will follow immediately in rear of the troops of that corps. So much of the bridge train of the Sixth Corps as may be necessary to bridge the Rapidan at Culpeper Mine Ford will proceed to Richardsville in rear of the Reserve Artillery, and, as soon as it is ascertained that the Reserve Artillery are crossing, it will move to Culpeper Mine Ford, where the bridge will be established. The engineers of this bridge train will at once open a road from Culpeper Mine Ford direct to Richardsville.

5. Major-General Hancock, commanding Second Corps, will send two divisions, with so much of the bridge train as may be necessary to bridge the Rapidan at Ely's Ford, and such artillery as may be required, at midnight of the 3d instant to Ely's Ford. The remainder of the corps will follow at such hour that the column will cross the Rapidan without delay. The canvas pontoon bridge at this ford will be taken up as soon as the troops of this corps have passed, and will move with it at the head of the trains that accompany the troops. The wooden pontoon bridge will remain. The Second Corps will enter the Stevensburg and Richardsville road at Madden's, in order that the route from Stevensburg to the plank road may be free for the Fifth and Sixth Corps. After crossing the Rapidan, the Second Corps will move to the vicinity of Chandler's or Chancellorsville.

6. It is expected that the advance divisions of the Fifth and Second Corps, with the wooden pontoon trains, will be at the designated points of crossing not later than 6 a.m. of the 4th instant.

7. The Reserve Artillery will move at 3 a.m. of the 4th instant, and follow the Second Corps, passing Mountain Run at Ross' Mill or Hamilton's, cross at Ely's Ford, take the road to Chancellorsville, and halt for the night at Hunting Creek.

8. Great care will be taken by the corps commanders that the roads are promptly repaired by the pioneers wherever needed, not only for the temporary wants of the division or corps to which the pioneers belong, but for the passage of the troops and trains that follow on the same route.

9. During the movement of the 4th and following days the commanders of the Fifth and Sixth Corps will occupy the roads on the right flank, to cover the passage of their corps, and will keep their flankers well out in that direction. The commanders of the Second Corps and Reserve Artillery will, in a similar manner, look out for the left flank. Whenever practicable, double columns will be used to shorten the columns. Corps commanders will keep in communication and connect with each other, and co-operate whenever necessary. Their picket-lines will be connected. They will keep the commanding general constantly advised of their prog-

ress and of everything important that occurs, and will send staff officers to acquaint him with the location of their headquarters. During the movement of the 4th instant headquarters will be on the route of the Fifth and Sixth Corps. It will be established at night between these corps on the Germanna plank road.

10. The infantry troops will take with them 50 rounds of ammunition upon the person, three days' full rations in the haversacks, three days' bread and small rations in the knapsacks, and three days' beef on the hoof. Each corps will take with it one-half its infantry ammunition, one-half the intrenching tools, one hospital wagon and one medicine wagon for each brigade, one-half the ambulance trains, and the light spring wagons and pack animals allowed at the various headquarters. No other train or means of transportation than those just specified will accompany the corps, except such wagons as may be necessary for the forage for immediate use (five days). The artillery will have with them the ammunition of the caissons only.

11. The subsistance and other trains, loaded with the amount of rations, forage, infantry and artillery ammunition, &c., heretofore ordered, the surplus wooden pontoons of the different corps, &c., will be assembled under the direction of the chief quartermaster of the army in the vicinity of Richardsville, with a view to crossing the Rapidan by bridges at Ely's Ford and Culpeper Mine Ford.

12. A detail of 1,000 or 1,200 men will be made from each corps as guard for its subsistence and other trains. This detail will be composed of entire regiments as far as practicable. No other guards whatever for regimental, brigade, division, or corps wagons will be allowed. Each detail will be under the command of an officer selected for that purpose, and the whole will be commanded by the senior officer of the three. This guard will be so disposed as to protect the trains on the march and in park. The trains are likewise protected by cavalry on the flanks and rear.

13. Major-General Sheridan, commanding Cavalry Corps, will direct the First Cavalry Division to call in its pickets and patrols on the right on the morning of the 4th instant, and hold itself ready to move and cover the trains of the army. It will picket and watch the fords of the Rapidan from Rapidan Station to Germanna Ford. On the morning of the 5th the First Cavalry Division will cross the Rapidan at Germanna Ford and cover the right flank of the trains while crossing the Rapidan and during their movements in rear of the army. The signal stations on Cedar, Pony, and Stony Mountains will be maintained as long as practicable.

14. The wooden pontoon bridges at Germanna Ford and Ely's Ford

will remain for the passage of General Burnside's army. That at Culpeper Mine Ford will be taken up, under the direction of the chief engineer, as soon as the trains have crossed, and will move with the train of its corps.

By command of Major-General Meade:

S. WILLIAMS
Assistant Adjutant-General.

APPENDIX C

Order for Movement, Army of the Potomac, May 4, 1864

Orders.   Headquarters, Army of the Potomac
May 4, 1864—6 p.m.

The following movements are ordered for the 5th of May, 1864:

1. Major-General Sheridan, commanding Cavalry Corps, will move with Gregg's and Torbert's divisions against the enemy's cavalry in the direction of Hamilton's Crossing. General Wilson, with the Third Cavalry Division, will move at 5 a.m. to Craig's Meeting House, on the Catharpin road. He will keep out parties on the Orange Court-House pike and plank roads, the Catharpin road, Pamunkey road (road to Orange Springs), and in the direction of Twyman's Store and Andrews' Tavern or Good Hope Church.

2. Major-General Hancock, commanding Second Corps, will move at 5 a.m. to Shady Grove Church and extend his right toward the Fifth Corps at Parker's Store.

3. Major-General Warren, commanding Fifth Corps, will move at 5 a.m. to Parker's Store, on the Orange Court-House plank road, and extend his right toward the Sixth Corps at Old Wilderness Tavern.

4. Major-General Sedgwick, commanding Sixth Corps, will move to Old Wilderness Tavern, on the Orange Court-House pike, as soon as the road is clear. He will leave a division to cover the bridge at Germanna Ford until informed from these headquarters of the arrival of General Burnside's troops there.

5. The Reserve Artillery will move to Corbin's Bridge as soon as the road is clear.

6. The trains will be parked in the vicinity of Todd's Tavern.

7. Headquarters will be on the Orange Court-House plank road near the Fifth Corps.

8. After reaching the points designated, the army will be held ready to move forward.

9. The commanders of the Fifth and Sixth Corps will keep out detachments on the roads on their right flank. The commander of the Second Corps will do the same on the roads on his front. These flankers and pickets will be thrown well out and their troops be held ready to meet the enemy at any moment.

By command of Major-General Meade:

S. WILLIAMS,
Assistant Adjutant-General.

APPENDIX D

Letter of Grant to Halleck

Headquarters, Wilderness, May 7,
1864—10 a.m.
(Received by mail from Alexandria,
Va., 10 p.m., May 12.)

Major Gen. H. W. HALLECK,
Chief of Staff:

We were engaged with the enemy nearly all day, both on the 5th and 6th. Yesterday the enemy attacked our lines vigorously, first at one point and then another, from right to left. They were repulsed at all points before reaching our lines, except once during the afternoon on Hancock's front and just after night on Sedgwick's front. In the former instance they were promptly and handsomely repulsed; the latter, Milroy's old brigade was attacked and gave way in the greatest confusion, almost without resistance, carrying good troops with them. Had there been daylight the enemy could have injured us very much in the confusion that prevailed; they, however, instead of getting through the break, attacked General Wright's division, of Sedgwick's corps, and were beaten back. Our losses to this time in killed, wounded, and prisoners will not probably exceed 12,000, of whom an unusually large proportion are but slightly wounded. Among the killed we have to deplore the loss of Generals Wadsworth and Hays. Generals Getty and Bartlett wounded, and Generals Seymour and Shaler taken prisoners. We have about 2,000 prisoners. They report General Jenkins killed and Longstreet wounded. I think the loss of the enemy must exceed ours, but this is only a guess based upon the fact that they attacked and were repulsed so often. I wish you would send me all the information you have from General Sherman, by Bull Run, and all the information from the James River expedition. At present we can claim no victory over the enemy, neither have they gained a single advantage. The enemy pushed out of his fortifications to prevent their position being turned, and have been sooner or later driven back in every instance. Up to this hour the enemy have not shown themselves in force within a mile of our lines.

U. S. GRANT
Lieutenant-General.

APPENDIX E

Letters of Lee to the Confederate Secretary of War

Headquarters, Army of
Northern Virginia,
Via Orange Court-House, May 6,
1864—8 p.m.
(Received Richmond, 4.45 p.m.,
May 7.)

SECRETARY OF WAR:

Early this morning as the divisions of General Hill, engaged yesterday, were being relieved, the enemy advanced and created some confusion. The ground lost was recovered as soon as the fresh troops got into position and the enemy driven back to his original line. Afterward we turned the left of his front line and drove it from the field, leaving a large number of dead and wounded in our hands, among them General Wadsworth. A subsequent attack forced the enemy into his intrenched lines on the Brock road, extending from Wilderness Tavern, on the right, to Trigg's Mill. Every advance on his part, thanks to a merciful God, has been repulsed. Our loss in killed is not large, but we have many wounded; most of them slightly, artillery being little used on either side. I grieve to announce that Lieutenant-General Longstreet was severely wounded and General Jenkins killed. General Pegram was badly wounded yesterday. General Stafford, it is hoped, will recover.

R. E. LEE.

Headquarters, Army of Northern Virginia,
May 7, 1864. (Received May 8.)

Hon. Secretary of War:

General Gordon turned the enemy's extreme right yesterday evening, and drove him from his rifle-pits. Among the prisoners captured were Generals Seymour and Shaler. A number of arms were also taken. The enemy has abandoned the Germanna Ford road, and removed his pontoon bridge toward Ely's. There has been no attack to-day; only slight skirmishing along the lines.

R. E. LEE

APPENDIX F

CHRONOLOGY OF EVENTS,
MAY 4–7, 1864

MAY 4

12:00–2:00 A.M.   The Army of the Potomac leaves its winter quarters near Culpeper Court House and marches for the crossings on the Rapidan. The spring campaign has begun.

2:00 A.M.   Wilson's cavalry arrives at Germanna Ford and disperses Confederate pickets. Engineers then begin to lay a canvas pontoon bridge.

5:00 A.M.	General Meade joins the army on the march.
6:00 A.M.	Griffin's leading division of Warren's Fifth Corps arrives at Germanna Ford.
7:00 A.M.	Griffin's troops begin crossing the river.
8:00 A.M.	General Grant joins the army on the march.
9:50 A.M.	Barlow's leading division of Hancock's Second Corps, having previously crossed the river at Ely's Ford, has arrived at Chancellorsville.
10:00 A.M.	Wilson's cavalry division has reached Wilderness Tavern, where it is awaiting the arrival of the leading troops of the Fifth Corps.
12:00 P.M.	Griffin arrives at Wilderness Tavern, allowing Wilson to proceed to Parker's Store. Also, A. P. Hill's Confederate Third Corps and Ewell's Confederate Second Corps have begun marching east from the vicinity of Orange Court House, following Orange Plank Road and Orange Turnpike, respectively.
1:15 P.M.	Grant and Meade, accompanied by their staffs, cross the river at Germanna Ford and establish army headquarters in an old farmhouse on the south bank. Also, Grant has just ordered General Burnside, commanding the Ninth Corps, to make a forced march and join the army as soon as possible.
2:00 P.M.	All of Hancock's Second Corps has arrived at Chancellorsville and is making camp.
3:05 P.M.	Warren's entire Fifth Corps is making camp at Wilderness Tavern.
4:00 P.M.	Longstreet's Confederate First Corps begins marching northward, from the vicinity of Gordonsville, in order to join the rest of Lee's army as soon as possible.
6:00 P.M.	Sedgwick's Sixth Corps has finished crossing the river at Germanna Ford and is in camp on the south bank.

MAY 5

5:00 A.M.	Meade's army breaks camp and begins to march south. Wilson's cavalry (minus the 5th New York, which is left behind to post Plank Road) leaves Parker's Store and rides toward Craig's Meeting House, two miles to the south.
6:00 A.M.	General Warren notifies Meade of the presence of a

	Confederate force on the turnpike, in front of his pickets.
7:00 A.M.	Meade informs Grant of the rebel troops in Warren's front.
7:30 A.M.	Meade suspends the march of his army.
8:00 A.M.	Wilson's cavalry engages Rosser's Confederate horsemen at Craig's Meeting House. Also, the advance of A. P. Hill's Confederate Third Corps is pushing the 5th New York down Plank Road, threatening the Federal left.
8:40 A.M.	Grant orders Burnside (who has not yet crossed the river) to close up with the Sixth Corps as soon as possible. Grant then leaves his headquarters of the previous day and rides toward the front.
10:00 A.M.	Grant and his staff arrive at the turnpike. Grant confers with Meade.
11:20 A.M.	General Getty's division of the Sixth Corps arrives at the Brock-Plank crossing and checks the advance of Hill's corps, saving the intersection and the Federal left flank.
11:40 A.M.	General Hancock, whose Second Corps is halted at Todd's Tavern, receives orders to advance northward up Brock Road to its junction with Plank Road.
11:50 A.M.	Warren curtly orders General Crawford, commanding the division on the left of the Fifth Corps, at the Chewning farm, to move to the right and connect with Wadsworth in order to close up the half-mile gap in the center of the corps. Crawford obeys, reluctantly.
12:00 P.M.	Confederate cavalry commander J. E. B. Stuart learns that Rosser's brigade is in trouble and rides to his relief.
12:15 P.M.	General Lee arrives at the Tapp farm, where he establishes Confederate headquarters.
12:45 P.M.	Hancock and his staff arrive at the Brock-Plank crossing, although his troops are not yet up.
1:00 P.M.	Warren's Fifth Corps advances westward and strikes Confederate General Ewell's Second Corps on the western side of Sanders' Field.
1:30 P.M.	Willcox's leading division of Burnside's Ninth Corps has crossed the Rapidan at Germanna Ford (although

the rest of the Ninth Corps is still some distance behind) and relieves Ricketts's division of the Sixth Corps in guarding the river crossing. Ricketts then rejoins the rest of Sedgwick's command.

2:00 P.M.   As Warren's attack on the turnpike reaches a climax, the leading elements of Hancock's Second Corps begin to arrive at the Brock-Plank crossing. There is a lull as the troops of Hancock, Getty, and A. P. Hill entrench.

2:40 P.M.   Hancock receives orders to attack down Plank Road.

2:45 P.M.   Wilson's division of cavalry has fallen back to Todd's Tavern, where it is now relieved by Gregg's fresh division. Gregg rides out Catharpin Road, where his men encounter Stuart's pursuing rebel horsemen. The clash that ensues lasts until nearly 6:00 P.M., at which time Stuart is compelled to retire.

3:00 P.M.   Warren's corps, having been driven back to the eastern side of Sanders' Field by a Confederate counterattack, regroups south of the turnpike. Wright's leading division of the Sixth Corps has connected with Warren's right and is attacking on the north side of the pike.

4:15 P.M.   Getty advances into the woods west of Brock Road and strikes Heth's division of Hill's corps. Wilcox's division of Hill's command has just arrived on the scene and is marching across the Chewning farm heights in order to connect Hill's left with Ewell's right. Ewell, meanwhile, is attacking the right of the Federal Sixth Corps.

5:00 P.M.   Hancock's men have advanced in support of Getty and a general attack is underway along Brock Road. General Alexander Hays is mortally wounded at the head of his brigade. Mott's division, just south of Plank Road, is routed, but the Confederates of Heth's division are still being heavily pressed on Plank Road. Lee orders Wilcox to abandon the Chewning farm and march to Heth's relief.

5:15 P.M.   As Hancock's battle continues to the south, Sedgwick attempts to flank Ewell's corps but is not successful; however, the fighting continues until 9:00 P.M., neither side gaining an advantage.

5:30 P.M.   Wilcox's Confederate division attacks Hancock and

	succeeds in reaching Brock Road, north of Plank Road, driving Ricketts's gunners from their pieces. Getty counterattacks and recaptures the guns.
6:00 P.M.	Wadsworth's Fifth Corps division marches south from the Lacy farm in order to unite with Hancock's Second Corps. In carrying out this movement, Wadsworth converges on Hill's exposed left.
7:00 P.M.	Wadsworth assaults Hill's largely unprotected left, but in the darkness and the confusion of the Wilderness, his division is halted by 125 men from the 5th Alabama.
8:00 P.M.	General Barlow, commanding the division on Hancock's left, sends in three brigades against Hill's right, but darkness prevents the attack from gaining success.

MAY 6

1:00 A.M.	Burnside's corps, having crossed the river, begins marching from the ford to a position on Hancock's right.
4:30 A.M.	Ewell's Confederates (Early's division) attack Sedgwick's Sixth Corps, but are repulsed. The fighting continues until 10:00 A.M.
5:00 A.M.	Hancock advances against Hill's uneven lines.
5:30 A.M.	Burnside's Ninth Corps arrives at the turnpike.
5:50 A.M.	Hancock's advance reaches the Tapp farm and threatens to cut Lee's army in half. Burnside has still not connected with Hancock.
6:00 A.M.	Longstreet's Confederate First Corps, having made an agonizing forced march from Gordonsville, arrives on the field. The Texas Brigade attacks Wadsworth's advancing force north of Plank Road, while Kershaw attacks the Federals south of the road. Also, Burnside has joined his corps on the turnpike.
6:30 A.M.	Benning's Georgians, of Field's division of Longstreet's corps, assault Wadsworth as the shattered Texas Brigade falls to the rear.
7:00 A.M.	Hancock orders General Gibbon, commanding the left wing of the Second Corps, to attack; unexplainably, only Frank's brigade advances while the rest of Gibbon's command remains idle. Also, Perry's (Law's)

brigade is relieving Benning's brigade in attacking Wadsworth.

7:45 A.M.   Perry routs Wadsworth's division.

8:00 A.M.   Webb's brigade marches to Wadsworth's rescue. Generals Wadsworth and Rice continue to rally what remains of their division. Burnside has finally arrived at the Chewning farm and is preparing to attack Hill's corps, which, having been relieved by Longstreet's First Corps, is now deployed across the Chewning farm heights.

8:30 A.M.   A brief lull settles over Hancock's front as the opposing forces re-form.

8:50 A.M.   Wadsworth renews the attack with troops on the north side of Plank Road. He has been reinforced by Carruth's brigade from Stevenson's detached division of the Ninth Corps. In the meantime, Burnside's main force has been ordered to connect with Hancock's right and is withdrawing from the Chewning farm area.

9:00 A.M.   Custer's Michigan Brigade of cavalry clashes with Rosser's troopers near the Furnace-Brock intersection.

9:10 A.M.   Gibbon reports to Hancock of the presence of an unknown force marching up Brock Road toward the Federal left. Hancock hears firing in that direction.

9:40 A.M.   Three brigades are sent from Hancock's right to reinforce Gibbon on the left.

10:10 A.M.   Hancock learns that the unknown force is a body of Federal convalescents following the route of the army. There is a lull as both Hancock and Longstreet reform. Longstreet plans a flank attack around the left of Hancock's assault force (under command of General Birney).

10:15 A.M.   Colonel Sorrel, commanding Longstreet's flanking force, leads his four brigades around Birney's left.

11:00 A.M.   Longstreet's flank attack begins as Sorrel smashes into Birney's left, taking the Federal troops completely by surprise.

11:30 A.M.   Custer's cavalry fight draws to a conclusion as Rosser abandons the field.

12:00 P.M.   Sorrel's flanking force converges on Plank Road and

Wadsworth's left, as Longstreet leads the divisions of Kershaw and Field in a supporting frontal assault. In a desperate attempt to save his position, Wadsworth leads the 20th Massachusetts in a suicidal attack down Plank Road into Kershaw's advancing force.

12:30 P.M. General Wadsworth and Major Abbott are mortally wounded. The 19th Maine moved into position on Wadsworth's left, allowing the safe withdrawal of that division. The retreating troops join the rest of Hancock's command behind the breastworks on Brock Road.

12:50 P.M. General Longstreet, riding down Plank Road at the head of his corps, is severely wounded by his own men. General Micah Jenkins is killed.

2:00 P.M. Burnside launches an attack against Longstreet's left. The attack does little more than keep the Confederates occupied.

3:00 P.M. Hancock is ordered to prepare to launch an attack at 6:00 P.M.

4:15 P.M. Lee launches a violent attack against Hancock's defenses on Brock Road. Although the Confederates rout Mott's division, south of the Brock-Plank junction, Carroll's brigade of Gibbon's division is able to drive the Confederates back and repair the break in Hancock's line. The attack is over by 5:00 P.M.

7:00 P.M. General John B. Gordon delivers a flank attack on the right of Sedgwick's Sixth Corps. The assault routs three of Sedgwick's brigades, but darkness prevents Gordon from achieving a great victory. During the night Sedgwick refuses his right, thus abandoning Germanna Ford.

MAY 7

6:30 A.M. Grant issues orders for the Army of the Potomac to make a night march toward Spotsylvania Court House. There is only skirmishing throughout the day. The Battle of the Wilderness is over.

8:00 P.M. Both Lee's and Grant's armies are on the move as they race for possession of Spotsylvania Court House.

NOTES

1. Shadows of the Past

1. E. B. Long, *The Civil War Day by Day: An Almanac, 1861–1865,* assisted by Barbara Long (Garden City, N.Y.: Doubleday and Co., 1971), p. 473; Bruce Catton, *A Stillness at Appomattox* (Garden City, N.Y.: Doubleday and Co., 1955), p. 38. Winfield Scott's commission as Lieutenant General was by brevet only.

2. Andrew A. Humphreys, *The Virginia Campaign of 1864 and 1865* (New York: Charles Scribner's Sons, 1883), p. 3.

3. Bruce Catton, *Grant Takes Command* (Boston: Little, Brown and Co., 1969), pp. 176–77.

4. Horace Porter, *Campaigning with Grant* (Bloomington: Indiana University Press, 1961), pp. 46–47. (Referred to hereafter as Porter, *Grant.*)

5. Ulysses S. Grant, *Personal Memoirs of Ulysses S. Grant,* vol. 2 (New York: Charles L. Webster and Co., 1885). Grant gives a detailed account of his plans for the spring campaign on pp. 124–32. (Referred to hereafter as Grant, *Memoirs.*)

6. Ibid., pp. 134–37.

7. Bruce Catton, *This Hallowed Ground* (New York: Pocket Books, 1976), p. 386.

8. Grant, *Memoirs,* p. 117.

9. For further reference to these figures, see Humphreys, *Virginia Campaign,* pp. 14, 408–11; and Adam Badeau, *Military History of U. S. Grant,* vol. 2 (New York: D. Appleton and Co., 1885), p. 94.

10. Humphreys, *Virginia Campaign,* p. 409; and Bell Irwin Wiley and Hirst D. Milhollen, *They Who Fought Here* (New York: Bonanza Books, 1959), p. 242.

11. Wiley and Milhollen, *They Who Fought Here,* p. 243.

12. For the orders for the march of the Army of the Potomac see U.S. War Department, *The War of the Rebellion: A Compilation of the Official Records of the Union and Confederate Armies* (U.S. Government Printing Office, 1881–1902), series 1, vol. 36, pt. 2, pp. 356–62, and 331–34 (hereafter referred to as *O.R.* 36).

13. Orders for the movement of the Second Corps, ibid., pt. 2, pp. 356–57.

14. Dispatch of Grant to Burnside, ibid., pt. 2, p. 337; and Edward Steere, *The Wilderness Campaign* (Harrisburg, Pa.: Stackpole Co., 1960), p. 37.

15. Catton, *Grant Takes Command,* p. 180, *Never Call Retreat* (Garden City, N.Y.: Doubleday and Co., 1965), p. 300.

16. Robert Penn Warren, ed., *Selected Poems of Herman Melville—A Reader's Edition* (New York: Random House, 1970), from the poem "The Armies of the Wilderness", p. 132 (hereafter referred to as Warren, *Selected Poems of Herman Melville*).

17. Morris Schaff, *The Battle of the Wilderness* (Boston: Houghton Mifflin Co., 1910), p. 86.

18. Quoted by Don Congdon, ed., *Combat: The Civil War* (New York: Castle Books, 1967), p. 472.

19. Schaff, *The Battle of the Wilderness,* p. 97. Details about Wilderness Tavern were brought to the attention of the author by David A. Lilley, a historian

with the Fredericksburg and Spotsylvania National Military Park, Fredericks-burg, Virginia.

20. Warren to Meade, *O.R.* 36, pt. 2, p. 378, Hancock to Meade, ibid., p. 374, Hancock to Williams, ibid., p. 375; also see Steere, *The Wilderness Campaign*, p. 51. The poem used here is from Warren, *Selected Poems of Herman Melville*, p. 134.

21. *O.R.* 36, pt. 2, p. 370.

22. St. Clair A. Mulholland, *The Story of the 116th Regiment Pennsylvania Volunteers in the War of the Rebellion: The Record of a Gallant Command* (Philadelphia: F. McManus, Jr. and Co., 1903), pp. 184–85 (hereafter referred to as Mulholland, *The 116th Pennsylvania*).

23. Congdon, *Combat: The Civil War*, p. 473.

24. Grant to Burnside, *O.R.* 36, pt. 2, p. 380.

25. Porter, *Grant*, p. 43.

26. Schaff, *The Battle of the Wilderness*, p. 67.

27. Wiley and Milhollen, *They Who Fought Here*, p. 70.

28. Douglas Southall Freeman, *R. E. Lee* (New York: Charles Scribner's Sons, 1962), 4: 524–25.

29. For a description of Ewell's line of march, see Report of Lieut. Gen. Richard S. Ewell, *O.R.* 36, pt. 1, p. 1068; Humphreys, *Virginia Campaign*, p. 23; Steere, *The Wilderness Campaign*, p. 73.

30. Humphreys, *Virginia Campaign*, p. 23.

31. Report of Lieut. Gen. James Longstreet, *O.R.* 36, pt. 1, p. 1054.

32. Humphreys, *Virginia Campaign*, p. 17.

33. *O.R.* 36, pt. 2, Taylor to Ewell, p. 948.

34. Catton, *A Stillness at Appomattox*, p. 62.

2. A Battle Develops

1. Robert S. Robertson, "The Battle of the Wilderness," *Civil War Times Illustrated*, April 1969, p. 7.

2. Richard Wheeler, ed., *Voices of the Civil War* (New York: Thomas Y. Crowell Co., 1976), p. 383.

3. Porter, *Grant*, p. 50.

4. For the projected movements of the Army of the Potomac on May 5, see *O.R.* 36, pt. 2, p. 371.

5. Wilson's orders can be found in *O.R.* 36, pt. 2, p. 371. It is clear that he did not follow them as he should have.

6. Schaff, *Battle of the Wilderness*, pp. 125–26.

7. Warren to Humphreys, *O.R.* 36, pt. 2, p. 413.

8. Ibid.

9. Steere, *The Wilderness Campaign*, pp. 98–99.

10. Meade to Grant, *O.R.* 36, pt. 2, p. 403.

11. Grant to Meade, ibid.

12. Badeau, *Military History of U. S. Grant*, pp. 96–97.

13. Locke to Griffin, *O.R.* 36, pt. 2, p. 416.

14. Crawford to Locke, ibid., p. 418.

15. Warren to Crawford, ibid.

16. Roebling to Warren, ibid.

17. Grant, *Memoirs*, p. 539.

18. For Grant's order to Burnside, see *O.R.* 36, pt. 2, pp. 423–24.

19. Porter, *Grant*, pp. 48–49.

20. Ibid., p. 50.

21. Steere, *The Wilderness Campaign*, pp. 88–94, 269–280.

3. Tempest in the Woodland

1. Melville, "The Armies of the Wilderness," p. 133.

2. Humphreys to Hancock, *O.R.* 36, pt. 2, p. 406.

3. Ibid., p. 407.

4. Hazard Stevens, "The Sixth Corps in the Wilderness," *Papers of the Military Historical Society of Massachusetts*, vol. 4 (Boston: Cadet Armory, 1895–1918), p. 180 (referred to hereafter as *MHSMP*).

5. Ibid., pp. 189–90.

6. This is strictly the author's opinion; however, the possibility exists in the fact that Brock Road led directly to Warren's exposed left flank.

7. The time of Hancock's arrival at the Brock-Plank crossing can only be estimated; however, Hancock states in his official report (*O.R.* 36, pt. 1, p. 318) that, upon receiving orders to proceed to that point, he started off at once. Since he received the orders at 11:40 A.M., it is reasonable to assume that he reached his destination in not much more than an hour's time. We know that all of Heth's troops were up at least by 2:00 P.M., for Wilcox's division, which was following Heth, began to arrive at that hour. See Humphreys, *Virginia Campaign*, p. 29.

8. Schaff, *Battle of the Wilderness*, p. 171; Steere, *The Wilderness Campaign*, p. 147.

9. Eugene Arus Nash, *A History of the Forty-Fourth Regiment New York Volunteer Infantry in the Civil War, 1861–1865* (R. R. Donnelly and Sons Co., 1911), p. 184; Steere, *The Wilderness Campaign*, p. 152; Schaff, *Battle of the Wilderness*, p. 151.

10. Steere, *The Wilderness Campaign*, p. 155.

11. Ibid., p. 156.

12. Schaff, *Battle of the Wilderness*, p. 149.

13. Humphreys, *Virginia Campaign*, pp. 15, 408.

14. Nash, *History of the 44th New York*, p. 184; Steere, *The Wilderness Campaign*, p. 161.

15. Schaff, *Battle of the Wilderness*, p. 154.

16. John J. Pullen, *The Twentieth Maine* (Philadelphia: J. B. Lippincott Co., 1957), p. 185.

17. O. B. Curtis, *History of the 24th Michigan of the Iron Brigade* (Detroit: Winn and Hammond, 1891), p. 231.

18. Jones's brigade suffered worst from the Federal attack and was entirely out of commission for the remainder of the day. See Steere, *The Wilderness Campaign*, p. 162.

19. Catton, *A Stillness at Appomattox*, p. 81.

20. Quoted in Congdon, *Combat: The Civil War*, p. 476.

21. Survivor's Association, *121st Regiment Pennsylvania Volunteers*, rev. ed. (Philadelphia: 1906), pp. 76–77.

22. John B. Gordon, *Reminiscences of the Civil War* (New York: Charles Scribner's Sons, 1902), pp. 239–41.

23. Schaff, *Battle of the Wilderness*, p. 158.

24. Steere, *The Wilderness Campaign*, pp. 155–56.

25. Pullen, *The 20th Maine*, pp. 187–90.

26. *O.R.* 36, pt. 1, p. 555, 557; Mary Genevie Green Brainard, *Campaigns of*

the One Hundred and Forty-Sixth Regiment, New York State Volunteers; Also Known as Halleck's Infantry, the Fifth Oneida, and Garrard's Tigers (New York: G. P. Putnam's Sons, 1915), p. 187 (hereafter referred to as Brainard, *146th New York*).

27. Brainard, *146th New York*, p. 91.
28. Ibid.
29. Walter Clark, ed., *History of the Several Regiments and Battalions from North Carolina in the Great War, 1861–'65*, vol. 1, (Raleigh: Published by the State, 1901), p. 150; Schaff, *Battle of the Wilderness*, pp. 162–64.
30. Brainard, *146th New York*, p. 195.
31. George R. Agassiz, ed., *Meade's Headquarters, 1863–65: Letters of Colonel Theodore Lyman from the Wilderness to Appomattox* (Boston: Atlantic Monthly Press, 1922), p. 90 (referred to hereafter as Agassiz, *Meade's Headquarters*).
32. Ibid., p. 91.
33. Steere, *The Wilderness Campaign*, pp. 176–78.
34. Ibid., pp. 178–80.

4. Carnage on Plank Road

1. Humphreys to Hancock, *O.R.* 36, pt. 2, p. 407.
2. Hancock to Humphreys, ibid., pp. 409–10.
3. Report of Major General Winfield S. Hancock, ibid., pt. 1, pp. 318–19; Mott was up by 4:00 P.M., as he is mentioned as having been sent in on Getty's left in Hancock's dispatch of 4:05 P.M. See *O.R.* 36, pt. 2, p. 410.
4. Humphreys to Hancock, ibid., pt. 2, p. 410.
5. Agassiz, *Meade's Headquarters*, pp. 91–92.
6. Hancock to Humphreys, *O.R.* 36, pt. 2, p. 410.
7. Report of Brigadier General George W. Getty, ibid., pt. 1, pp. 676–77, Report of Brig. Gen. Frank Wheaton, ibid., pp. 681–82; Steere, *The Wilderness Campaign*, p. 197.
8. Schaff, *Battle of the Wilderness*, p. 183.
9. Freeman, *R. E. Lee*, 3: 278; Steere, The Wilderness Campaign, p. 223.
10. Stevens, "The Sixth Corps in the Wilderness," p. 191.
11. Report of Colonel L. A. Grant, *O.R.* 36, pt. 1, p. 697.
12. Steere, *The Wilderness Campaign*, p. 224.
13. Colonel Grant's report, *O.R.* 36, pt. 1, p. 697.
14. Catton, *A Stillness at Appomattox*, p. 73.
15. Wheaton's report, *O.R.* 36, pt. 1, pp. 681–82.
16. Grant, *Memoirs*, p. 194.
17. Schaff, *Battle of the Wilderness*, pp. 186, 219–20.
18. Catton, *A Stillness at Appomattox*, p. 88.
19. D. G. Crotty, *Four Years in the Army of the Potomac* (Grand Rapids, Mich.: 1874) p. 126.
20. Report of Colonel Robert McAllister, *O.R.* 36, pt. 1, pp. 487–88.
21. Agassiz, *Meade's Headquarters*, p. 92.
22. Schaff, *Battle of the Wilderness*, pp. 187–88.
23. Steere, *The Wilderness Campaign*, p. 228.
24. Stevens, "The Sixth Corps in the Wilderness," p. 193.
25. Hancock's report, *O.R.* 36, pt. 1, p. 320, Getty's report, ibid., p. 677.
26. Lyman to Meade, ibid., pt. 2, p. 411.

27. J. H. Lane, "Battle of the Wilderness—Report of General Lane," *Southern Historical Society Papers*, 9:125–26 (referred to hereafter as *SHSP.*)

28. Glenn Tucker, *Hancock the Superb* (Indianapolis: Bobbs-Merrill Co., 1960), pp. 198–99.

29. Hancock's report, *O.R.* 36, pt. 1, p. 319.

30. Brooke's report, ibid., p. 407.

31. Mulholland, *The 116th Pennsylvania*, p. 186.

32. Schaff, *Battle of the Wilderness*, p. 198; William Woods Hassler, *A. P. Hill: Lee's Forgotten General* (Chapel Hill: University of North Carolina Press, 1979), p. 191.

33. Rufus R. Dawes, *Service with the Sixth Wisconsin Volunteers* (Marietta, Ohio: E. R. Alderman and Sons, 1890), p. 261.

5. *"He Won't Be Up—I Know Him Well!"*

1. Miller, *Photographic History of the Civil War* 10:202; Catton, *A Stillness at Appomattox*, p. 38.

2. Steere, *The Wilderness Campaign*, pp. 243–44; Report of Brig. Gen. Emory Upton, *O.R.* 36, pt. 1, pp. 665–66, Report of Major Henry R. Dalton, ibid., pp. 659–60, Report of Brig. Gen. Daniel Bidwell, ibid., p. 719.

3. Upton's report, *O.R.* 36, pt. 1, pp. 665–66.

4. Ibid.

5. Ibid., p. 666.

6. Report of Brig. Gen. Armistead Long, Chief of Artillery, Second Corps (Confederate), ibid., p. 1085; Steere, *The Wilderness Campaign*, p. 250.

7. Thomas W. Hyde, *Following the Greek Cross; or, Memories of the Sixth Army Corps* (Boston: Houghton Mifflin Co., 1894), pp. 184–85.

8. Ewell's report, *O.R.* 36, pt. 1, p. 1070; Steere, *The Wilderness Campaign*, p. 245.

9. Report of Colonel Oliver Edwards, *O.R.* 36, pt. 1, p. 672.

10. George T. Stevens, *Three Years in the Sixth Corps* (Albany: S. R. Gray, 1866), pp. 310–11.

11. Report of Brig. Gen. William H. Morris, *O.R.* 36, pt. 1, pp. 722–23, Report of Brig. Gen. Truman Seymour, ibid., p. 728.

12. Seymour's Report, ibid., p. 728.

13. Dawes, *Service with the 6th Wisconsin*, p. 261.

14. Frank Wilkenson, "Spotsylvania: Reflections How Men Die in Battle," *Civil War Times Illustrated*, April 1983, p. 18.

15. Schaff, *Battle of the Wilderness*, p. 220.

16. Quoted by Charles D. Page, *History of the Fourteenth Regiment, Connecticut Volunteer Infantry* (Meridian, Conn.: Horton Printing Co., 1906), p. 242.

17. A. T. Brewer, *History Sixty-First Regiment Pennsylvania Volunteers, 1861–1865* (Pittsburgh: Art Engraving Printing Co., 1911), pp. 82–83.

18. Catton, *A Stillness at Appomattox*, pp. 76–77.

19. John W. Urban, *Battlefield and Prison Pen; or, Through the War, and Thrice a Prisoner in Rebel Dungeons* (Hubbard Brothers, 1887), p. 396.

20. Schaff, *Battle of the Wilderness*, p. 216; Hassler, *A. P. Hill: Lee's Forgotten General*, pp. 192–93.

21. D. Augustus Dickert, *History of Kershaw's Brigade, With Complete Roll of Companies, Biographical Sketches, Incidents, Anecdotes, Etc.* (Newberry, S.C.: Elbert H. Aull Co., 1899), p. 344.

22. Ewell's report, *O.R.* 36, pt. 1, p. 1071; Steere, *The Wilderness Campaign,* pp. 258, 313–14.

23. Schaff, *Battle of the Wilderness,* p. 225.

24. Meade to Grant, *O.R.* 36, pt. 2, pp. 404–05.

25. Rowley to Meade, ibid., p. 405.

6. *"Longstreet Slants Through the Hauntedness!"*

1. Porter, *Grant,* p. 56.

2. Steere, *The Wilderness Campaign,* pp. 297, 313.

3. Morris's report, *O.R.* 36, p. 1, p. 722, Dalton's report, ibid., pp. 659–60, Report of Brig. Gen. Henry Hunt, Chief of Artillery (Federal), "Extracts from Journal of," ibid., p. 290; Steere, *The Wilderness Campaign,* p. 296.

4. Bidwell's report, *O.R.* 36, pt. 1, p. 719, Seymour's report, ibid., pp. 728–29, Report of Colonel J. Warren Keifer, ibid., p. 732.

5. Stevens, *Three Years in the 6th Corps,* p. 309.

6. Fredericksburg and Spotsylvania National Military Park, *Troop Movement Maps of the Battle of the Wilderness, May 6, 1864,* prepared by Ralph Happel, January 1962. (Referred to hereafter as *FNMP.*)

7. Steere, *The Wilderness Campaign,* pp. 294–95; *O.R.* 36, pt. 2, p. 441. Meade's dispatch to Hancock indicates Wadsworth's force as 5,000 strong.

8. *FNMP;* Report of Brig. Gen. Samuel S. Carroll, *O.R.* 36, pt. 1, pp. 446–47, Getty's report, ibid., p. 677.

9. *FNMP.*

10. Steere, *The Wilderness Campaign,* p. 311.

11. Report of Lt. Col. C. W. Tyler, 141st New York, *O.R.* 36, pt. 1, p. 477; Freeman, *R. E. Lee,* 3:286.

12. Agassiz, *Meade's Headquarters,* p. 94.

13. Lyman to Meade, *O.R.* 36, pt. 2, p. 439.

14. Hancock to Humphreys, ibid.

15. Getty's report, ibid., pt. 1, p. 677, Carroll's report, ibid., pp. 446–47.

16. Steere, *The Wilderness Campaign,* pp. 332–33, 337.

17. Report of Brig. Gen. Lysander Cutler, *O.R.* 36, pt. 1, p. 611; *FNMP.*

18. *FNMP;* Humphreys, *Virginia Campaign,* pp. 43–44.

19. Stevens, "The Sixth Corps in the Wilderness," p. 196.

20. Crotty, *Four Years in the Army of the Potomac,* pp. 127–28.

21. Melville, "The Armies of the Wilderness," p. 135.

22. Humphreys, *Virginia Campaign,* p. 38.

23. William Wallace, "Operations of Second South Carolina Regiment in Campaigns of 1864 and 1865," *SHSP* 7:128; Steere, *The Wilderness Campaign,* pp. 339–41.

24. Dickert, *History of Kershaw's Brigade,* p. 346.

25. Wallace, "Operations of Second South Carolina," *SHSP* 7:128; Schaff, *Battle of the Wilderness,* p. 249.

26. Getty's report, *O.R.* 36, pt. 1, p. 678.

27. Report of L. A. Grant, ibid., pp. 698–99.

28. *FNMP.*

29. Ibid.; Steere, *The Wilderness Campaign,* p. 349.

30. C. S. Venable, "The Campaign from the Wilderness to Petersburg: Address of Col. C. S. Venable . . . before the Virginia Division of the Army of Northern Virginia, . . . Richmond, Oct. 30th, 1873," *SHSP* 14:525–26.

31. Quoted by Harold B. Simpson, *Hood's Texas Brigade: Lee's Grenadier Guard* (Waco, Tex.: Texican Press, 1970), pp. 400–01.

32. Schaff, *Battle of the Wilderness*, p. 252.

33. Ibid.

34. Pullen, *The 20th Maine*, p. 183.

35. Quoted by Page, *The 14th Connecticut*, pp. 241–42.

36. Lyman to Meade, *O.R.* 36, pt. 2, p. 440.

37. Lyman to Meade, 6:30 A.M., ibid.

38. Report of Major General Ambrose E. Burnside, ibid., pt. 1, p. 906, Report of Brig. Gen. Robert B. Potter, ibid., p. 297; Schaff, *Battle of the Wilderness*, pp. 230–32.

39. Humphreys to Hancock, *O.R.* 36, pt. 2, p. 440.

40. Hancock to Humphreys, ibid., pp. 440–41.

41. Hancock's report, ibid., pt. 1, p. 321; Schaff, *Battle of the Wilderness*, pp. 241–42.

42. McAllister's report, *O.R.* 36, pt. 1, pp. 488–89.

43. Henry N. Blake, *Three Years in the Army of the Potomac* (Boston: Lee and Shepard, 1865), p. 281.

44. Circular, *O.R.* 36, pt. 2, p. 439.

45. Schaff, *Battle of the Wilderness*, p. 296.

46. Quoted by Page, *History of the 14th Connecticut*, p. 243.

47. William F. Perry, "Reminiscences of the Campaign of 1864 in Virginia," *SHSP* 7:53; the dispatch of Warren to Humphreys (*O.R.* 36, pt. 2, p. 449) indicates that Kitching had 2,400 men.

48. Perry, "Campaign of 1864," *SHSP.* The order of Perry's regiments is given throughout the report, pp. 49–56.

49. Cutler's report, *O.R.* 36, pt. 1, p. 611; *FNMP.*

50. Report of Brig. Gen. Alexander Webb, *O.R.* 36, pt. 1, pp. 437–39, Getty's report, ibid., p. 677; Schaff, *Battle of the Wilderness*, pp. 256–57.

51. Perry, "Campaign of 1864," *SHSP* 7:57.

52. Lyman to Meade, *O.R.* 36, pt. 2, p. 442.

7. A Specter Appears on Hancock's Left

1. Meade to Hancock, *O.R.* 36, pt. 2, p. 441.

2. Hancock's report, ibid., pt. 1, p. 321.

3. Hill's troops were the only Confederates in the area at that time. See Steere, *The Wilderness Campaign*, p. 375.

4. Burnside's report, *O.R.* 36, pt. 1, p. 906.

5. Schaff, *Battle of the Wilderness*, pp. 257–58; Lyman to Meade, *O.R.* 36, pt. 2, p. 442.

6. *FNMP;* Steere, *The Wilderness Campaign*, map 21, p. 372.

7. *O.R.* 36, pt. 1, p. 352.

8. Ibid.

9. Humphreys to Hancock, ibid., pt. 2, p. 442.

10. Ibid., p. 443.

11. Humphreys to Hancock, ibid., p. 442, Platt to Humphreys, ibid., p. 451, Hancock to Williams, 10:30 A.M., ibid., p. 444.

12. Ibid., pt. 1, p. 353.

13. J. H. Kidd, *Personal Recollections of a Cavalryman with Custer's Michigan Cavalry Brigade in the Civil War* (Ionia, Mich.: Sentinel Printing Co., 1908), p. 264; Steere, *The Wilderness Campaign*, p. 275.

14. Kidd, *Personal Recollections of a Cavalryman*, p. 264.

15. Custer's report, *O.R.* 36, pt. 1, p. 816.
16. Kidd, *Personal Recollections of a Cavalryman*, pp. 265–67.
17. Ibid., p. 267.
18. Ibid., pp. 267–68.
19. Ibid., p. 269.
20. Ibid., p. 270.
21. Ibid., pp. 270–71.
22. Custer to McClellan, *O.R.* 36, pt. 2, p. 466.
23. Porter, *Grant*, p. 59.
24. Humphreys to Warren, *O.R.* 36, pt. 2, pp. 451–52.
25. Hancock's report, ibid., pt. 1, pp. 323–24; James Longstreet, *From Manassas to Appomattox* (Bloomington: Indiana University Press, 1960), pp. 561–62.
26. Longstreet, *From Manassas to Appomattox*, p. 563.
27. G. Moxley Sorrel, *Recollections of a Confederate Staff Officer* (New York: Neale Publishing Co., 1905), pp. 241–42. These were probably not Longstreet's exact words.
28. Longstreet, *From Manassas to Appomattox*, p. 562; Perry, "Campaign of 1864," *SHSP*, 7:59.
29. Sorrel certainly did not start out until after Smith returned at 10:00 A.M.; he was in position on Birney's left by 11:00 A.M. This indicates swift movement on the part of Sorrel, especially when the nature of the terrain and the overall difficulty of the maneuver are taken into consideration.
30. Douglas Southall Freeman, *Lee's Lieutenants*, vol. 3 (New York: Charles Scribner's Sons, 1944), pp. 360–61 n.
31. McAllister's report, *O.R.* 36, pt. 1, p. 489.
32. Longstreet, *From Manassas to Appomattox*, p. 562; Steere, *The Wilderness Campaign*, map 23, p. 396.

8. "You Rolled Me Up Like a Wet Blanket . . . "

1. *FNMP*; Getty's report, *O.R.* 36, pt. 1, p. 678, Wheaton's report, ibid., p. 682, McAllister's report, ibid., p. 489.
2. McAllister's report, *O.R.* 36, pt. 1, p. 489.
3. Longstreet, *From Manassas to Appomattox*, p. 562.
4. Colonel Grant's report, *O.R.* 36, pt. 1, p. 562.
5. Agassiz, *Meade's Headquarters*, p. 96.
6. Lyman to Meade, *O.R.* 36, pt. 2, p. 444.
7. George A. Bruce, *The Twentieth Regiment of Massachusetts Volunteer Infantry, 1861–1865* (Boston: Houghton Mifflin and Co., 1906), p. 353; Schaff, *Battle of the Wilderness*, pp. 258–59.
8. Schaff, *Battle of the Wilderness*, p. 271; Platt to Humphreys, 12:45 P.M., *O.R.* 36, pt. 2, p. 452.
9. Sorrel is quoted in Paul M. Angle and Earl Schenk Miers, *Tragic Years, 1860–1865*, vol. 2 (New York: Simon and Schuster, 1960), p. 799.
10. Mark DeWolfe Howe, Jr., ed., *Touched with Fire: Civil War Letters and Diary of Oliver Wendell Holmes, Jr.* (Cambridge: Harvard University Press, 1947), pp. 40–41, 56.
11. Bruce, *20th Massachusetts*, p. 353; Schaff, *Battle of the Wilderness*, p. 259.
12. J. D. Smith, *The History of the Nineteenth Maine Regiment of Volunteer Infantry, 1862–65* (Minneapolis: 1909), pp. 142–43; Webb's report, *O.R.* 36, pt. l, p. 438.
13. Longstreet, *From Manassas to Appomattox*, p. 563.

14. Ibid.
15. Ibid., p. 564.
16. Ibid.
17. Ibid., p. 563–64.
18. Ibid., p. 566.
19. Wilbur Thomas attempts to give Longstreet the credit he deserves in his biography, *General James "Pete" Longstreet, Lee's "Old War Horse": Scapegoat for Gettysburg* (Parsons, W.Va.: McClain Printing Co., 1979).
20. Longstreet, *From Manassas To Appomattox*, p. 565.
21. C. W. Field, "Campaign of 1864 and 1865 Narrative of Major-General C. W. Field," *SHSP* 14:545.
22. Longstreet, *From Manassas to Appomattox*, p. 568.
23. Hancock's report, *O.R.* 36., pt. 1, p. 353.
24. Comstock to Grant, ibid., pt. 2, p. 460.
25. Rawlins to Burnside, ibid., p. 461.
26. Lyman Jackman and Amos Hadley, eds., *History of the Sixth New Hampshire Regiment in the War for the Union* (Concord, N.H.: Republican Press Association, 1891), pp. 221–23; *FNMP.*
27. Potter's report, *O.R.* 36, pt. 1, p. 928.
28. Perry, "Campaign of 1864," *SHSP* 7:61–62.
29. Jackman and Hadley, *History of the 6th New Hampshire*, p. 221.
30. Ibid., pp. 222–23.
31. Steere, *The Wilderness Campaign*, map 24, p. 414.
32. Ibid., p. 415.

9. *"We Fairly Howled Them Down"*

1. Lyman to Meade, *O.R.* 36, pt. 2, p. 444. Lyman indicates that Hancock had a continuous line by 2 P.M., although it was not well enough organized to attack.
2. Hancock's report, ibid., pt. 1, pp. 323–24.
3. *FNMP*; Carroll's report, *O.R.* 36, pt. 1, p. 447; Schaff, *Battle of the Wilderness*, pp. 290–91; Steere, *The Wilderness Campaign*, map 25, p. 424. One has only to compare these sources to see how they conflict in regard to the positions of Hancock's brigades just prior to Lee's attack of 4:15 P.M.
4. Report of Capt. Edwin B. Dow, Sixth Maine Battery, *O.R.* 36, pt. 1, pp. 513–14; *FNMP.*
5. Steere, *The Wilderness Campaign*, map 25, p. 424.
6. Meade to Hancock, *O.R.* 36, pt. 2, pp. 444–45.
7. Agassiz, *Meade's Headquarters*, p. 97.
8. Quoted in Wheeler, *Voices of the Civil War*, p. 388.
9. Steere, *The Wilderness Campaign*, p. 425; Schaff, *Battle of the Wilderness*, p. 291. Schaff indicates that the Texas Brigade aided Henagan's South Carolinians in the attack, but it was Anderson's Georgians who were the supporting force. This can readily be seen by consulting Steere, *The Wilderness Campaign*, map 25, p. 424.
10. Dow's report, *O.R.* 36, pt. 1, p. 514.
11. Ibid.
12. Hancock's report, ibid., p, 324.
13. Hancock to Meade, ibid., pt. 2, p. 445–46.
14. Ibid., p. 446.
15. Humphreys to Hancock, Ibid., p. 447.

16. Report of Brig. Gen. John B. Gordon, *O.R.* 36, pt. 1, p. 1077.
17. Ibid.
18. Ewell's report, ibid., p. 1071; Steere, *The Wilderness Campaign*, pp. 432–33.
19. Ewell's report, *O.R.* 36, pt. 1, p. 1071.
20. Ibid.
21. Steere, *The Wilderness Campaign*, p. 440.
22. Seymour's report, *O.R.* 36, pt. 1, p. 729.
23. Bidwell's report, ibid., p. 719.
24. Brewer, *History of the 61st Pennsylvania*, p. 85.
25. Morris's report, *O.R.* 36, pt. 1, p. 723; E. M. Haynes, *A History of the Tenth Regiment, Vt. Vols.: With Biographical Sketches*, 2d ed. (Rutland, Vt.: Tuttle Co., 1894), p. 99.
26. Upton's report, *O.R.* 36, pt. 1, p. 666.
27. Gordon's report, ibid., p. 1077.
28. Quoted in Steere, *The Wilderness Campaign*, pp. 448–49.
29. Quoted in Catton, *Grant Takes Command*, p. 200.
30. Ibid., pp. 200–01.
31. Schaff, *Battle of the Wilderness*, pp. 318–19.
32. Quoted in Catton, *A Stillness at Appomattox*, p. 89.
33. Report of Major Henry R. Dalton, *O.R.* 36, pt. 1, p. 660; Steere, *The Wilderness Campaign*, map 27, p. 452.
34. Porter, *Grant*, p. 70.
35. Steere, *The Wilderness Campaign*, pp. 451–53.
36. Sheridan to Humphreys, *O.R.* 36, pt. 2, p. 515.
37. Schaff, *Battle of the Wilderness*, pp. 327–28.
38. Grant to Meade, *O.R.* 36, pt. 2, p. 481.
39. Freeman, *R. E. Lee*, 3:299–300.
40. Ibid., 3:301–02.
41. Long, *The Civil War Day by Day*, p. 494.

BIBLIOGRAPHY

General Historical Works

Angle, Paul M., and Miers Earl Schenck. *Tragic Years, 1860–1865.* 2 vols. New York: Simon and Schuster, 1960.

Battine, Cecil. *The Crisis of the Confederacy.* London: Longmans, Green and Co., 1905.

Boatner, Mark M., III. *The Civil War Dictionary.* New York: David McKay Co., 1959.

Catton, Bruce. *Grant Takes Command.* Boston: Little, Brown and Co., 1969.

Catton, Bruce. *Never Call Retreat.* Garden City, N.Y.: Doubleday and Co., 1965.

Catton, Bruce. *A Stillness at Appomattox.* Garden City, N.Y.: Doubleday and Co., 1955.

Coffin, Charles Carleton. *Four Years of Fighting.* Boston: Ticknor and Fields, 1866.

Congdon, Don, ed. *Combat: The Civil War.* New York: Castle Books, 1967.

Dowdey, Clifford. *Lee's Last Campaign.* Boston: Little Brown and Co., 1960.

Fuller, J. F. C., *Grant and Lee: A Study in Personality and Generalship.* 2d ed. Bloomington: Indiana University Press, 1957.

Hotchkiss, Jed, and Evans, Clement A., eds. *Confederate Military History: A Library of Confederate States History . . .* Vol. 3. Atlanta: Confederate Publishing Co., 1899.

Long, E. B. *The Civil War Day by Day: An Almanac, 1861–1865.* Assisted by Barbara Long. Garden City, N.Y.: Doubleday and Co., 1971.

Lord, Francis A. *Civil War Collector's Encyclopedia: Arms, Uniforms, and Equipment of the Union and Confederacy.* Harrisburg, Pa.: Stackpole Co., 1963.

Miers, Earl Schenck. *The Last Campaign: Grant Saves The Union.* Philadelphia: J. B. Lippincott Co., 1972.

Miller, Francis T., ed. *The Photographic History of the Civil War.* 10 vols. New York: Review of Reviews Co., 1911.

Naisawald, L. Van Loan. *Grape and Canister.* New York: Oxford University Press, 1960.

Pollard, Edward A. *The Last Year of the War.* New York: Charles B. Richardson, 1866.

Stewart, A. M. *Camp, March, and Battlefield.* Philadelphia: 1865.

Swinton, William. *Campaigns of the Army of the Potomac: A Critical History of Operations in Virginia, Maryland, and Pennsylvania, from the Commencement to the Close of the War, 1861–5.* New York: Charles B. Richardson, 1866.

Swinton, William. *The Twelve Decisive Battles of the War.* New York: Dick and Fitzgerald, 1867.

Warren, Robert Penn, ed. *Selected Poems of Herbert Melville: A Reader's Edition.* New York: Random House, 1970.

Wheeler, Richard, ed. *Voices of the Civil War.* New York: Thomas Y. Crowell Co., 1976.

Wiley, Bell Irwin and Milhollen, Hirst D. *They Who Fought Here.* New York: Bonanza Books, 1959.

Books Dealing Specifically with the Battle of the Wilderness

Robinson, Leigh. *The South before and at the Battle of the Wilderness.* Richmond, Va.: James E. Gooder, 1878. Address before the Virginia Division of the Army of Northern Virginia, Richmond, Va., November 1, 1877.

Schaff, Morris. *The Battle of the Wilderness.* Boston: Houghton Mifflin and Co., 1910. By far the most interesting account of the battle, written by one of Meade's ordnance officers.

Steere, Edward. *The Wilderness Campaign.* Harrisburg, Pa.: Stackpole Co., 1960. The most detailed account of the campaign to date.

Public Documents, Reports, Etc.

American Historical Association. *Annual Report of the American Historical Association.* Vol. 1. 1908.

Clark, Walter, ed. *History of the Several Regiments and Battalions from North Carolina in the Great War, 1861–'65: Written by the Members of the Respective Commands.* 5 vols. Raleigh: Published by the State, 1901.

Dwight, T. F., ed. *Papers of the Military Historical Society of Massachusetts.* Vol. 4. Boston: Cadet Armory, 1895–1918.

Southern Historical Society Papers. Vols. 6, 7, 9 and 14. Richmond, Va.: The Society.

U.S. War Department, *The War of the Rebellion: A Compilation of the Official Records of the Union and Confederate Armies.* 128 vols. Washington, D.C.: Government Printing Office, 1881–1902. Series 1, volume 36, parts 1 and 2 give various accounts of the Battle of the Wilderness; part 1 contains the reports of operation and part 2 contains the dispatches.

Biographies, Autobiographies, Memoirs, Etc.

Alexander, Edward Porter. *Military Memoirs of a Confederate.* Bloomington: Indiana University Press, 1962.

Badeau, Adam. *Military History of U. S. Grant.* 3 vols. New York: D. Appleton and Co., 1885.

Cleaves, Freeman. *Meade of Gettysburg.* Norman: University of Oklahoma Press, 1960.

Dowdey, Clifford, ed. *The Wartime Papers of Robert E. Lee.* Boston: Commonwealth of Virginia, 1961.

Early, Jubal A. *Autobiographical Sketch and Narrative of the War between the States.* Philadelphia: J. B. Lippincott Co., 1912.

Freeman, Douglas Southall. *Lee's Lieutenants.* 3 vols. New York: Charles Scribner's Sons, 1944.

Freeman, Douglas Southall. *R. E. Lee: A Biography.* 4 vols. New York: Charles Scribner's Sons, 1962.

Grant, Ulysses S. *Personal Memoirs of Ulysses S. Grant.* 2 vols. New York: Charles L. Webster and Co., 1885.

Hassler, William Woods. *A. P. Hill: Lee's Forgotten General.* Reprint. Chapel Hill: University of North Carolina Press, 1979.

Longstreet, James. *From Manassas to Appomattox.* Bloomington: Indiana University Press, 1960.

McFeely, William S. *Grant: A Biography.* New York: W. W. Norton and Co., 1981.

Meade, George. *The Life and Letters of George Gordon Meade, Major General United States Army.* 2 vols. New York: Charles Scribner's Sons, 1913.

Porter, Horace. *Campaigning with Grant.* Bloomington: Indiana University Press, 1961.

Taylor, Emerson Gifford. *Gouverneur Kemble Warren: The Life and Letters of an American Soldier, 1830–1882.* Boston: Houghton Mifflin and Co., 1932.

Thomas, Wilbur. *General James "Pete" Longstreet, Lee's "Old War Horse": Scapegoat for Gettysburg.* Parsons, W.Va.: McLain Printing Co., 1979.

Tucker, Glenn. *Hancock the Superb.* Indianapolis: Bobbs-Merrill Co., 1960.

Regimental Histories, Soldiers' Reminiscences, Etc.

Agassiz, George R., ed. *Meade's Headquarters, 1863–1865: Letters of Colonel Theodore Lyman from the Wilderness to Appomattox.* Boston: Atlantic Monthly Press, 1922.

Anderson, John. *The Fifty-Seventh Regiment of Massachusetts Volunteers in the War of the Rebellion, Army of the Potomac.* Boston: E. B. Stillings and Co., 1896.

Blake, Henry N. *Three Years in the Army of the Potomac.* Boston: Lee and Shepard, 1865.

Brainard, Mary Genevie Green. *Campaigns of the One Hundred and Forty-Sixth Regiment, New York State Volunteers; Also Known as Halleck's Infantry, the Fifth Oneida, and Garrard's Tigers.* New York: G. P. Putnam's Sons, 1915.

Brewer, A. T. *History Sixty-first Regiment Pennsylvania Volunteers, 1861–1865.* Pittsburgh: Art Engraving Printing Co., 1911.

Bruce, George A. *The Twentieth Regiment of Massachusetts Volunteer Infantry, 1861–1865.* Boston: Houghton Mifflin and Co., 1906.

Caldwell, J. F. J. *The History of a Brigade of South Carolinians Known as "Gregg's" and Subsequently as McGowan's Brigade.* Philadelphia: King and Baird, 1866.

Casler, John O. *Four Years in the Stonewall Brigade.* 2d ed. Marietta, Ga.: Continental Book Co., 1951.

Cogswell, Leander W. *A History of the Eleventh New Hampshire Regiment Volunteer Infantry in the Rebellion War, 1861–1865.* Concord, N.H.: Republican Press Association, 1891.

Comstock, Cyrus B. Diary (unpublished). Division of Manuscripts, Library of Congress, Washington, D.C.

Crotty, D. G. *Four Years in the Army of the Potomac.* Grand Rapids, Mich.: 1874.

Curtis, O. B. *History of the 24th Michigan of the Iron Brigade.* Detroit: Winn and Hammond, 1891.

Davis, Charles E., Jr. *Three Years in the Army: The Story of the Thirteenth Massachusetts Volunteers from July 16, 1861, to August 1, 1864.* Boston: Estes and Lauriat, 1894.

Dawes, Rufus R. *Service with the Sixth Wisconsin Volunteers.* Marietta, Ohio: E. R. Alderman and Sons, 1890.

Dickert, D. Augustus. *History of Kershaw's Brigade, With Complete Roll of Companies, Biographical Sketches, Incidents, Anecdotes, Etc.* Newberry, S.C.: Elbert H. Aull Co., 1899.

Field, C. W. "Campaign of 1864 and 1865: Narrative of Major-General C. W. Field." *SHSP* 14: 542–63.

Floyd, Fred C. *History of the Fourtieth (Moazart) Regiment New York Volunteers, Which was Composed of Four Companies from New York, Four Companies from Massachusetts, and Two Companies from Pennsylvania.* Boston: F. H. Gilson Co., 1909.

Gibbon, John. *Personal Recollections of the Civil War.* New York: G. P. Putnam's Sons, 1928.

Gordon, John B. *Reminiscences of the Civil War.* New York: Charles Scribner's Sons, 1902.

Harris, W. H. "Report of General Harris Concerning an Incident of the Wilderness." *SHSP* 7: 131.

Haynes, E. M. *A History of the Tenth Regiment, Vt. Vols.: With Biographical Sketches.* 2d ed. Rutland, Vt.: Tuttle Co., 1894.

Howe, Mark DeWolfe, Jr., ed. *Touched with Fire: Civil War Letters and Diary of Oliver Wendell Holmes, Jr.* Cambridge: Harvard University Press, 1947.

Humphreys, A. A. *The Virginia Campaign of 1864 and 1865.* New York: Charles Scribner's Sons, 1883.

Hyde, Thomas W. *Following the Greek Cross; or, Memories of the Sixth Army Corps.* Boston: Houghton Mifflin and Co., 1894.

Jackman, Lyman, and Hadley, Amos, eds. *History of the Sixth New Hampshire Regiment in the War for the Union.* Concord, N.H.: Republican Press Association, 1891.

Kidd, J. H. *Personal Recollections of a Cavalryman with Custer's Michigan Cavalry Brigade in the Civil War.* Ionia, Mich.: Sentinel Printing Co., 1908.

Lane, J. H. "Battle of the Wilderness—Report of General Lane." *SHSP* 9: 124–29.

Law, E. M. "From the Wilderness to Cold Harbor." In *Battles and Leaders of the Civil War.* Vol. 4, pp. 118–44. New York: Thomas Yoseloff, 1956.

Mulholland, St. Clair A. *The Story of the 116th Regiment Pennsylvania Volunteers in the War of the Rebellion: The Record of a Gallant Command.* Philadelphia: F. McManus, Jr., and Co., 1903.

Nash, Eugene Arus. *A History of the Fourty-Forth Regiment New York Volunteer Infantry in the Civil War, 1861–1865.* Chicago, R. R. Donnelley and Sons Co., 1911.

Nevins, Allan, ed. *A Diary of Battle: The Personal Journals of Colonel Charles S. Wainwright.* New York: Harcourt, Brace and World, 1962.

Page, Charles D. *History of the Fourteenth Regiment, Connecticut Volunteer Infantry.* Meridian, Conn.: Horton Printing Co., 1906.

Perry, William F. "Reminiscences of the Campaign of 1864 in Virginia." *SHSP* 7: 49–63.

Pullen, John J. *The Twentieth Maine.* Philadelphia: J. B. Lippincott Co., 1957.

Rhodes, John H. *The History of Battery B, First Regiment Rhode Island Light Artillery in the War to Preserve the Union, 1861–1865.* Providence: Shaw and Farnham, 1894.

Roe, Alfred S. *The Tenth Regiment Massachusetts Volunteer Infantry, 1861–1864.*
    Springfield, Mass.: Tenth Regiment Veteran Association, 1909.
Sheeran, James B. *Confederate Chaplain: A War Journal.* Milwaukee: Bruce Pub-
    lishing Co., 1960.
Simpson, Harold B. *Hood's Texas Brigade: Lee's Grenadier Guard.* Waco, Tex.:
    Texican Press, 1970.
Smith, J. D. *The History of the Nineteenth Maine Regiment of Volunteer Infan-
    try, 1862–65.* Minneapolis: 1909.
Sorrel, G. Moxley. *Recollections of a Confederate Staff Officer.* New York: Neale
    Publishing Co., 1905.
Stevens, George T. *Three Years in the 6th Corps.* Albany: S. R. Gray, 1866.
Stevens, Hazard. "The Sixth Corps in the Wilderness." *MHSMP* 4: 176–203.
Survivor's Association. *121st Regiment Pennsylvania Volunteers.* Rev. ed.
    Philadelphia: 1906.
Taylor, Colonel Walter H. *Four Years with General Lee.* Bloomington: Indiana
    University Press, 1962.
Thomson, O. R. Howard, and Rauch, William H. *History of the "Bucktails"
    Kane Rifle Regiment of the Pennsylvania Reserve Corps (13 Pennsylvania
    Reserves, 42 of the line).* Philadelphia: Electric Printing Co., 1906.
Urban, John W. *Battlefield and Prison Pen: or, Through the War, and Thrice a
    Prisoner in Rebel Dungeons.* Hubbard Brothers, 1887.
Venable, C. S. "The Campaign from the Wilderness to Petersburg: Address of
    Col. C. S. Venable . . . before the Virginia Division of the Army of
    Northern Virginia, . . . Richmond, Oct. 30, 1873," *SHSP* 14: 522–42.
Waitt, Ernest Linden. *History of the Nineteenth Regiment Massachusetts Volun-
    teer Infantry, 1861–1865.* Salem, Mass.: Salem Press, 1906.
Wallace, William. "Operations of the Second South Carolina Regiment in Cam-
    paigns of 1864 and 1865." *SHSP* 7: 128–31.
Webb, Alexander S. "Through the Wilderness." In *Battles and Leaders of the
    Civil War.* Vol. 4, pp. 152–69. New York: Thomas Yoseloff, 1956.
Wilcox, C. M. "Four Years with General Lee—A Review of General C. M.
    Wilcox." *SHSP* 6: 71–77.
Woodbury, Augustus. *The Second Rhode Island Regiment: A Narrative of Mili-
    tary Operations in Which the Regiment Was Engaged from the Beginning
    to the End of the War for the Union.* Providence, R.I.: Volpey, Angell and
    Co., 1875.

Magazine Articles

Cullen, Joseph P. "The Battle of the Wilderness." *Civil War Times Illustrated,*
    April 1971, pp. 4–12, 43–47.
Robertson, Robert S. "The Battle of the Wilderness." *Civil War Times Illustrated,*
    April 1969, pp. 5–9, 45–46.
Wilkenson, Frank. "Spotsylvania: Reflections How Men Die in Battle." Edited
    by Albert Castel. *Civil War Times Illustrated,* April 1983, pp. 16–19.

Maps

Department of Biology and Air Survey and Design, American University,
    Vienna, Virginia. *Map of the Wilderness Battlefield with Overlay,* Histor-

ical features compiled by Michael Jeck. On display at Fredericksburg and Spotsylvania National Military Park.

Fredericksburg and Spotsylvania National Military Park. *Troop Movement Maps of the Battle of the Wilderness, May 5–6, 1864.* Prepared by Ralph Happel, January, 1962. Five Maps.

INDEX